Responding to the West

 PUBLICATIONS SERIES

General Editor
Paul van der Velde

Publications Officer
Martina van den Haak

Editorial Board
Wim Boot (Leiden University); Jennifer Holdaway (Social Science Research Council); Christopher A. Reed (Ohio State Faculty); Anand A. Yang (Director of the Henry M. Jackson school of International Studies and Chair of International Studies at the University of Washington); Guobin Yang (Barnard College, Columbia University)

The *ICAS Publications Series* consists of Monographs and Edited Volumes. The Series takes a multidisciplinary approach to issues of interregional and multilateral importance for Asia in a global context. The Series aims to stimulate dialogue amongst scholars and civil society groups at the local, regional and international levels.

The *International Convention of Asia Scholars* (ICAS) was founded in 1997. Its main goals are to transcend the boundaries between disciplines, between nations studied, and between the geographic origins of the Asia scholars involved. ICAS has grown into the largest biennial Asia studies event covering all subjects of Asia studies. So far five editions of ICAS have been held respectively in Leiden (1998), Berlin (2001), Singapore (2003), Shanghai (2005) and Kuala Lumpur (2007). ICAS 6 will be held in Daejeon (South Korea) from 6-9 August 2009.

In 2001 the *ICAS secretariat* was founded which guarantees the continuity of the ICAS process. In 2004 the *ICAS Book Prize* (IBP) was established in order to create by way of a global competition both an international focus for publications on Asia while at the same time increasing their visibility worldwide. Also in 2005 the *ICAS Publications Series* were established.

For more information: www.icassecretariat.org

Responding to the West

Essays on Colonial Domination and Asian Agency

Edited by
Hans Hägerdal

Amsterdam University Press

 Publications Series

Edited Volumes 5

Cover design: JB&A raster grafisch ontwerp, Delft
Layout: The DocWorkers, Almere

ISBN   978 90 8964 093 2
e-ISBN 978 90 4850 820 4
NUR   692

© ICAS / Amsterdam University Press, Amsterdam 2009

Table of Contents

List of Figures and Tables

Introduction: New Paths of Colonial History

Hans Hägerdal

On 26 February 1687, the Dutch yacht *Negombo* departed from the roadstead of Batavia, the Asian hub of the still relatively vital and expansive Dutch East India Company, or VOC. On board was the Company official Arend Verhoeven, who had been appointed resident or *opperhoofd* of the unprofitable trading post of Kupang in West Timor. Verhoeven may have been less than enthusiastic about his promotion; of the last eight residents, six had died of illness at the unhealthy place, and one had been dismissed on complaints from the locals. With him on the *Negombo* went Dasi, *raja* of the small princedom of Lamakera on Solor, to the north of Timor. Dasi was an activist prince who did his utmost with the limited resources at hand, forging a comprehensive network on the easterly islands nowadays known as Nusa Tenggara Timur. This was to become one of the cornerstones of his policy and was to make him indispensable to the Dutch in their rather fragile outpost in westernmost Timor, and he visited the Dutch authorities in Batavia from time to time.

After a lengthy sea trip, delayed by the doldrums, the vessel finally reached Solor in April. There Verhoeven found a snake's nest, where supposed allies of the Company turned violent, murdering a Dutch representative there and clashing with a group of somewhat more loyal allies. Reaching the coastal village of Lamakera, Dasi asked if he could take his goods ashore, which Verhoeven gladly agreed to do, 'the more so since we were salvaged from a great stench and filth.' As he prepared to go ashore, the irascible Verhoeven told him not to stay long, since the Dutch intended to sail on towards Kupang as soon as the wind was right. Dasi suggested to the resident that he should at least show him the honour to let him spend five or six days with his wife whom he had not seen for many months. Verhoeven retorted that Dasi knew the orders given by Batavia all too well, and that the *raja* was ordered go to Kupang with the resident to assist in quelling the political troubles on Rote, another island under VOC suzerainty. As the grumbling Dasi stepped back onto the barge that would take him ashore, Verhoeven asked the raja pointedly whether he intended to provide the *Negombo* with tugboats, and whether he intended to follow him to Kupang or not. Contemptuously, Dasi snarled, 'You are just a new resident, and you should not act so sternly; or else we will complain about you, as we did about the other one, and see that you are recalled.' Verhoeven barked back at Dasi, but there was not much else he could do. The raja was too important a tool in the maintenance of Dutch interests via his many connections in this part of the Archipelago. However, Verhoeven, like so many residents who came before and after him on Timor, had fallen victim to the dreaded "Timorese fever" by November of the same year. Dasi, meanwhile, lived to a ripe old age, dying in 1701 after a modestly successful career covering almost half a century.[1]

The story, culled from a contemporary *Dagregister* or book of daily annotations, may offer a glimpse into the assertiveness that indigenous people or groups could occasionally display vis-à-vis the colonial establishment within the system. The type of early colonialism represented by the VOC was for the most part indirect or informal, which provided opportunities for those subjected to colonial authority to argue their case with some degree of success. Most places, especially during the last century of Western colonial dominance, may have offered less opportunity in that respect. Still, it must be remembered that colonialism as a historical phenomenon is multifaceted and has engendered a very broad spectrum of relationships between ruler and ruled, between coloniser and colonised, between foreigner and indigenous, between whites and peoples of colour.

The economic and strategic aspects of European colonial expansion have been the subjects of serious scholarly analysis at least since the days of Karl Marx. Moreover, there is no denying that historians since the rise of Asian and African nationalisms have devoted attention to the agency of those who were subjected to colonial domination in its various forms. Still, for a long time much of this was confined to aspects of national or anti-colonial struggles rather than the exploration of communication and negotiation in a social science history context. For example, it has been argued that the historiography of Indian nationalism has been decidedly elitist since the beginning despite its emancipatory ambitions (Guha 2000: 1). The ambitious publication *Subaltern Studies* surfaced in India in the 1980s and was devoted to writing a history from the underside of nineteenth- and twentieth-century India; however, its tradition of historical materialism has not escaped criticism either.

In the last decades, three lines of research in particular have informed the study of colonial relationships. The first is the field of postcolonial studies that has emerged in the wake of the seminal work of Edward Said (1978). Said succinctly pointed out that orientalism, or the textual output about the 'orient', enjoyed an incestuous relationship with the Western exercise of power over the non-Western world. This implied a mutually supportive relationship between power and knowledge, and a historiography that produced essentialised statements on the 'orient'. In effect, postcolonial study critically analyses the hierarchical power relationships that encompass the production of what is alleged to be scientific knowledge. It may thereby set out to destabilise the Western discourse of modernity. It also explores the connection and interaction between coloniser and colonised, and catches their respective constituent roles (Slater 1998; Prakash 2000).

Secondly, global and transnational history has gained ground. The field began to be explored by pioneers like William McNeill in the 1960s, and has dealt with comprehensive world system theories such as the one offered by Immanuel Wallerstein, which sees the world as an expanding system of inter-linked economic connections. There are also revisionist models that challenge the assumed trend of an expanding Western world towards 'the rest' (Frank 1998). Lately, this brand of historiography has endeavoured to apply a broad spectre of methods outside the traditional historical field, such as microbiology, linguistics, geography, etc., as exemplified by the work of Jared Diamond (1997). By seeing the processes of global history in a broader perspective than the 'traditional' political and economic history, it is possible to regard colonialism as an asymmetric interaction rather than just a movement from centre to periphery. The point of global history may not be to grasp the world as a whole, or to make it a history of globalisation, but rather to discern the mutual influences of various regions and cultures of the world (Casalilla 2007: 676).

Thirdly, certain perspectives and methodologies of social science history have gone global. Scholarly networks and conferences nowadays encompass widely different geographical areas and academic subfields (Burke 2001). Studies of colonial history have benefited from approaches that integrate culture, economics, class, gender, body, emotions, environment, microbiology and other issues. This is especially true as the rich possibilities that the colonial archival resources offer are right now being explored; a good recent example is the study of trade and society in colonial Malacca by Nordin Hussin (2007), which uses local documents to reconstruct the interactions in a colonial context that is in fact not so 'colonial' in character as commonly thought. Recent studies of colonial relations have pointed out that technology flows could very well have moved from local subjugated peoples to the colonising community, casting a radically new light on the forms of interaction that took place in an era of European expansion (a term that becomes only partly applicable to the situation) (Ransel 2007: 633-634).

The present volume offers nine essays originally presented as papers on the ICAS 4 and ICAS 5 conferences, in 2005 and 2007 respectively. They all deal with situations and milieus influenced or dominated by a Western colonial presence. The texts include descriptions of a wide range of efforts and strategies of indigenous groups to arrange their lives in the face of the non-indigenous impact. In this, the authors charter a wide array of ways to take advantage of, negotiate with, interact with, resist or portray the non-indigenous authorities. Chronologically, the nine studies cover the period from the 1700s to the immediate postcolonial period after World War II, in other words, going from an early and largely indirect form of colonial domination to a more direct type of authoritarian governance, and finally to the demise of the system. Geographically, the essays include studies on India, Southeast Asia, Japan and Australia.

In the first essay, 'The future of the Past, the Past of the Future: History in Southeast Asia', *Vincent Houben* takes up the intriguing historiographical connection between the past, the present, and the future. Using examples taken from Vietnam, Malaysia and Indonesia, he shows that the preoccupation with the future was an integral part of the representations of the past in Southeast Asia during the colonial period. Manuscripts from Java from the nineteenth century written in a traditional context evoke a future without colonialism. This is interestingly paralleled by twentieth-century, postcolonial cases from the three nations, where the creation of official histories becomes a way for the national elites to plot the future. Far from being neutral, political landscapes, past and future are loaded with meaning.

Next, *Ram Krishna Tandon* studies 'European Adventurers and Changes in the Indian Military System', where he focuses on the political confusion that characterised the South Asian subcontinent in the eighteenth century. In the wake of the European trading companies, a number of Western adventurers entered India, engaging in business activities to earn a quick fortune, but also offering their service as 'hired guns'. Compared to the old military systems, they presented a radically different input to the Indian political and military establishment of the time. This no doubt added to the modernisation of the military in the princely states that dotted the subcontinent, by attempting to arm the Indian military so that it would be the equal of European armies, and giving it a Western touch.

The third text brings us back to the theme of historiography. My own essay, 'The exile of the *Liurai*: A Historiographical Case Study from Timor', examines a dramatic event in the early colonial Dutch trading post on Timor. A local Timorese ruler (a *liurai*) fled from Portuguese Timor in 1749 and sought refuge in the Dutch area of jurisdiction. When he tried to defect from his new Dutch protectors three years later, he was arrested and exiled to Batavia by the colonial authorities. What makes this case interesting is that it is commemorated not only by contemporary records, but also by oral tradition recorded in the twentieth century. A comparison between the two types of sources provides widely different perspectives that highlight the indigenous Timorese processes of commemoration and history making.

Early colonial perceptions of racial relations form the theme of *Sandra Khor Manickam*'s essay, 'Africans in Asia: The Discourse of "Negritos" in Early Nineteenth-century Southeast Asia'. The term *Negrito* or *Negrillo* has been known since the seventeenth century, and was used by European travellers and colonial officials to denote various groups of people in the Archipelago considered smaller and darker than peoples of the Malay type. Manickam investigates how this label (of questionable scientific utility) was applied initially by scholars working with the discourses of race in early nineteenth-century Europe. She points out the interactions between stereotypes of Africans, slaves and tribal groups, and how these groups were visualised in Southeast Asia.

Rachana Chakraborty's essay 'Women's Education and Empowerment in Colonial Bengal' continues the theme of colonial cultural hegemony. The British rulers of India, in their civilising mission, ascribed the backwardness of the Indian woman to local religion and culture. The movement for female education as a discourse of modernity attempted to coalesce the conventional Indian wife and mother with the Victorian notion of womanhood. Chakraborty highlights this by studying the genesis and development of women's education in Bengal from the nineteenth century to 1947. This protracted struggle for educational emancipation brought them into the vortex of another struggle, namely the one for empowerment, which remains an unfinished agenda.

The implications of colonial lifestyles are studied by *Victoria Haskins*, in her essay 'Her Old *Ayah*: The Transcolonial Significance of the Indian Domestic Worker in India and Australia.' Using the life and colonial trajectory of her ancestors in the nineteenth century as a point of departure, she explores the construction of respectable white womanhood under British colonisation. Haskins uses the term transcolonial construction when discussing the emotional economy of colonial memories of the beloved and nurturing servant. The Indian nursemaid or *ayah* would provide a template for the 'fashion' of engaging young indigenous women as maids in both Australia and the United States in the first half of the twentieth century.

The period after 1945 provides some striking cases of the agency of indigenous groups in the course of the decolonisation process, and also an example of 'colonialism after colonialism', which concerns the last three essays of the book. In his text 'The Chinese, the Indians and the French Exchange Control during the French Indochinese War, or How to Endure, Fight and Mock the Colonial Power (1945-1954)', *Daniel Leplat* follows the intriguing paths of Asian money trafficking networks during the violent last days of French Indochina. The background of this trafficking was the official over-valuation of the Indochinese cur-

rency, the piastre. Leplat shows in detail how the members of the Indian and Chinese diasporas managed to free themselves to some extent
from the constraints of colonial financial policy, and to make some
profit by selling their assistance to members of the colonial community.

In 'Living the Colonial Lifestyle: Australian Women and Domestic
Labour in Occupied Japan 1945-1952', *Christine de Matos* returns to the
subject of domestic labour, this time in a quasi-colonial milieu. During
the allied occupation of Japan, a significant number of Australian women came to live in Japan for a period of years, as nurses, teachers
and the wives of soldiers. They became a symbol and agent of 'civilisation', adopting the role of coloniser-occupier with enthusiasm. The
most potent symbol and practice of this was the domestic labourer, the
'housegirl' or 'houseboy'. De Matos explores the power dynamics of the
occupier-occupied relationship of female occupiers and domestic labourer, and by implication, the interaction between race, class and gender. She shows how the women easily adopted a colonial/imperialist
discourse rather than one based on democratisation and emancipation
– the ostensible aims of and justification for the Occupation.

Finally, *Bambang Purwanto* in his essay 'Decolonisation and the Origin of Military Business in Indonesia' explores the dynamics of indigenous economic activity in a turbulent time of decolonisation. As he
points out, those who have studied the role of Indonesian military business have tended to see it as a phenomenon of the New Order after
1966, or at best, something that originated in the 1950s. Purwanto
challenges this notion by tracing the business activities back to the revolution in 1945-1949, and then follows the development up to the takeover of Western corporate interests in 1957-1959. He argues that the
process of decolonisation provided the basis for subsequent military involvement in business, at length, supporting the more sophisticated
military business format that has been visible since the 1960s.

In conclusion, the nine texts in this volume set out to explore the diversity of human relationships that was forged by the colonial presence. This is done through a fresh application of concepts, perspectives, theories and methodologies, many of them taken from the fast
developing area of social science history. Taken together, the essays reveal, on the one hand, the variety of devices by which colonials wielded
and maintained physical and mental authority over the dominated societies, but also the numerous ways that the latter could use to respond
to colonialism. The response might be economic, such as the trafficking in Indochinese piastres in a time of decolonisation, or it could be
literary, like the inclusion of the colonials in a historiographical framework in nineteenth-century Java. It could also be an interaction that
took place on colonial terms but entailed an element of emancipation,

such as the issue of women's education in colonial Bengal. For all its features of structural oppression, colonialism – needless to say – was not a one-way communication process; its study requires an analysis of the ever-shifting constituent roles of coloniser and colonised.

Note

1   VOC 8310, in Nationaal Archief, The Hague, no. 1.04.02, sub. 18 April 1687.

The Future of the Past, the Past of the Future: History in Southeast Asia

Vincent Houben

1 Entanglements of histories and futures

The future in Southeast Asia is intimately linked to its past as well as its present. Starting from any present anywhere, both the past and the future can only be conceived of in relational terms. One has to imagine overlaps between past and present / present and future or think in the form of forward/backward strings of events, processes and structures condensed into preconditions and consequences. Looking backwards in time has developed into the science of history, while looking forward is often felt as a much more haphazard practice undertaken by non-scientific actors such as politicians, administrative planners and even fortune-tellers. Yet, the past cannot do without the present, as the present without the future, the future without the past and even the past without the future.

Screening through titles of studies on Southeast Asia, the multi-directionalities and asymmetrical linkages between past, present and future become apparent. The present is historicised through a past that is perceived, told, written, framed, mapped but also handed down, transmitted, remembered, recalled as well as examined, interpreted or explained. The future, however, is viewed, faced, approached or bridged in the form of trajectories, prospects and challenges. So it seems that as a general rule the human past needs to be maintained as an ordered space to assist in the structure and stability of the present, whereas the future is primarily linked to change, risk and contingency. This is primarily a function of linear, forward-moving perceptions of time, which sees the present state of (post)modernity as the outcome of a specific development of the past, prefiguring a future that is partly predetermined by the presence of the past but also open to the new and unexpected.

However, the connections between future-past-present become multidirectional and highly charged if other perceptions of time are taken into consideration. Hopes or fears of the future certainly impact on present-day peoples' attitudes, while the past only acquires meaning through our preoccupations in the present, and the future is supposed to be shaped via the experiences or 'lessons' learned in the past, whereas the past is conceived of as containing the seeds of the future.

Yet, these kinds of multiple connections only display the 'secure' time modes. In contrast, many temporal entanglements are also charac-terised by instability, insecurity, crisis and even a psychological state-of-mind called 'angst'. Angst lies beyond fear, because what one fears can be named and is therefore calculable, whereas angst refers to an un-controllable and unspecific feeling of threat. Coming to terms with trau-matic episodes of the past as well as with some angst about the future shows how crisis-prone and charged the connections between past, pre-sent and future often are, both on an individual and a collective level.

Past, present and future are entangled but what are the specific pro-cesses involved and how can these be captured by using specific terms? Recent literature offers some clues to these questions. One approach is to use optical terms – that of reflecting and mirroring, which is more sensate than the concepts of imagining and envisioning.[1] These terms clarify that we are looking at the past as well as the future in the form of a space through a lens from a certain angle, which per definition means biased. A second approach uses the language of power: The past is empowered, the future is confronted, and history is revived in order to be able to face the future.[2] A third approach infuses quality into temporal dimensions: The past has been turbulent and the future is uncertain.[3] Human agency is contained in it.

In this short essay, an attempt is made to show how past and future interact in the spatial settings of what is conveniently called Southeast Asia. The core conceptual instrument in approaching this theme is that of 'representations of social order'. Representations can be defined as notions or ideas that define the world and allow people to organise it, historically, socially and politically. They reflect certain cultural predis-positions but, at the same time, open up cultural, spatial as well as temporal dimensions that allow for the construction of social orders in which subjects as well as objects can be positioned. Representations are forms of knowledge that allow people to establish their world and can-not be reduced to something that lurks between us and reality. Repre-sentations create a social order but, at the same time, they are part of it. Representations are not simply 'depictions' of the past or the future, but resources for the creation of meaning vis-à-vis the past and the fu-ture, which enable the individual as well as multiple actors and even whole societies to act both within and beyond the confines of the pre-sent. By imposing meaning on the past through expectations of the fu-ture and the other way around, cultural practices establish, maintain or contest a particular social order.[4] Two dimensions of one major strand of representation are considered here: the way in which the future has been embedded in the past during the *colonial* and *postcolonial* eras in Southeast Asia. I will concentrate on Vietnam, Malaysia and Indonesia.

2   Futures of the colonial

The preoccupation with the future was an integral part of representations of the past in colonial Southeast Asia. Studying prophetic writing
in Javanese history, Nancy Florida translated the *Babad Jaka Tingkir*, an
anonymous nineteenth century text that describes the transition of
Hindu-Buddhist realms in the East to the dominance of Islam in Central Java 250 years earlier. She notes:

> (T)his text does *not* chronicle a dynastic history preoccupied with
> the doings of kings and their armies in a linear narrative fash-
> ion. Rather this poem interrupts the dominant genealogical style
> of the dynastic chronicle to treat the past episodically, to gener-
> ate a novel genealogy of the future. ... Rather than register a re-
> cuperation of past reality in the name of 'objective truth' ... *or* a
> reinscription of the imagined pasts of dynastic presents with an
> eye to continuing traditional status quos ... this text constructs
> an alternative past which, countering its oppressive colonial pre-
> sent, would move towards more autonomous, perhaps even lib-
> erating, futures (Florida 1995: 10).

The text was apparently written circa 1850 on the island of Ambon by
someone from the entourage of the exiled king of Surakarta, Pakubuwana VI.[5] Instead of using a traditional linear narrative, it was composed as a series of episodic fragments. Within the context of the absence of a genuine scion of the royal Mataram house being on the
throne, the text dwells on 'other powers, which arise – repeatedly – at
the edges or margins of society'. It refers to the Jayabaya tradition, said
to be the prophecies of a Hindu Javanese king on the future of Java in
the form of eight eras to come. Contrary to *babad* tradition, however,
the marginalised figures do not move toward the centre but remain obscure. Writing history (Jav. *mengèti*) also has a connotation of bringing
about a desired future (Florida 1995: 270-274, 315, 397).
    One can ask whether the *Jaka Tingkir* text was an exceptional way of
writing pre-colonial history, set within a troubled colonial present and
thus provoking a breakthrough into the future. I argue that this is not
the case. Even in the major Javanese chronicle on the history of Java,
the *Babad Tanah Jawi*, prophecies (*pasemon*) were regularly integrated
into earlier parts of the story as ways to foreshadow later 'predestined'
events. The constant rewriting and extension of the so-called major *babad* had the intention of being in control of both present and future by
wielding power over the past (Wieringa 1999: 244-263). Nor was this
phenomenon of future orientation limited to Javanese history writing.
In the Acehnese *Hikayat Potjoet Moehamat*, the story of a conflict be-

tween two contenders of the throne unfolds after the younger one has a dream with a 'concealed meaning' in which the land is thrown into chaos but then regains order. At the same time, the record of events omits the conjunctions between them (Siegel 1976: 322, 327). A discussion of the Malay *hikayat* style likewise referred to the feature of temporal phrases that are attached to individual events but not placed within an overarching temporal framework. Contrary to Western perceptions of the past as a line of events that heads towards the present as a privileged point, in the *hikayat* events are temporally flat and recounted when they come up. This does not preclude a sense of future though. On the contrary, as Shelly Errington demonstrated: 'Thus to be spoken about in future ages provides an impulse for action, drawing the *hikayat*'s figures into the future' (Errington 1979: 38). The episodic nature of time in pre-colonial chronicles from Java and the Malay world was linked to their function of being sung before an audience. The social meaning the sounds acquired through their performance was a central feature and in this way *hikayat* history was transferred towards the future.

The social meaning of the future was transported in other ways than through historical chronicles and their performance. Throughout Southeast Asia, ordinary rural people recounted stories of expectation, which acquired a sense of immediacy and relevance in times of crisis. In Java, the premonitions of Jayabaya, a Kedhiri king, were well known. G.P. Rouffaer, a Dutch scientist who stayed in Central Java during the years 1889 and 1890, retrieved and translated a Jayabaya manuscript from the Solo Residency archive. It shows history as an alternation of periods of prosperity and order versus times of chaos. The story contains predictions (*pralambangan*) that are linked to the specific times when an old century turned into a new in the Javanese time reckoning. A fragment of the Rouffaer text reads as follows:

> In the year 1900 the realm shall decay and as a consequence of the will of the Almighty a brave European king will come, accompanied by countless armies, to which all kings will have to bow, without being able to resist him. Java will also succumb to him and he will be ruling there for a long time and in a stringent manner, and establish himself immovably. In these times the king of Rum in Constantinople will sit in a State Council and say to his prime-minister: *patih*, it is known to me that there are no longer ruling princes in Java, all having been forced to submit to a European ruler. Leave with all your armies and chase this usurper from there. If you won't succeed you are not entitled to go there. The *patih* and his people will leave for Java

and drive the European king out. The people will thereafter be happy, live peacefully and united.[6]

Jayabaya prophecies were circulated widely in Java and certainly fed into the future expectations of the people. Similar prophetic expectations were contained in an Islamic vocabulary (al-Mahdi), whereas in the Philippines they were of Christian provenience (Pasyon). Millenarian and messianic movements in Southeast Asia have been studied extensively by authors like Michael Adas, Sartono Kartodirdjo, Ray Ileto and others.

Ideas of a future beyond colonialism were therefore prevalent in indigenous societies and certainly served as a threat to the colonial order. Therefore, manuscripts and pamphlets referring to the future were meticulously collected by colonial authorities, creating fear among Europeans that ideas might lead to social action, as it sometimes but certainly not always did. The pasts contained in *babad*, *hikayat* and millenarian traditions were, however, far from ordered and singular. The dynastical chronicles were connected to oral traditions, which circulated widely but were manifold in their meaning, whereas narratives of expectation on a change of eras had a timeless 'empty' quality. Like the past, the future was therefore a reservoir of dreams that were beyond control and unspecific with regard to time and space.

3   Projecting nationalist pasts

The first decades of the twentieth century fundamentally changed the representations of past and future in Southeast Asia. The key to this development was modernity, which, in the words of Anthony Giddens, separated time and space and therefore opened up the social order to time-space 'zoning'. The historicity associated with modernity depended on a new, unitary kind of 'insertion' into time and space (Giddens 1990: 16, 20-21). The major vehicle of Southeast Asian modernity was the idea of nation. Nationalism intertwined representations of pasts and futures into a linear scheme and gave it a single meaning.

Whereas history in nineteenth-century Vietnam had, besides providing legitimacy for the ruling dynasty, the function of strengthening 'timeless' Confucian ethical principle. But in the beginning of the twentieth century, this began to change because intellectuals such as Phan Boi Chau and Phan Chu Trinh, began adopting the idea of linear progress. The major philosophical change, however, was promoted by the Vietnamese who had been to France and had been exposed to Western philosophy. Tran Huu Do, who had a keen understanding of Hegelian dialectics but gained little recognition, and Ho Chi Minh belonged to this group.[7] A similar development took place in Indonesia, where a small urban intelligentsia received a Western education and were exposed to Western versions of history. In a similar vein, on the Malay Peninsula, the Malay College in Melaka introduced the subject of *tawarikh* ('history in dates') in 1918, which led to the writing of new sort of *hikayat* (Khoo Kay Kim 1979: 301, 307).

Both history and the future were encapsulated by the project of the nation and their representations needed to be modelled on the social order strived for. A fundamental qualitative change was that from then on the future was the main orientation. Just as there were multiple modernities (Eisenstadt 2002), there existed multiple ways to imagine the national future. The nationalist movements of Southeast Asia often contested not only colonialism but also each other. One could distinguish between secular, religious and Marxist versions of projecting the past into the future, but all of them were characterised by hybridity emanating from transfers between the old, the novel and the outside turned inward.

When Ai Quoc (Ho Chi Minh) secretly returned to his home country in 1941, he sat in a cave at Pac Bo typing letters to the people to be published in the Indochinese Communist Party's newspaper, in an attempt to fuse anti-traditionalism with a nationalistic version of the history of Vietnam. He combined historical dialectics on a teleological basis with the idea of a timeless Vietnamese tradition, thus creating the mould for all subsequent nationalist historiographies (Marr 1981: 284-286). His pamphlet titled 'The History of Our Country' (*Lich su nuoc ta*), published in 1942, was very important. The major lesson of history, besides stressing the importance of resistance to foreign intervention, was that the people should be united. An appended list of dates where he tried to predict the year of Vietnamese independence ended with 1945 (Duiker 2000: 251-253, 260).

Early Indonesian nationalists also argued for a united stance on the basis of a nationalist past, and were, in fact, inspired by Dutch histories of pre-colonial Java published around 1920 (Reid and Marr 1979: 288-289). Sukarno was the chief architect of Indonesian national history. He set out his ideas on history and the future of Indonesia in a defence speech read out in court in 1930, titled 'Indonesia accuses' (*Indonesië klaagt aan!*), which was further complemented by a pamphlet in 1933 on the attainment of Indonesian independence (*Mentjapai Indonesia Merdeka*). A recent biographer of Sukarno labelled his 1930 defence speech as a 'cogent set of Indonesian arguments, though always closely wedded to the vernacular of European and other Western sources of political thought' (Hering 2002: 190). Sukarno adopted a simple but 'classic' three-stage temporal model of Indonesian history: glorious past – dark present – shining future. The glorious future of the Indonesian people was, so he argued, already contained in its great past since history showed that the Indonesian nation was on a par with any Western one (Reid and Marr 1979: 290-291). In the 1933 brochure, these ideas were expanded upon but further strengthened by connecting the present struggle against the Dutch colonialists to a mythic past from the Ramayana repertoire, in which Ramawidjaja killed the overseas demon Dasamuka (Hering 2000: 227). During the preparatory meetings that eventually led to Indonesian Independence in June 1945, Sukarno came up with the idea of *Pancasila* and again referred to the 1933 pamphlet, stating that political independence (*kemerdekaan*) was a golden bridge (*jembatan emas*), on the far side of which the Indonesians would rebuild their own society (*kita sempurnakan kita punya masyarakat*).[8]

Islamic and Marxist projections of a national future were quite different, although both were part of a global movement set within a utopian frame of thought. The Arab-Islamic sense of history has been based on *tarikh*, or the study of events or occurrences with the goal of establishing their nature and position in time (Johns 1979: 58). Religion proved to be a powerful vehicle to inscribe the future of the nation and the importance of so-called Islamic movements within Malayan as well as Indonesian nationalism is well-known. The promise of eternal happiness after one's resurrection and final judgement constitutes an essential message of salvation. The modernist religious renewal movement of the late nineteenth century propagated the idea of the unity of all Muslims and the need to strip local Islam of the customs that prevented its progress towards its pure origins. Ideas on how to accommodate Islam within the framework of independent statehood diverged, making it a political issue of critical importance. However, pre-Islamic messianism or the belief among Muslim peasants that the reappearance of al-Mahdi would signal the advent of the Day of Judgement continued to be strong. The same was true for mysticism, which allows for the immediate experience of the Creator's presence, which transgresses time.

The Marxist goal of studying history was in order to change it. At the same time, as argued by Tan Malakka in Indonesia, Marxism was not a dogma but a guide for action (Marr 1979: 333; Poeze 2007: 851). Communism, like Islam, had a global presence and a messianic message. It claimed that history was governed by material dialectics that would come to an end with a revolution that would spell the collapse of capitalism, leading to a dictatorship of the proletariat and the establishment of a stateless communist society. The teleological characteristics of history were in this manner linked to concrete expectations for the future – a highly effective mix for mobilising the poor rural masses of Southeast Asia. The Vietnamese communist party proved to be more successful in the end than the Indonesian communist party (PKI). But the hybrid ways in which they combined Marxist-Leninist orthodoxy with pre-existing popular expectations was common to both.

The PKI attracted a huge following in the 1951-1965 period but was not so much based on anti-imperialism or social justice but, as Ruth McVey argued, the idea that 'by associating and thinking in a new way one could again gain strength and become, in the end, invincible ... The essential symbol in this appeal was modernity' (McVey 1979: 344). In 1957, a historical analysis by D.N. Aidit was published under the title *Indonesian Society and the Indonesian Revolution (Masjarakat Indonesia dan Revolusi Indonesia)*. Only the 'correct' interpretation of history, could determine the proper action for the future. History was not an account of past events but a 'pattern of organising thought. It provided a past which was a model for the future not simply in terms of recommended action but in categories of perception, presenting certain ways of looking at things and excluding others' (McVey 1979: 349). The past was essentially national and the role of the Indonesian communist party was to liberate a country that was independent in name only. However, the communists in the 1920s continued to invoke local utopianism, as the Jayabaya prophecy was linked to the Soviet Union and revolution with the coming of the Ratu Adil (Tarling 2001: 374).

4   Plotting future from the present

In some societies, like in Mongolia, the past is up front while the future lies far behind because the former remains visible, while the latter is not.[9] However, in contemporary society in Southeast Asia, the future lies ahead. In Malay, it is *masa depan*, time that lies before. The connotation of *tuong lai* in Vietnamese is different, however, because it signifies what one has not yet done but wants to do next.

The central idiom of the post-independence national existence is focussed on the future, like the present in post-World War II Southeast Asia had, at least in the beginning, which did not have much to offer in the form of political stability and economic prosperity. Since the independent states in Southeast Asia could not immediately realise popular expectations of social and economic improvement, they had to resort to occupying the future as a tool for legitimating existing power relations. A crucial way of representing this has been through 'development', essentially a continuation of a central project of the late-colonial state. The most obvious way was by the introduction of planning. Through planning the future could be grasped, its underpinning statistics could be presented as 'objective' goal orientation.

Planning, however, presupposed a certain national stability, which was lacking in Indonesia of the 1950s. Therefore, President Sukarno, in his public speeches, prolonged the revolution. After a stage of survival (1950-1955), a new period commenced, that of the socio-economic revolution, with as its objective a just and prosperous society, phrased as 'tata-tentram-kerta-rahardja', which alludes to the golden age announced by the puppet master (dalang) of the wayang.[10] After 1965, political stability was guaranteed by the military, so the revolutionary rhetoric was dropped. Economic progress under the Suharto regime was represented through state planning. From 1969 until 1994, five Rencana Pembangunan Lima Tahun (Five-year Plans) were announced, with different foci ranging from infrastructure to industry and from transmigration to education. In the official language, development became the most frequently used term of the New Order, Suharto himself being hailed as its 'father' (bapak pembangunan).

Development planning in Malaysia, a relatively affluent country in the region, has not been particularly effective. As K.S. Jomo argued, postcolonial planning has provided only limited blueprints, whereas private sector activities cannot be planned. The nature of the planning here has been more political: 'Development policies, plan allocations as well as implementation reflect the nature, role and orientation of the state' (Jomo 1999: 86-87). In 1991, Mahathir launched his Vision 2020, a program that would turn Malaysia into a fully developed country. He stressed that this vision was not 'just a slogan' but 'a framework for action', which included the application of science and technology but also 'attitude and value changes' (Kidam and Hamim 1999: 339).[11] However, in the midst of the 1997 Asian financial crisis, during a conference in Tokyo, he deplored the destructive role of the so-called new capitalists: 'So what is going to be the future, the future of Asia? Actually there is not going to be much of a future for Asia, at least a future that is distinctly Asian' (Kidam and Hamim 1999: 155). The doom after the boom did not materialise, however, since the Asian economies began to recover after 1999.

A second way of plotting the future is through the creation of official histories, which are condensed into central representations upholding the postcolonial national social order. Collective memory is constructed through central discursive topoi, which are infused with a temporal extension within a demarcated territory – royalty, unity, culture, and religion. History is supposed to have extended itself beyond a centre or core region. Moreover, in many Southeast Asian countries, myths of a golden age, decisive turning points such as battles, key sacrificial events, and heroes with exemplary characters all play a major role. These historical representations are, however, contested by foreign professional historians, critical home historians living abroad and from below, in the form of local and regional histories that remain largely unwritten (Houben 2008). Furthermore, official histories are revealing in the sense of what has been 'forgotten' or censored, with the aim of making sure that future is not destabilised by memories of a troubled past.

An extreme example of national history as tool for regime justification has been Indonesia under Suharto rule. The key theme of Sukarno's version of the past has been the progression towards a brighter future. During the New Order, a new vision of history was promulgated, with Nugroho Notosusanto as its main composer. It converted the armed forces into the main historical player as it defended the nation at critical junctures in the past, notably during the Indonesian independence struggle and, in 1965, during the supposed communist coup attempt. According to Katharine McGregor, history was confiscated from the Indonesian people to become the story of military triumphs, representing the New Order as the apex of history (Mc Gregory 2007: 217). Yet, more than ten years after the fall of Suharto, a new official version of Indonesian history has not taken its place.

The persistence of official historical myths is shown by the official representations of the Nhan Van-Giai Pham affair during the middle of 1956, which consisted of a number of intellectuals and writers who openly addressed the contemporary domestic problems of the DRV. Dissenting views were briefly tolerated by the party leadership, only to be suppressed later on. In the official historiography, these events were then turned into an anti-socialist conspiracy, a myth that has survived until the present day, although, since the beginning of Doi Moi (the economic renovation policy), those who participated in this movement have been unofficially rehabilitated. Dissenting private memories are tolerated as long as they do not enter the public sphere. Meanwhile, official renderings of history display a greater variety than in the past (Großheim 2007).

These examples show how the future is configured both in a forward trajectory (planning) and backwards by ensuring an official domination over public memory. Numbers that designate how the future will be and historical myths that allow people to understand the collective past are a means to extending state control beyond the confines of the contemporary social order. These kinds of control are neither uncontested nor stable in themselves but they have proven to be socially effective and enduring in character.

5   Concluding remarks: controlled pasts, contingent futures?

This essay has attempted to make a few statements on how the future is represented in history writing in Southeast Asia. The question has been raised about how the past and the future interact in this region and what it means for the establishment, maintenance or contestation of a social order. Past and future are not neutral mental landscapes; on the contrary they are loaded with meaning for those who are living consciously in the here and now. Distinguishing between colonial, national and postcolonial social orders has offered some general clues on how representations of past and future are entangled. Indigenous history texts during the colonial era frequently addressed the future as did millenarian traditions, but both the past and the future were framed within an overall decontextualised time structure. Modernity encouraged the emergence of linear national pasts and futures. Chronology and movement towards the future comprised its essential characteristics. Future orientations combined with a control over history in the form of planning and official historiographies were aimed at regime legitimation, and have been the dominant modes of representation during the postcolonial period.

Thus far, this essay may have created the impression that it supports the received view that modernity, transferred directly or indirectly from the West, has overtaken pre-colonial, culturally specific notions of how past and future are intertwined. This kind of argument does not suffice, however. First, this kind of generalisation ignores the intricacies of transfer. Let me illustrate this with a Javanese notion about contents (isi): the contents may change but the vessel (wadhah) remains is the same. Western notions of modernity were selectively transferred and fused with indigenous figurations, giving rise to distinct Indonesian, Malaysian and Vietnamese representations of the modern, an intermediate space in which the boundaries between source and outcome, between indigenous and modern have become indistinguishable.

Secondly, the incorporation of the future into a present that is a continuation of the past is not wholly a function of modernity. Writing, talking or knowing about the past has always been a way of inscribing the future. Although the ability of the state to establish and control a dominant version of the entanglements of past and future have become stronger, alternative representations on how past events open up possible futures have been and continue to exist. Thirdly, stabilising the future through myth making about the past makes the representations that anchor the existing social order resistant to change. Recurrent crises between past-future representations and social orders that are entangled in the processes of transformation heighten contingency, a phenomenon that can hardly be interpreted as solely a function of modernity.

Notes

1   For instance: Vedi R. Hadiz (2001), 'Mirroring the Past or reflecting the Future?:
    Class and Religious Pluralism in Indonesian Labor' in: Robert W. Hefner (ed.), *The
    Politics of Multiculturalism*. Honolulu: University of Hawai'i Press.
2   For instance: Andrew Strathern (2004), *Empowering the Past, Confronting the Future:
    the Duna People of* PNG (2004); John Kleinen (1999), *Facing the Future, Reviving the
    Past: A Study of Social Change in a Northern Vietnamese Village*. Singapore.
3   See: Milton Osborne (2000), *The Mekong: Turbulent Past, Uncertain Future*. New
    York.
4   These are among the leading ideas that underpin the Berlin research cluster 640.
    See: www.repraesentationen.de.
5   On the flight and exile of Pakubuwana VI, see: Vincent Houben, *Kraton and Kumpe-
    ni. Surakarta and Yogyakarta 1830-1870* (Leiden: KITLV Press 1994) 33-37.
6   KITLV Collection G.P. Rouffaer H 391.
7   David Marr has written extensively on this. See: *Vietnamese Tradition on Trial 1920-
    1945*. Berkeley: University of California Press 1981.
8   *Risalah Sidang Badan Penyelidik Usaha-Usaha Persiapan Kermerdekaan Indonesia* etc.
    (Jakarta: Sekretariat Negara R.I. 1995) 65; see also: Hering 2002: 353.
9   Information by Ines Stolpe, a member of the SFB 640 team.
10 *The Rediscovery of Our Revolution*. Address by the President of the Republic of Indone-
    sia on the 17 of August 1959 (Jakarta: Ministry of Information) 1959: 12.

European Adventurers and Changes in the Indian Military System

Ram Krishna Tandon

Introduction

Eighteenth-century India witnessed a very significant transitional epoch. The traditional glory and greatness of the Mughals was tottering and about to a fall into a state of degeneration and decay. Peace and stability had been eroded. Centrifugal tendencies began raising their heads and inexorable forces were seen as rapidly converging, one upon the other, leading to an inevitable dissolution. Aurangzeb, the last mighty Mughal, breathed his last in 1707, but during his reign, the Marathas had already raised their heads and he had to fight them for more than 20 years. None of his successors were capable of defending his vast empire. This resulted in the emergence and rise of many other independent local powers in both North and South India. These local powers consisted of the Marathas in Poona, Indore, Gwalior and Gujarat, the Nizam in Hyderabad, the Jat in Bharatpur and the Sikhs in Punjab. The Mughal Emperor was basically nothing more than a shadow of royalty and the country was in a state of flux. The political vacuum thus created provided very favourable conditions for the influx of foreign powers. The invasion of Nadir Shah in 1739, followed by a series of attacks by Ahmad Shah Abdali between 1748 and 1761, dealt a deadly blow not only to the tottering Empire of Delhi but also to the Marathas.

At this juncture, the Europeans in India began to get involved in the politics of the local rulers. These Europeans came to India on the pretext of engaging in trade and commerce, and in order to save their trading interests they took up arms and started to take political control over the area. They raised armies based on the European pattern and when they fought the Indian rulers, the difference between a European-trained army and the Indian traditional army was obvious. The Indian rulers understood that their armies were no match for these European-trained armies; thus they needed to build an army based on the European model.

The question was, who would raise a European-style army for these Indian rulers? It turned out to be European adventurers who made themselves available and were ready to sell their swords to whomever paid the highest price; consequently, they were employed by the Indian rulers for raising these European-style armies.

The objective of this essay is to examine the role played by these European adventurers in bringing about a change in the military system that was prevalent in India by this time, by raising army units based on the European model, and by demonstrating their superiority over the existing Indian military system. In this way the process of westernisation of the Indian military system began.

This essay will look at the following issues in chronological order:
A. The European military system during the eighteenth century
B. The Indian military system during the eighteenth century
C. European adventurers: their background, both military and non-military
D. Armies raised by these adventurers and the changes that the armies of the Indian states underwent
E. Conclusion.

A.   The European military system during the eighteenth century

Eighteenth-century Europe underwent large-scale social, political, economic and industrial changes. Britain, France, Russia, Austria, Holland, Portugal and Prussia were the major powers in Europe and had interests outside Europe. Despite different forms of government, these European powers had one thing in common and that was 'to maintain boundaries of the state; to expand them, if possible or desirable, by diplomacy of war to maintain internal justice and to protect the established Church' (Rude 1972: 103). During this period Europe became a model for both military and non-military affairs.

Religion, which in the past had played a major role in European wars, received a setback and social, political, economic, industrial and technological developments were becoming the major factors in the shaping of the nature of war and in turn the military system. The best brains society had to offer were engaged in the cause of economic expansion and thus only the unemployed and unproductive sectors of society were available to serve in the armies. 'The officers were found almost exclusively from the nobility' (Howard 1976: 69) and the other ranks from the riff-raff of society. For example, the army of King Fredrick William I (1713-40) recruited as much riff-raff as possible from the peasants, who were sent back to their farms during the sowing and harvest seasons. They were paid a pittance and encouraged to supplement their pay by practicing trade in their barracks.

Professionalism also entered warfare during this period. The officers were the servants of the state and were guaranteed regular employment and wages. They dedicated themselves to the service of their respective states. This professionalism clearly discriminated between the military and civilian elements of society.

The army in Europe during this period could best be described as a state within the state. They were the symbol of state power. They maintained a subculture of routine, ceremonies, habits, dress and music, in other words, a way of life known as soldiering. It would not be out of place to mention here that traces of these practices could be seen in the British army in far more recent history. The officers who stood in direct relationship to the Crown led aristocratic lifestyles, while other ranks were recruited from all over Europe by impressments or bounty, disciplined by the lash, drilled until they were able to perform like automatons, and were kept in order by the watchdog class. This regimentation made it possible for these recruits to stand at attention for hours while the enemy fired at them from point blank range (Howard 1976: 70).

The army, as a rule, was kept at a distance from society because the rulers feared that they would create terror among the common people or that they might desert, which was a common problem of the era. And thus came the concept of cantonments.

The way troops were organised was almost the same throughout Europe. The armies were organised in infantry battalions and regiments; the cavalry in companies and regiments, whereas squadrons were the fighting formations. In advance of any attack, the artillery would be placed in the centre, the infantry on their right and left wings and the cavalry on both flanks.

The first half of the eighteenth century saw the expansion of the army and during campaigns there was a rigid sense of discipline in the order to facilitate the execution of the battle. Importance was given to the personnel and material aspects of the army. Large armies meant that roads and weather conditions were major determinants in the operation plans. New types of light troops were raised. These troops were irregular, lacked discipline and were used for overrunning or holding an area and were counted upon to gain intelligence. The light troops consisted of a mix of infantry and cavalry and were known as legions, and they used to provide security for the marching army or forced into direct battle if necessary (Spaulding 1937: 538).

In the second half of the eighteenth century, we see a new pattern of warfare emerging. The citizens' armies replaced the professional armies (Earle 1944: 49).The rigid discipline became even more rigorous. This concept of discipline was common throughout Europe. Frederick the Great's Prussian military system and army became the model for the rest of Europe. The 'Prussian soldier, through incessant, brutal, rigid drill and discipline, including cadenced steps, became an automation' (Dupuy and Dupuy 1977: 664). His cavalry was used for shock effect in the field and for reconnaissance off the battlefield. He stressed the importance of mobility over firepower. At the beginning of a battle, his army used to stand still like chessmen. And thus, battle became a methodical affair. Gilbert combined the advantage of dispersion and concentration with those of mobility and called it 'Grand Tactics', which were adopted by Napoleon later on (Montross 1946: 449).

B.   The Indian military system during the eighteenth century

The Portuguese were the first Europeans to arrive in 1498 on the West Coast of India. They confined themselves to Goa, Daman and Diu and only left India in 1961. Then came the British, followed by the French and the Dutch. During this period, there were two main military systems in India. One was that of the Mughals and the other was that of the Marathas and others like the Jats, Rajputs, etc. who more or less followed the Mughal military system. The Mughal armies were feudal in character. The Nobles were given a *Mansab* (rank) and were ordered to maintain a fixed number of troops and produce them whenever they were needed. For this service, they were given a piece of land. The troops were commanded by these *mansabdars* (military rank holders) and the loyalty of troops depended on the loyalty of the *mansabdar*. The army consisted of infantry, cavalry, artillery, elephants and camel troops. The actual number of non-combatants in the army was much larger than the number of combatants. The armies were huge and when they were on the march, it was like a moving city with its various types of fighting and non-fighting professionals. The camp life was luxurious and the number of women who came along was large. Armies were usually in arrear of payment. Though the Mughals were fond of their artillery, being the first to use firearms in North India in the first battle of Panipat in 1526, their firearms were old-fashioned. Heavy as well as light guns were employed. Battles would normally start with heavy artillery shelling followed by a cavalry charge, followed by the infantry. Once the battles began, more emphasis was placed on personal bravery. The commander sat on a big elephant, directing the battle and if he was not seen on the elephant for some reason it usually decided the battle. The guns and an army's numerical strength were the main factors in winning a battle. Elephants and forts played an important role in the military system. A huge Mughal army would have cumbersome artillery drawn by horses and bulls and even by elephants. The huge, luxurious character of the Mughal army came at the expense of flexibility and mobility. But this army allowed the Mughals to remain the masters of India for more than 150 years; the Mughal army had no equals in India.

The other major military system in India at that time was that of the Marathas. The Marathas inhabited the regions of Nasik, Poona, Satara, parts of Ahmadnagar and Sholapur and the western corner of Aurangabad, a total area of some 28,000 square miles (Sarkar 1973: 1-2) in today's Maharastra and the Konkan area of the Western Ghats. This area includes three mountain ranges: the Sahyadari, Satpura and the Vindhyas, with numerous valleys and forests. The Chinese traveller Hiuen Tsang noted that the Marathas were warlike and proud, but also grateful and vengeful when the occasion warranted (Sen 1958: 1).

The Maratha family of Bhonsle came into the limelight in the court of Ahmadnagar and one of its descendants Shivaji was the founder of the Maratha Kingdom in Maharashtra. He associated a brave race from the Poona area, the Mavle, and began his military career with them. The Marathas' military system consists of two parts: one, under Shivaji, the founder of the Maratha Empire, and the other that arose after his death. The core of Shivaji's army was his Mavle infantry who had their own arms such as swords, shields and bows and arrows. His cavalry consisted of two categories, those with state horses – the Bargies or Paga – and his own horses, the Silehdars. Both the infantry and cavalry comprised an efficient organisation of units and an efficient payment system. Swiftness, speed and mobility were their specialty and they were experts in guerrilla-type warfare and in the use of swords, bows and arrows and spears. A chain of about 240 forts was a major component of Shivaji's military system (Majumdar 1977: 566). These forts were the fabric of his empire, and they served as his saving grace in the days of adversity (Ranade & Telang 1961: 64-65). The artillery was the weakest branch of the army of Shivaji. Meanwhile, the Marathas purchased their guns from European merchants, who, alas, sold them mostly inferior weapons. Shivaji also had a large fleet of ships to protect the coast of his empire. He understood the danger that the Europeans posed from the sea. Therefore, Shivaji's foresight led him to protect his people, punish his enemies, and develop his ports, as well as a share of maritime trade and the freedom of the sea. 'So he combined the forts and ships' (Sarkar 1984: 262).

Shivaji had a council of ministers who ran the administration known as Astha Pradhan (Peshwas, Amatya, Sachiv, Mantri, Senapati, Sumant, Panditrav and Nayadish); excluding Panditrav and Nayadish, the other 'six ministers were bound in consonance with the needs of the time, to conduct military operations when required' (Sardesai 1946: 280). A very strict discipline was followed in the army and any breach of discipline was very severely punished. In his battles, Shivaji resorted to hit and run tactics known as *Gamini Kava*. This army was so light that it could cover 40 to 50 miles in a single march. Night attacks and mobility were his main tactics. His army was expert in the art of harassment and cutting off the enemy's supply lines and can be compared to the strategy of indirect approach, developed by Liddle Hart after World War I.

After Shivaji's death, the political situation in the Maratha Empire changed. The real power came into the hands of the Peshwas, the prime ministers, and the king became a nominal figurehead (Nadkarni 1966: 221). The Peshwas adopted a policy of war in North India. This led to a major change in army organisation and fighting techniques because they had to cover very long distances and thus the cavalry became more important. The induction of non-Marathas into the army brought major organisational changes and affected the discipline in the army. Now the Marathas adopted field-battle techniques to replace the *Gamini Kava*.

Non-Marathas, including Arabs, Siddis and Abyssinians, were also recruited for the Peshwa infantry, and a trend toward an infantry trained along the European model became the fashion of the time. These European-trained troops were called *Gardi* troops, who were supposed to be superior to the more traditional Indian soldiers. But, in the Battle of Panipat in 1761, the *Gardi* troops failed miserably. These Hindustani *Sepoys* were paid much less compared to those from other counties.

The Peshwa's policy of distant expeditions required more cavalry troops. Furthermore, the Peshwas took advantage of the weak Mughal administration and successfully plundered the area and levied taxes or *Chauth*. The introduction of the concept of plundering meant the influx of a large number of undesirable people into the cavalry. The cavalry regiments, however, still included large numbers of non-combatants like the rest of the army's units.

The artillery, as a branch of the Maratha army, began taking shape with the Portuguese being the main suppliers of powder, cannon balls, sulphur, lead and other military supplies at the right price. Local attempts were also made to manufacture ammunition and artillery themselves. But the main suppliers of the Peshwas' artillery remained the Europeans. The Peshwas also purchased a lower grade of newer weapons without ever mastering their operation, which left them dependent on others.

The Peshwas extended their power beyond the Maratha territories, but this meant giving insufficient attention to their forts and gradually the forts lost their importance and utility and thus, by 'course of events and the neglect of the state rendered incapable, for different reasons, of doing any service in [the] later half of [the] 18th century' (Ranade & Telang 1961: 185).

The Peshwas' navy during this time also reached new heights when led by one of the Marathas' naval chiefs, Kanhoji Angre. But after his death the European powers took advantage of conflicts between his surviving sons, and a chapter of Maratha naval history was closed. In fact, the Peshwas never truly grasped the essence of naval strategy (Bhagwat 1977: 426).

The Peshwas adopted a method of warfare that was not really suited to their character. Their army was always in arrear as far as paying the wages of the troops, much like that of the Mughals. And the Peshwas' armies eventually became similar to those of the Mughals, embracing luxury, pomp and show, which inevitably affected their mobility, flexibility and speed, which had been the main characteristic of the Maratha army.

C.   European adventurers: their background – both military and non-military

During the eighteenth century, India was in a state of constant turmoil – involving war and internal disorder. The Mughal Empire's decay provided an opportunity for the oppressed native chiefs to begin engaging in revolutionary efforts. But even while they were fighting against the Imperial Crown of the Mughals, they were also fighting and bickering among themselves. Thus India was broken up into a number of warring states. Apart from these local warring states, the European nations (or powers, as they were technically not nations, but rather companies engaging in business-war on behalf of their respective national governments) were also milking India for their own purposes. The Dutch exploitation faded away over time and the Portuguese influence was limited to their possessions of Goa, Daman and Diu. This ultimately left the English and the French as the only players in the battle for supremacy. These two European powers took advantage of the native rivalries in an almost continuous state of warfare, and began to exploit India's riches for the benefit of their European investors. Their national rivalry hid behind the agencies of France (the Compagnie des Indes) and England (the British East India Company), which was given the power of making both war and peace with any non-Christian power (a new charter in 1661 authorised the English company to wage war or make peace with any non-Christian power and to send warships, civilians and troops to its factories in India). Both the English and the French had their own armies composed of both European and native troops. The emergence of a British political entity arose from the prevailing friction between the English and French in India. The anarchy that followed the downfall of the Mughals paved the way for British rule.

In this state of chaos and anarchy, a number of European adventurers came to India to seek their fortunes, with sword in hand. They were French, English, Scottish, Irish, German, Dutch and Portuguese, who lived by their guts, swords and wits, and assumed the ranks of colonels and generals by themselves, changed their names and employers according to their own convenience, and fought for the highest bidders (Bhatia 1977: 118). They not only raised armies but also periodically sold them; they commanded their own retinues of infantry and cavalry troops ready for hire to the highest bidder. They were comprised of a broad mix of people, with some having distinguished military records while others were totally inexperienced. Furthermore, they sought service with various Indian chiefs, raised armies for them, and fought their battles. Some were deserters from European armies or navies; while others were escaping their debts. Others included the idle wanderers or those who belonged to the respectable classes of by-gone eras, while others came from the lower classes. Some of them had bright, honourable and colourful personalities while others had the most shameful or colourless pasts. Some were hard living and hard fighting, while others were of the easy living and pleasure-seeking sort.

All these adventurers with their variety of backgrounds, different characters and qualities, sought to enter the service of the native chiefs, i.e., the Maratha chiefs, the Mughal emperor Nawab of Awadh, the chiefs of Deccan and later on the Sikhs. They organised and commanded armies, helped the native chiefs in winning battles, conquered kingdoms, overthrew princes, ruled provinces, won distinction, mustered power and amassed considerable wealth. They also shared some of the lifestyle features of these Indian chiefs. It is not an exaggeration that the careers of these military adventurers would not have been possible anywhere else than India in the eighteenth century, when anarchy prevailed. The political turmoil allowed for the establishment of power and supremacy and this became instrumental in the building up of a very favourable environment for these adventurers.

These European military adventurers varied greatly in terms of their backgrounds, motives and personalities. The adventurers, who had military training and battle experience in their home countries, came to India to serve with the army units posted to India. They eventually deserted and joined local leaders to help to raise an army based on the European model. Others had no military background, but hopped a ship sailing for India in any way they could, and during the voyage to India, learned something from the other soldiers on board, deserted as soon as they landed in India, assumed their own ranks and found employment with some native ruler. There was a common feeling in India during that time that every white person was a good soldier and an expert in training and raising troops based on the European model.

D. Armies raised by these adventurers and changes in the environment of the armies of Indian states

The Marathas were the first to establish contacts with the Europeans. Apart from being dependent upon the French and the Portuguese for their supply of guns, cannons and ammunition (Sen 1958: 85), Shivaji also permitted the French to build a factory at Rajapore and employed Portuguese agents to purchase artillery from them (1679). Advice given in tactical matters by the French Governor Martine to the Marathas at the time of their war with the Mughals (1692) showed how long the Marathas already had contact with the French (Hatalkar 1958: 48). It was at this time, in the late seventeenth century, that the hybridisation process of the Indian and European armies began.

In the battle of St. Thome (1746), the French officer M. Paradis, commanding 230 soldiers and 700 *sepoys* without any artillery, attacked an Indian force of 10,000 men and defeated them on the field of battle (Mason 1974: 29-30). This shows the discipline, skill, and inventiveness of the few defeating poor leadership and the masses of untutored troops (Malleson 1885: 6). It proved that an attack by properly trained men could usually defeat the army of an Indian prince ten times as large. It would be incorrect to believe that the Marathas who were engaged in an expansion of their political authority would have not noticed this course of events at that time.

By the middle of the eighteenth century, every power in South India was aware that both the French and English had a military secret and this appeared to be their unique training system. The best thing one could hope for was to be able to persuade these adventurers to join their army to properly train their troops. As early as 1751, the Maratha chief Balaji Baji Rao, the Peshwa, was defeated by troops sent into battle by the Nizam (Mughal), who had been trained by Bussy and the French. In order to boost the morale of the general public and the army of the Nizam (Mughal), a general review of the French troops was arranged during this campaign, on 14 October 1751. The uniforms of the French soldiers, their discipline and manoeuvres had a magical effect on all those who witnessed the review (Hatalkar 1958: 88). This would have certainly led the Marathas to realise that there was something new in the way of fighting a war. The Peshwa, Balaji Baji Rao tried to hire Bussy away from the enemy, but Bussy refused, thus, the best Rao could do was to recruit two Muslim officers who had been trained by Bussy. Muzzarafar Khan and later Ibrahim Khan were used by Rao to train his troops using the French method. These soldiers later became known as *Gardi* troops. The Maratha victory in the Battle of Udgir, 1760, was to a great extent due to these newly trained troops.

In this way, the superiority and myth of the European soldier became firmly established. Almost all of the Marathas chiefs fell under this European influence and endeavoured to employ military adventurers who were mercenaries willing to undertake any work for a fee. The Nawabs of Bengal were far ahead with this as they had already employed an adventurer named Sombre as early as in the 1750s. The Rana of Gohad, Nizam, and Haider Ali also recruited various adventurers.

There is a long list of European adventurers who joined the native states to help them to raise more effective armies. But there are a few who were able to develop a new military system, while others merely followed them. A study of some of these adventurers who influenced India's military system is presented in the following sections.

De Boigne

In 1784, Mahadaji Sindhia, the powerful chief of the Maratha Confederation, through Mr. Anderson, the British resident attached to his court, invited De Boigne, a French adventurer, to join his army. He was commissioned by Mahadaji Sindhia to raise two battalions of disciplined infantry with suitable artillery.

Benoit La Boigne, who is commonly known as De Boigne, was born in Cambrery in Savoy on 8 March, 1751. He was educated in his local college and could speak French, Italian and Latin. He started his career as an ensign in the Irish Brigade of France, the Brigade known for its discipline. Later, he joined the Greek Regiment of Empress Catherine of Russia, was taken as a prisoner of war by the Turks, was sold as a slave in Constantinople and was relieved only after his parents paid the ransom. He again joined the Russian Army as a major. In 1777, he started for India to make his fortune and landed in Madras in March, 1778. In India, he joined the 6th Regiment of the Madras Native Infantry as a *Subedar* and served for three years, then went to Calcutta and proceeded to Delhi to meet the Mughal Emperor, but could not do so as the prime minister was in Agra, so he proceeded for Agra. Mahadaji Sindhia was busy capturing Gwalior, which was in the possession of the Rana of Gohad who had a battalion of disciplined infantry purchased from the French adventurer Midoc. The battalion was commanded by a Scotsman named Sangster. De Boigne tried to join the service of the Rana of Gohad but failed as his demand for Rs. 100,000 for raising five battalions of infantry was refused by the Rana of Gohad. De Boigne also tried to join the service in the state of Jaipur but failed. Mahadaji offered him service. He was supposed to raise two battalions of infantry with suitable artillery based on the model of the East India Company. De Boigne employed other European adventurers like John Hassing, a Dutchman, and Fremont, a Frenchman to command the battalion. Sangster, who was in the service of the Rana of Gohad and was expert of cannon casting, was also employed by De Boigne as Superintendent of the Arsenal. Soon thereafter, he started manufacturing artillery and small arms. Thus, within five months, he had properly drilled two battalions with proper uniforms, weapons, and other field equipment and prepared them to take the field. These trained battalions proved their importance along with the conventional Maratha army in the battles of Lalsot and Chaksana.

In 1790, De Boigne was asked by Mahadaji Sindhia to raise a brigade of ten battalions with a suitable train of cavalry and artillery. All were to be disciplined in the European style and commanded by European officers (Cotton 1927: 95). He had with him Sangster and Fremont from France and Hessing from Holland. He also appointed Perron, Baours, Pedron and Rohan, all French, and two Englishmen, Sutherland and Roberts. They would all eventually command battalions. These battalions had uniforms like those of the East India Company with blue Pagris. Some Pathans wearing Persian blue uniforms were also recruited (*Central Gazetteer* 1908: 111). Their arms were sword, shield and matchlock. Later on, bayonets would replace swords. The commands were all in English. In De Boigne's army, every operation was carried out with precision and routine; the men marched and manoeuvred using the methods that were prevalent in the European armies (Compton, 1892: 50). By 1793, De Boigne had three Brigades ready and the number of European officers increased to 300. They were of different nationalities – French, English, German, Swiss, Italian, Irish, etc. Ten per cent of them were commissioned officers and the rest were drill sergeants and artillerymen recruited from people who had deserterted from Company service (Compton 1892: 68).

Perron

Pierre Cuillier, famous as Perron, was a Frenchman born in 1755. He started his career as a businessman, then joined a cannon foundry and mastered the art of cannon casting. He landed in India in 1780 on a French ship, as a common sailor or petty officer. Just after landing on the Malabar Coast he deserted and, in 1781, took up employment in the Rana of Gohad's army under the command of the adventurer Sangster, who was assisted by two other Europeans, Tom Leggs and Michael Filose. Later he joined the Raja of Bharatpur under Lastineau and took part in the Battles of Agra and Chaksana. He lost his military employment at a time when Lastineau fled from the battlefield. In 1790, he joined the first brigade of De Boigne and took command of the Burhanpur Battalion, and took part in the battles of Patan and Merta. Thus, he joined the army of the Marathas and when De Boigne resigned he was put in charge of the army of Daulat Rao Sindhia. Later on, Perron, along with Major Pedron and Sutherland, captured the Delhi and Agra Forts and won the confidence of Sindhia. He became increasingly more powerful and by 1800 commanded four brigades along with a number of European officers who served under him.

George Thomas

Born in 1756, into a very poor family of Tipperary, George Thomas had no formal education. He fled home and reached India in 1781. After serving the Polygars of Karnataka he joined the Army of the Nizam of Hyderabad under the command of François Raymond. He left the Nizam forces and joined Begun Samru's forces in 1787, then left her and raised his own band of 250 mounted men. He trained them and eventually joined Appa Khadi Rao, who asked him to raise a battalion of 1,000 men. In order to finance this he received the revenues from the Jagir (fiefs) of three districts. He established a Jagir at Hansi and collected a huge sum.

John Parker Boyd

An American born in Massachusetts in 1764, he served in the American Army in 1783 and reached India in quest of fortune. Ahilya Bai Holkar of Indore had a contract with Boyd for raising a battalion of infantry on the European pattern in 1793 (*District Gazetteer* 1908). In 1795, he took part in the battle of Kharda, fighting on the Nizam of Hyderabad's side with a force of 1,800 trained men. He later raised two battalions for Peshwa Baji Rao II.

It was not only Maratha or Jat or Muslim rulers who employed these adventurers but later, in the early nineteenth century, the Sikhs also employed the European adventurers to modernise their army. Ranjit Singh's army employed a very large number of European officers, for instance. Ranjit Singh wanted to have an effectively controlled military system that merged the best foreign elements with best aspects of indigenous war tactics. The European adventurers were in much demand as technical experts in artillery and ordinance. The most famous of the Europeans in the Sikh army were Allard, Ventura, Court, Fort, Holmes, etc.

E.   Conclusion

In the eighteenth century, the Mughal successor states attempted to modernise their armies. Both the Indian kingdoms and the British led East India Company (EIC) attempted to set up hybrid military organisations (Roy 2005: 651). Maharaja Sindhia, one of the Peshwa Chiefs, began his expedition of North India in the post-Panipat (1761) period. At this juncture, he thought of employing a European adventurer in his army and hired De Boigne, and asked him to raise two battalions. Once European trained battalions entered the Maratha army, their numbers seemed to increase almost daily. Over the years, they became an integral part of the Maratha army. Practically all of the Maratha chiefs employed Europeans. The raising of trained battalions was a costly affair, so the Marathas started assigning *Jaidads* (lands) to these adventurers to meet expenses. Thus, the adventurers gradually became almost independent but remained part of the army under the Maratha chief, although on the battlefield, they were in command. Apart from the Marathas, Muslims, Rajputs and later Sikhs employed European adventurers in order to raise trained battalions and modernise their armies.

It must be noted here that the impact of the military system of these adventurers can only be seen and understood via the surveys and analyses of their participation in the various battles. The Battle of Lalsot (1787) between the Rajputs and the Mughal Emperor's army under Mahadaji Sindhia, who had trained battalions under De Boigne, proved that well-trained and disciplined infantry battalions could even face cavalry charges. The training they underwent developed confidence among the troops and the scientific method of warfare was considered superior to the conventional method. The Battles of Chaksana (1788) proved the superiority of calm discipline over mad valour, and the triumph of war science over sheer numbers. The Battle of Agra (1788) and the Battle of Patan (1790) again proved the importance of training and discipline. The Battle of Merta (1790) showed that highly disciplined troops and tactical formations had saved the day. The importance of planning, to make ample provisions for essential amenities like water in desert battles and the significance of a well-planned transport system carrying ammunition to the frontlines was proven.

The unconscious acceptance of the superiority of these adventurers who inspired a positive interpretation and adaptation of their military strategies had a very significant impact on the armies.

A new type of administrative skill developed in how the various units of the army – infantry, cavalry and artillery – were organised. So-called Rasalas were attached to every infantry unit for skirmishing purposes. Artillery pieces of different calibres were also allotted to the infantry brigades. This made the infantry unit self-supporting. Apparently this was not due to the material additions to the Indian Army, but rather to the impact of the European adventurers on the existing military system. The II and III Brigades of De Boigne were examples of this.

Furthermore, a proper and efficient transport system for the conveyance of the troops, the equipment, the sick and water and even replacement of horses eventually also developed.

The adventurers also gave the native armies the concept of uniform, insisting that the troops wear uniforms. The infantry wore red and black leather accoutrements, and blue turbans. The cavalry appeared in green and red turbans and cummerbunds (English Records 1936: 397). One could imagine the scene with two different armies, one properly dressed in uniform and the other in personal clothes (almost similar in design) of various colours. Apart from the aesthetic influence that uniforms had on the troops, there was also the development of a sense of belonging, unity and discipline.

The concept of training was also entirely new when it was introduced by the adventurers. Every able-bodied man in India who wanted to join the army, learned to use a weapon that he knew from childhood. Horseback riding was also common in society. Thus anyone who was physically fit could join the infantry and if he could ride a horse, he ended up in the cavalry. The use of muskets and guns was just a matter of experience but with the arrival of the European adventurers, discipline and training were stressed. Through continuous training the troops were so disciplined that they could remain immobile even in the face of a heavy cavalry charge. The battle of Agra, Chaksana and Patan are examples of their discipline. Intense drilling enabled the *sepoy* to maximise the use of their weapons in the minimum amount of time. Shooting practise and a perfect order of firing increased the speed of fire. In more modern terms, the adventurers introduced the man-machine system. The training allowed the *sepoy* to develop his powers of endurance, patience, confidence, obedience, vigilance and alertness, which resulted in increased efficiency and the development of a sense of belonging and team work, which had been lacking in the older Indian military system.

The native army's weapons and equipment were of a heterogeneous character. They used bows and arrows, swords, spears and shields, daggers and firearms. Their guns were large and heavy and gun carriages were clumsy. Cannons were also never made of any precise calibre. The cannon balls were of the same composition as ordinary firearms. These adventurers brought concrete changes and introduced new weaponry. Sometimes narrow-bladed straight rapiers with gauntlet hilts could be seen on the battlefield, which was an obvious western influence (Pant 1970: 187).

De Boigne also established an arsenal at Gwalior where there were iron mines for the casting of cannon balls and a gunpowder factory in Agra. Saltpetre and sulphur were imported from Bikaner under the supervision of another adventurer, Sangster, whom we met earlier (Hutchinson 1964: 126). The role of the adventurers was obvious in the way the arsenals were properly managed.

In South India, the Marathas in the early period adopted a type of guerrilla warfare where the infantry was more important than the cavalry. Later on during the Peshwa period, when they had conquered land extending to the north, the cavalry became more important. The Maratha light cavalry was, however, not very effective against heavy artillery and a well-trained infantry supported by cavalry in the heat of the battle. They lacked that Western-style of doing battle and had no concept of discipline and training. Speed and sheer numbers were their only weapons. Here the adventurers joined the Marathas and trained the infantry battalions properly in the use of fire weapons and artillery manned by European gunners. This Western style of training and tactical formations became a part of the Maratha army and marked the hybridisation of Western and Eastern warfare strategies.

Battle plans were another element that the adventurers added to the Maratha army. The importance of an efficient transport system was also emphasised, which meant the introduction of carrying ammunition up to the frontlines and providing drinking water for the *sepoys* in the desert. During the Battle of Merta marching in formation became a clear element of their disciplined approach. The co-ordination of communication between the various wings of the army was also a new addition.

All these tactics and the above-stated battle preparations and plans were, no doubt, introduced into the Indian military system by the European adventurers. But in the end, the British prevailed because, in the eighteenth century, 'India tried to acquire the superior methodology and weapons of the stronger, i.e., the Europeans (the British) and the British won because they retained their military superiority' (Bryant 2004: 431).

The Exile of the *Liurai*:
A Historiographical Case Study from Timor

Hans Hägerdal

1   History in a non-literate society[1]

The methodological problems of writing the history of non-literate societies have been extensively debated since the groundbreaking studies
of Jan Vansina in the 1960s. The techniques of obtaining vital sociological and historical information from oral tradition have not least been
developed in the study of the African past, where the lack of written
sources up to the nineteenth century necessitate the evaluation of this
type of material. Vansina himself initially believed that oral tradition,
i.e., stories spanning a time perspective beyond living memory, could
be judged according to a modification of the sound principles of historical criticism developed by Western historians in the late nineteenth
and early twentieth centuries. Thus, comparisons between variants of
oral stories, analysis of the techniques of transmission, and observation
of circumstances of narration, could lead to conclusions about past
events and structures.[2] Such studies have since thrived in research
about pre-modern Africa, and the methods of analysis have developed
accordingly. In recent decades, and presumably in the footsteps of the
'linguistic turn' that has influenced the humanities, many scholars take
a much more careful stance than (the early) Vansina with regard to oral
materials. The traps appear to be more formidable than conceived by
an older generation of scholars, and the chances of reinterpretations
and reinventions of 'historical' traditions are such that a reconstruction
of events older than a few generations proves to be adventurous. The
historical consciousness of a group, and hence its representation of
past events, is highly dependent on the political and social structures
of recent times pertaining to such a group.[3] On the other hand, in the
footsteps of postmodern and postcolonial debate the processing of oral
indigenous data in former colonial societies becomes vital in order to
challenge Western narratives. The oral collective memory of these societies reflects on the past historical landscape in terms that serve as a
corrective to colonial perspectives and judgments on the same past.

Occasionally we are in the fortunate position to have access to two
categories of materials dealing with the early history of a specific area:
a corpus of oral traditions not influenced by written documents, and a

corpus of contemporary archival sources. This is the case in Africa with
a few geographical areas like Congo and Angola, which have engendered several detailed scholarly studies over the years. At first glance,
Asia may seem to be fundamentally different: a vast region that is largely covered by more or less literate societies since long ago. If we nar-
row the scope to the extensive maritime areas of Southeast Asia, most
of the historical cultures in the western part of the island world have a
tradition of written historiography, albeit with frequent legendary and
mythologised features. In the eastern part, more or less corresponding
to eastern Indonesia and Timor Leste, by contrast, many of the societies are traditionally non-literate. Local princedoms often have a substantial corpus of 'historical' traditions, including origin stories, princely pedigrees and tales about particular events and persons. An interesting question is naturally how these traditions compare in content
and perspective with archival documents. As it turns out, this question
can partly be answered due to the long-term presence of literate foreign
communities.

2   The Timorese scene

It is well known that the Dutch East Indies Company (Verenigde Oost-
Indische Compagnie, VOC) established a power base in maritime Asia,
especially in what is present-day Indonesia, in the early seventeenth
century. Although based in Batavia or Jakarta, it maintained its extensive commercial and political network via a system of alliances and
conquests in various coastal places, where fortified trading posts were
constructed. One such outpost was Fort Concordia at Kupang, in the
westernmost part of Timor, which was first set up in 1653. The Dutch
had had contacts with Timor since 1613 because of the potential lucrative sandalwood trade, since the best sandalwood in Southeast Asia
grew on Timor. However, they discovered rivals here in the seafaring
Makassarese people from Sulawesi, and above all, the Portuguese traders, missionaries and soldiers who had been established in eastern Indonesia long before the Dutch. The Dutch and the Portuguese lived in
a state of intense enmity until 1663, when a peace treaty was made
public. By this time, the Portuguese possessions of Southeast Asia
were reduced to parts of Timor and neighbouring islands. Although
they were otherwise victorious against the Portuguese adversaries, the
Dutch were at a disadvantage in the Timor area, where their territory
was initially limited to a minor stretch of land in West Timor.[4] The
commercial opportunities for the VOC were quite limited, and they
kept the Kupang post mainly for strategic reasons (Coolhaas 1968: 255;
Hägerdal 2007: 7-8). The Company garrison usually consisted of no

more than 40 to 50 men, and for larger enterprises they had to trust their Timorese allies. The VOC officials nevertheless kept meticulous records of their activities.

Timorese society during the VOC period (seventeenth and eighteenth centuries) was a low-technological, highly localised one with a poor infrastructure, based on genealogical groups and divided into numerous minor princedoms that tended to ally themselves with either the VOC or Portugal. Timorese society was not influenced by Indian models or by Islam to any degree. Catholicism made inroads in the first half of the seventeenth century, although in a rather superficial way, and the society remained illiterate and only very marginally touched by Western material culture. Advanced metalwork, high-quality pottery and firearms were unknown to this traditional society and these items had to be imported, initially in exchange for sandalwood.

At the same time, the political structures of Timorese society were rather elaborate, following a complicated pattern of hierarchical relations. Much of this escaped the early Dutch and Portuguese colonialists of the seventeenth and eighteenth centuries, but modern ethnographical studies have revealed the complexities of traditional Timorese politics. Among the Atoni people, who dominate West Timor, there were kinship-based villages on the local level, which were, however, not densely settled but made a scattered impression on early visitors. Prominent clan heads known as *amaf* (fathers) were important in the various localities in a traditional Atoni domain, holding authority over lesser clans. These *amaf*, in turn were ruled by a small number (sometimes four, in accordance with the Timorese tendency of ritual quadrupartition) of *amaf naek* (great fathers) whose functions varied from domain to domain. In some places, they held authority over the land in part of the domain, overseeing rituals and the harvesting of tributes and gifts (*poni* and *tuthais*) for the ruler. In other places, they were less resourceful (McWilliam 2002: 66-67). Dutch sources usually knew these chiefs as lesser and grander *temukung* – a term derived from the Malay-Javanese *temenggung*. At the apex of the domain was a ruler, known as *atupas, neno anan, liurai* etc. The Dutch usually termed them *radja, vorst* (ruling prince) or *koning* (king). Their position was strictly hereditary and sometimes described in colonial texts as despotic. However, the system also kept checks on the executive powers of the ruler. In most domains, the ruler was a deliberately inactive figure, whose main task was 'eating, drinking and sleeping' at the centre of the realm. By resting at the centre, the lord symbolically kept the system in place. A ritual opposition between the 'male' and 'female' (*mone – feto*) permeates Timorese socio-political relations, and here the ruler is counted as female (not withstanding his or her actual sex) (Fox 1982). An actively ruling, 'male' part, known as *usif* or, in Dutch, *rijksbestierder*, was usual-

Figure 1   *Historical map of Timor*

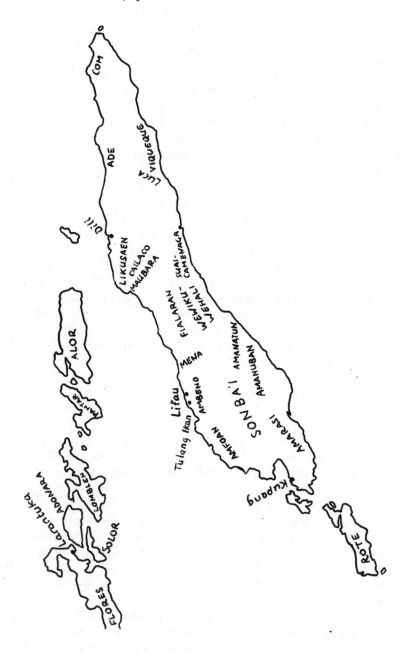

ly found by the ruler's side. Later in history, he was known by the Por-
tuguese-derived term *fettor*. There was normally a second *usif* family at
the side of the principal one, who took part in the governance of the
realm. Moreover, in some realms, there was a *pah tuaf* or lord of the
land, whose ancestors had once possessed the land but ceded it to the
current ruling family, but who still entertained an honoured position.[5]

At the dawn of colonial influence on Timor, in the seventeenth century, there were some eight domains in the Atoni area in the west:
Sonba'i, Amanuban, Amanatun, Amarasi, Amabi, Amfo'an, Ambeno
and Mena. The Tetun-speaking realm Wewiku-Wehali dominated the
centre of the island, Belu, while the eastern part was divided into some
40 to 50 smaller domains.[6] The population of these domains was not
more than several thousand people each, in a few cases maybe just
over 10,000. Although the Dutch and Portuguese termed these domains 'kingdoms' it is doubtful that they were kingdoms in any mean-
ingful sense. In spite of their complex structure, they did not have the
means of resource mobilisation or indeed the manpower to act as
states. They fall instead within the category of chiefdoms. However, the
numerous domains were not on an equal footing; instead, there was a
marked hierarchy among them. From the then contemporary colonial
and later ethnographic records, it appears that a larger, even Timor-
wide political network was centrally located on Wewiku-Wehali in
south-central Timor. The 'female' lord, the Maromak Oan (the son of
God) was the central ritualistic figure and was revered across the island. Under him, we find three *liurai* ('surpassing the earth'), namely
those of Wehali in the centre, Sonba'i to the west and Likusaen (alter-
natively Suai-Camenaça) in the east (Schulte Nordholt 1971: 391; Hägerdal 2007: 8; Fobia 1984: 9). Wewiku-Wehali was in particular acknowledged as the highest in status by the Tetun-speaking domains in
central and eastern Timor. This does not mean that it ever constituted
an 'empire' in the literal sense; rather, it might have been a vehicle for
conflict resolution and deliberation among the numerous domains.

Sonba'i was thus the most prestigious polity of West Timor. According to various legends recorded in the nineteenth and twentieth centuries, the first Sonba'i ancestor was a brother of the *liurai* of Wehali who
went to the Atoni territory of West Timor. There he met the daughter
of Nai Ke Kune, a powerful chief in the mountainous interior, and he
eventually married her. He thereby assumed authority over the land
held by the Kune family, who were reduced to *pah tuaf*, with honoured
but impotent positions.[7] The other Atoni domains, Ambeno, Amfo'an,
etc., related themselves genealogically to the lord of Sonba'i, though
they were not actually politically obedient to him. The importance of
Sonba'i and Liurai (i.e., Wehali) in the mental universe of the Atoni is
seen by innumerable references. For example, the two basic means of

nutrition, maize and rice, are known as Liurai-Sonba'i (Schulte Nordholt 1971: 55, 91).

History had a deep significance in this type of society, albeit in a
rather different way than in Western society. Timorese society until the
twentieth century was more or less illiterate, so there were no written
chronicles, like the Malay *hikayat* or the Javanese-Balinese *babad*. There
was, however, a rich treasure trove of oral tradition stories, which could
be related via folk stories or via institutionalised history telling. The traditional domains kept speakers, *mafefa*, in their employ; these people
had the task of representing the ruler and maintaining the traditional
regulations and stories. Similarly, there were non-hereditary historians
who kept track of origin stories, genealogies, etc., which were important for the self-definition of the ruling strata of the domain.

In certain aspects, the scope of these histories is structurally reminis-
cent of the types of Indonesian historiography prevalent in the literate
parts of the archipelago. The social importance of origins is an overarching concern, whether we are dealing with a Timorese oral story or
a written *hikayat* or *babad* account. It was essential to establish the
coming of the ruling dynasty to a particular realm, and to set out the
original relationship between the dynastic founder and the various *usif*
and *amaf naek*. Historically, there were numerous migrations of Timorese groups from one part of the country to another, and these migrations were extensively treated in the oral stories and combined with local topography. A succession of geographical place names was connected to the stage of progress of a group by means of folk etymology.
Another parallel concerns the structure of the genealogies. While in
reality a dynastic succession seldom descends from father to son in
more than a limited number of generations, Indonesian historiography
frequently simplifies history. It prefers to present a straight line of des-
cent that leaves out brother-to-brother or uncle-to-nephew successions.
In the oral accounts of Timorese spokesmen, this genealogical stream-
lining occurs in nearly all cases that I have investigated, where comparisons can be made to Dutch or Portuguese documentary data. A third
parallel is the chronological uncertainty that applies to particular historical episodes. A story about an event occurring under a particular ruler
or generation might be retold in another story where it applies to another ruler. By carefully comparing different stories, one may notice
certain probabilities, but the uncertainty is likely to persist if the episode cannot be substantiated by European documents.[8]

Occasionally there are episodes that are told by a number of storytellers recorded in modern time, which can be checked against detailed
colonial records. The small Dutch outpost in Kupang in westernmost
Timor produced relatively abundant records about its own activities, records that are to a large extent preserved in the Nationaal Archief in

The Hague. These records include diaries, letters, and the minutes of legal proceedings, budget accounts and reports for the VOC hub in Batavia. The Portuguese materials have been less systematically preserved. Whenever a Timorese polity had dealings with the Dutchmen, we can thus usually follow the events in some detail. This is not to say that European records are above suspicion. The residents or *opperhoofden* of the VOC fort were, for the most part, placed on Timor on a temporary basis, and thus most of them understood little about the local customs or history. This ignorance was coupled with a relatively negative view of the Timorese and their way of life. The latter were frequently denigrated in the documents for being rough, mendacious, lazy, cowardly, etc. Thus, we do not obtain any unbiased or particularly well-informed picture from the colonial material. The advantage, however, is that these records are from that period of time, and were written in the context of a bureaucratic company whose leaders needed facts and not fiction about what was going on in Timor.

On the following pages, I will investigate a case that is frequently mentioned in late Timorese as well as contemporary Dutch records. By such an investigation, we are able to clarify how a particular event is commemorated in the two types of sources – one posthumous, sympathetic and indigenous, and one contemporary, negative and foreign. The differing perspectives may throw light on the construction and function of history in a small-scale non-literate society, and demonstrate how colonial narratives can be challenged by alternative perspectives. The case occurred in the year 1752 and concerns the ruler of the indigenous domain Sonba'i.

3   Sonba'i in early colonial history

The prestigious Sonba'i polity had a chequered history during the course of colonial history. It is mentioned in European sources dating from as early as 1649. By then, it was already a domain with expansive ambitions, actively supported by the Portuguese. At this time, the Portuguese – who were actually a *mestiço* group, also known as the Topasses – were establishing their direct authority over Timor's northwestern coast, with their main port at Lifau in the present-day Oecusse-Ambeno enclave.[9] For a time it seemed that the Sonba'i were destined to conquer a large part of Timor with Portuguese backing. However, in 1655, it suddenly switched sides and entered into an alliance with the VOC, newly established in Kupang. As it turned out, this reversal of loyalties did little to help the Sonba'is' position. They were defeated by the Portuguese and their clients in 1657-1658 and part of the population fled to Kupang under miserable conditions (De Roever 2002: 249-267).

The defeat in effect led to a split of the Sonba'i into two separate domains. The refugees settled in the vicinity of Kupang where they formed the Lesser Sonba'i (Sonba'i Kecil) group, which was loyal to the Dutch until the demise of the colonial state in the 1940s. Those who stayed in the mountainous interior of West Timor, by contrast, became subservient to the Portuguese, forming the Greater Sonba'i (Sonba'i Besar) group. The colonial powers gave the rulers of the two Sonba'i domains the lofty title of 'emperor' (keizer, imperador), which indicates that the Dutch and Portuguese both understood the importance of maintaining control over the ritually prestigious princes.[10] The main political forces of the respective domain were the usif families, the executive regents who were 'male' in relation to the 'female' monarch.[11] The united Sonba'i domain in the mid-seventeenth century was governed by usif of the Oematan family. When the main branch of the Oematan fled to Kupang in 1658, members of the Kono family soon replaced him.[12] The Usif Kono (Uis Kono, Amakono) was elevated with the assistance of the Portuguese; while at his side was a branch of the Oematan clan who assumed the position of second usif.[13] The Kono family had their main stronghold in the region known as Miomaffo or Amakono, while the Oematan family dominated the Mollo region. The Greater Sonba'i realm was mostly known to the colonial powers as 'Amakono' due to the importance of the Usif Kono.

Although Portuguese colonial rule was eventually restricted to East Timor plus the Oecusse-Ambeno enclave, its focus initially lay in the Atoni areas in the west, in what is today largely Indonesian Timor. Amakono-Greater Sonba'i was considered to be a cornerstone of Portuguese rule in the second half of the seventeenth century, together with Amarasi, Amanuban and Ambeno. Nevertheless, Greater Sonba'i often proved to be a disgruntled and rebellious client. The emperors of Greater and Lesser Sonba'i often entertained clandestine contacts, where the former might warn the latter over impending Portuguese attacks on the Kupang area. There were also cases of open rebellion against Portuguese rule, as in 1711-1713, and attempts to meddle in Portuguese fractional strife, as in 1673 and 1722. The exacting of tributes and forced deliveries of sandalwood and other products, appear to have caused considerable dissatisfaction among some of the Atoni domains, and not least Sonba'i.

The relationship between the colonial groups on the island was complicated. After 1663, the United Provinces of the Netherlands were at peace with Portugal. To actually implement this peace treaty on the other side of the globe was another matter. Although the main colonial bases at Kupang and Lifau did not commit direct acts of aggression against each other, there was a great deal of manoeuvring and warfare by proxy. The respective allies or vassals of the two powers were constantly pitted against each other, meaning that soldiers of the two Sonba'i domains sometimes met on the battlefield. It was a low-level type of warfare with a few assaults, minor skirmishes and headhunting raids rather than actual full-scale battles. Inside the Portuguese camp there was a major conflict after 1702 that further complicated the situation. The *mestiço* population who upheld the authority of Portugal in the initial colonial phase was challenged by the appointed representatives of the Estado da Índia, the official colonial apparatus in Asian waters. For certain periods, the Estado-appointed governor of Lifau fought outright wars with the *mestiços* and routinely accused the Dutch in Kupang of scheming against the Portuguese positions (Matos 1974: 84-101; Hägerdal 2007: 7, 10, 14-16; Boxer 1947).

4 The crisis of 1748-1749 in written and oral history

While some of these accusations were apparently unfounded, things indeed came to a head in 1748. The ruler of Amfo'an-Sorbian, a domain in the northwestern part of Timor, had hitherto acknowledged the King of Portugal as his overlord. Now, however, he suddenly turned to the Dutch in Kupang and asked them for assistance in his planned rebellion against his old masters, referring to severe Portuguese oppression. The VOC post had long-standing orders from Batavia to avoid meddling in the troubles afflicting the Portuguese sphere. This time, however, neither Kupang nor Batavia was completely averse to a weakening of Lusitanian influence on the island (Generale missiven 1997: 652, 779). At any rate, Amfo'an-Sorbian violently attacked the core area of the *mestiços* in late 1748, which was a somewhat reckless undertaking since the *mestiços* and Lifau's governor were at relative peace at that time.

The *mestiço* leader or *tenente general*, Gaspar da Costa, reacted to the attacks with a desperate sense of brutality. He began threatening the other Atoni vassals to prevent them from joining the rebels. This policy did not work, however. The domain of Amanuban was the next to defect to the VOC. In view of this, Gaspar da Costa arrested a brother of the Greater Sonba'i emperor and some other grandees, to apparently keep them hostage. These arrests were accompanied by acts of violence whereby 120 Sonba'is were killed. The Emperor Bau (Baob), with the Christian name Dom Alfonso Salema, now took to evacuating the old homeland and fled to Kupang. He was accompanied by 2,305 armed men with wives and children in tow, comprising a total of more than 10,000 people.[14] The Amanuban and Sonba'i refugees were cheerfully

received by the Dutch and their allies in the Kupang area in the early
days of 1749.[15]

These events are mentioned in some detail in oral stories recorded
by the Timorese scholar F.H. Fobia, mainly in the 1960s. These stories
were edited down to a digest that was published in a chronicle-like
manuscript, *Sonba'i dalam kisah dan perjuangan* (1984). According to
this material, Bau or Baob Sonba'i was indeed an important ruler or
liurai of the 'kingdom' of Sonba'i (also known as Oenam) who was able
to strengthen the realm for a while. Sonba'i had not experienced any
subjugation under the Portuguese until this time. Now, however, the
Portuguese attempted to secure his person by inviting him to a meeting. Knowing the untrustworthiness of the Portuguese, Baob Sonba'i
declined to show up, and as a consequence, a war broke with the Portuguese. In the beginning, the Sonba'i troops were able to push back
the Portuguese positions to the point where they were verging on re-
treating off of Lifau and Oecusse. After bringing in reinforcements
with modern weapons, however, the enemy turned the tables on Sonba'i. The religious authority of the Catholic padres was so great that
several grandees chose to submit to the might of Portugal. Baob Sonba'i's troops eventually surrendered to the enemy. The ruler himself
fled to a place called Oeluan where he hid in a dry rice paddy with his
wives and extended family but he was captured in the end. Meanwhile,
many people fled westward because of the Portuguese attacks.

At this point, Fobia's digest proves to be somewhat muddled, perhaps as a consequence of his attempt to write down the data of several
oral spokesmen. In his version, the *liurai* was taken together with some
others to the foreign stronghold of Kupang to hold them accountable
for not having surrendered earlier. Curiously, Kupang is mentioned
here as a Portuguese place. At any rate, the informants interviewed by
Fobia agreed that Baob Sonba'i went toward Kupang, and that numerous followers had accompanied him. Along the way, he was joined by
people involving solemn ceremonies. The story about his progress does
not give the impression that he travelled to Kupang as a Portuguese
prisoner. Instead, the text asserts that he went to request that the Portuguese take responsibility for their policies, since they had forced the
population to cut sandalwood trees and to deliver beeswax and other
goods. At Fatule'u, he helped the local *amaf* to distribute land for agriculture. He stopped in other places to open up the dry rice paddies during the right time, and continued his journey only when the harvest
had been reaped.

Finally, Baob Sonba'i reached Kupang, which is, from now on, understood to be a Dutch port rather than a Portuguese one. He en-
camped at the spring of Airnona, which was also known as Oel-Feot-
nainu-pehkin, the spring where the princesses washed their hair. The

sisters of the *liurai*, Bi Sulat Sonba'i and Bi Aolasi Sonba'i, who accompanied him on his journey, are alluded to here. One of them became the ancestress of the Nisnoni family, which ruled Lesser Sonba'i from the late eighteenth century onwards.[16]

More than two centuries passed between this event and the final recording of indigenous accounts. Fragments of these events were mentioned in a few inaccessible Dutch publications, which were probably unknown to the Timorese storytellers.[17] Thus the two sources must be considered independent of each other, although substantial portions of the oral stories clearly refer to the same events as the Dutch reports. The threatening attitude of the Portuguese, and their ambition to control the princely family by force, are mentioned in both sources. The same goes for the eventual defeat of Sonba'i, the exodus of his people westward, and the eventual arrival of Bau or Baob Sonba'i to Kupang.

It is also important, however, to note the omissions and obvious factual errors in the oral accounts. First, the entire context of the war is missing; no mention is made of the role of Amfo'an-Sorbian, let alone Amanuban, in the events leading up to the clash. This is a rather typical feature of traditional Indonesian historiography in general. Dynastic histories, which followed the vicissitudes of a ruling line, were profoundly parochial in their perspective, meaning that the role of other polities in a chain of events was reduced or omitted. The actions of the other Atoni domains were quite simply dispensable, since the aim of the accounts was to point out conditions important to the understanding of the subsequent dynastic position of Sonba'i, in particular, its temporary retreat to Kupang and its approaching the Dutch.

Second, it goes without saying that Kupang was not a Portuguese port. It is also surprising that at least one version picked up by Fobia lets Baob Sonba'i be captured by the Portuguese and sent thither, while he actually fled from the Portuguese and he and his people joined the Dutch. There is confusion between different external groups that is not uncommon for Timorese traditions. The basic and important 'fact' remains that a migration from the highlands in the interior to the coastal site Kupang did indeed occur, which had important implications for subsequent Sonba'i history. The itinerary where the *liurai* moves from place to place, opens up rice paddies, etc. is also a typical Timorese historiographic device, where conditions at various locations are traced back to the historical progress of a polity.[18]

5   Forgotten showdown

The events following the arrival of the Greater Sonba'i in Kupang are among the more dramatic in the recorded history of Timor. The *mestiço*

leader Gaspar da Costa considered it essential to force the important
Sonba'i polity back to its old settlement. The rather meagre Portuguese
records from this period show their concern that the emperor had
slipped away to join his Dutch rivals. Da Costa assembled an army of
mestiços and still-loyal vassals, recruited from the entire island. According to an oral story recorded by Fobia, the decision was made at a
grand meeting of Timorese chiefs in Nunheun, the centre of the Ambeno domain south of Oecusse (Fobia 1984: 83). The Dutch estimated
the army to be between 40,000 to 50,000 men, which is probably a
gross exaggeration, but it was surely sizeable. A new emperor was appointed to lead the Sonba'is who had stayed behind in the old homeland, a certain Bastiano, who allied himself with Da Costa (Haga 1882:
393). What exactly Da Costa was up to is not altogether clear. Witnesses
later asserted that he intended to exterminate the stronghold of the 'cat
eyes', meaning the white Dutchmen, and convert them into parasol car-
riers – a symbol of subservience in the Southeast Asian context. He
would then turn against the white Portuguese in Lifau and dispose of
them as well.[19] The Portuguese documents, on the other hand, only
say that he pursued the fugitive Sonba'is. The governor of Lifau tried
to discourage him, but to no avail (Castro 1867: 208; Haga 1882: 401).

The campaign ended in an enormous disaster. When the Portuguese
army approached Kupang, the Dutch authorities managed to prevent a
panic among their Timorese allies. Da Costa's forces built stone re-
doubts at Penfui to the east of the town, but were slow to take advantage of the initial shock among the VOC side. Instead, a multi-ethnic
Dutch army consisting of 500 men – Europeans, Solorese, Rotenese,
Sawunese, mardijkers (non-whites in the VOC service) – marched out
of Kupang on 9 November 1749. They were followed at some distance
by their hesitant and fearful Timorese allies. The VOC troops steadily
attacked the stone defences and took them by storm, one after another.
The weakness of the large but non-uniform Portuguese army was immediately demonstrated, since large contingents fled the field at the beginning of the battle. Timorese warriors had no interest in extended
campaigns in distant places, let alone major pitched battles, and their
motivation to fight for the mestiço leader was apparently limited. At the
end of the day, Gaspar da Costa lay dead along with thousands of his
followers including the ill-fated Bastiano.[20]

The battle of Penfui had far-reaching consequences for the political
map of Timor. The defecting domains of Amfo'an-Sorbian, Amanuban
and Greater Sonba'i were confirmed as new VOC allies, and a number
of Atoni and Tetun domains soon followed suit and acknowledged the
Dutch. From being limited to a small area around Kupang, the Dutch
sphere soon encompassed a major part of Timor – or so it seemed.
The lands adhering to the mestiços were limited to some tiny territories

in the north of West Timor. The white governor in Lifau was careful to distance himself from the enterprise of Da Costa, and made no initial attempt to impede the Dutch expansion.

The oral Sonba'i histories say nothing at all about the battle of Penfui and its aftermath. The battle itself is mentioned in other traditions, but it seemed to have no place in the stories about Baob Sonba'i. Once again, we must consider that Penfui, however important in a Timor-wide perspective, had no direct consequence for the dynastic and geographical position of Sonba'i. They had already arrived in Kupang by that time, and remained there until some time after the battle. Once again we are reminded of the parochial outlook of the Timorese, and indeed much of Indonesian historiography.

6   The confrontation

The events of 1749 seemed to reserve a bleak future for the Portuguese on the island. Daniel van der Burgh, the resident of Kupang, was an activist who worked incessantly for the rest of his short life to minimise the Portuguese sphere of influence. The Atoni domains submitted to the VOC, but the Tetun princes of the centre and east of Timor also began to withdraw from the Estado da Índia. The ritually prestigious lord of Wewiku-Wehali approached the Dutch a couple of years after the battle of Penfui, and with him went a considerable number of local lords who acknowledged him as their symbolic leader.[21]

However, the Portuguese *mestiços* and their remaining clients displayed a perseverance not untypical of the small Lusitanian colonial settlements in Asia. Resistance against the Dutch centred on Noemuti in the highlands, which had previously been a possession of Sonba'i, but which had later been taken over by anti-Dutch elements. Moreover, the governor of Lifau and the new *mestiço* leader João Hornay got into touch with some of the rulers who had recently switched sides, and attempted to win them back (Matos 1974: 419-420). In 1751, Hornay handed a letter to a Chinese man who resided on Timor, and asked him to deliver it to the Emperor of Sonba'i in utmost secrecy, although the Dutch ultimately found out. The contents of the letter stated that the emperor and his forces would be completely crushed unless he once again became a subject of the Crown of Portugal.[22]

By Spring 1752, the VOC had plenty of indications that something was not right among their new allies. Apart from Sonba'i, there was trouble with Amarasi, a domain that had defected from the Portuguese side immediately after the battle of Penfui. Incited by João Hornay's promises of pardons if they returned to the Portuguese, the two kingdoms reportedly became allies. They planned to embark on an exodus from their present settlements close to Kupang, and along the way they were to receive muskets, bullets and gunpowder from the Portuguese governor in Lifau to further their ends. Furthermore, the plotters promised to bring along the people of Amanuban, who were also former Portuguese subjects, and if they resisted they would be cut down.

On 19 March 1752 the urgent issue was discussed in a *landvergadering* in the Dutch fort, that is, a meeting where the local VOC council and the allied princes convened. At the meeting, the emperor and most of his grandees were ordered to stand outside the venue. After due deliberation it was decided that it would be best to arrest the emperor, his son Sane, and his main sub-regents. The emperor was informed and arrested on the spot. The pro-Dutch allied rulers sent out their retainers in order to urge the Sonba'i people who had already withdrawn to return. A forceful order was issued by the VOC that the refugees were not to be violently assaulted – the tradition of headhunting in this part of Southeast Asia could otherwise lead to killings and atrocities.

In April it was reported that most of the Sonba'i people had been subdued. The various sub-regents reportedly wished for nothing more than to be brought directly under the VOC's command. Ten Sonba'i grandees then made a solemn oath before the Dutch *opperhoofd* that was based on their animist religion. As for the captive, Alfonso Salema alias Baob Sonba'i, he was sent via the next available ship to VOC headquarters in Batavia together with his eldest legitimate son Sane and six sub-regents.[23] The exiles were sent to the Island of Edam off Batavia; but, alas, their subsequent fate was never documented. Eventually a rumour had it that the Sonba'i lord had been beheaded.[24] The Sonba'is, who had formerly been under his rule, were now temporarily governed by local VOC authorities. Later they were restored to power under a younger son of the exiled ruler. Four years after this incident, the Sonba'i elite lodged complaints against the deceased resident Daniel van der Burgh, who had supposedly acted in some corrupt and despicable way. When he was imprisoned, the ruler would have handed over part of his gold treasure to Van der Burgh to regain his freedom. The resident, it was asserted, simply took the gold and then proceeded to exile the royal prisoner anyway.[25]

Later that same year, the Amarasi domain was brutally attacked by VOC forces and their native allies. In a bloody showdown, the Amarasi forces were routed and the ruler made the cruel decision to order the guards to kill him and more than a hundred women and children who remained behind in his stronghold.[26] The events of 1752 seemed to demonstrate that the VOC system of governance, successful in the immediate surroundings of Kupang for over a century, failed to secure the loyalty of the former allies of Portugal. The VOC documents complain about the ungrateful attitude of Sonba'i and Amarasi who repaid their good intentions with malicious plots. As far as can be seen from a study of the original documents, Sonba'i left the Portuguese side in 1748/49 mainly due to the individual despotic rule of the *mestiço* leader Gaspar da Costa. After his fall, the emperor and his chiefs had second thoughts about all those Portuguese symbols of authority, such as the Portuguese kingdom and Catholicism.[27] To this were added severe abuses on the part of the VOC. These abuses were emphasized four years later by a Batavian commissioner sent to Timor (Van der Chijs 1872).

The two remaining sons of the leader in exile reigned in turns, namely Don Bernardo (reign 1752-1760) and Tafin Sonba'i (reign 1760-68). The Dutch authorities kept them under close watch to prevent any further misadventures. Tafin, however, was suspected in particular of being involved in plots against the Dutch. The VOC policy of forcing contingents of their new allies to pan for gold in the highland rivers led to a lot of dissatisfaction while producing preciously little gold (Müller 1857 II: 138-139). All this led to the emergence of political networks that circumvented the control of colonial authorities. Tafin's son Kau Sonba'i (reign 1768-1819) inherited the two domains of Greater and Lesser Sonba'i. In 1782, however, he hastily fled Kupang for the highlands, reputedly because the Dutch *opperhoofd* plotted against him (Heijmering 1847: 193). The two Sonba'i domains once again went their separate ways, and a pro-Dutch side-branch of the family called Nisnoni henceforth governed the Kupang congregation. As for Greater Sonba'i it remained an important inland realm for the next century, practically independent from the Dutch colonial apparatus and sometimes waging war against the latter with impunity (Kartodirdjo et al. 1973: 429-430). Due to internal dissention the realm broke up in smaller domains by the late nineteenth century. Colonial forces captured the last titular ruler in 1906, although a surviving branch was permitted by the colonial administration to govern the Dutch-created *landschap* (territory) of Mollo from 1930 to 1959 (Doko 1981: 28-29; Fobia 1984: 100-121).

7   A posthumous perspective of the confrontation

The story of the arrest and exile of the ruler can also be told from quite another perspective. During the twentieth century an indigenous oral account was recounted at least three times. One version, by a member of the Sonba'i clan, was recorded by the missionary Piet Middelkoop in 1927, and published in 1938 along with a Dutch translation. A second version, or rather a digest of several versions, was recorded by F.H. Fobia and documented in his unpublished 1984 manuscript. A local grandee in Kauniki, the one-time residence of the Sonba'i rulers, told the third version to Australian scholar Peter Spillett in 1998.[28] The essentials of the story are similar in each case, although the three versions add and subtract various details. The storytellers cannot have been influenced by the published Dutch historiography, which barely mentions the event.[29]

The oldest version, the one recorded by Middelkoop, tells of the early migrations of the Sonba'i, who eventually arrived in Camplong in the Fatule'u region. The Portuguese are not mentioned in this context; the account seems to suggest that the Sonba'i chiefs arrived there in order to clear fields for agriculture.

A lord called Bau [Baob] Sonba'i stayed there; he stood up and went to Kupang, and stayed at Kiu Tuta [Bakunase, south of Kupang]. He searched for lands to put him on equal terms with the Company [VOC]. As he remained behind there, Bau Sonba'i begat three children, two girls and a boy named Tafin Sonba'i; the girls were named Bi Sul Sonba'i and Bi Au Lais Sonba'i.[30]

Bau Sonba'i's territory was enormous. The Company requested he come to Kupang. Then he [the VOC resident] took a blowpipe and turned it toward him, and said: 'If you are a ruler, then crawl through the blowpipe barrel, and come out the other end as Sonba'i'. Sonba'i responded: 'Good, I will crawl in there first, and then you shall follow me'. The ruler then performed his trick – I do not know how – and was turned into a snake. He crawled into the hole and came out the other end. He then gave the blowpipe back to the Company and said: 'Crawl in'. But the gentleman could not do it.

Then they made ten wax candles; the Company made them. Then they lit them at one end, and they blazed like a lamp. He was told to 'take these candles between your teeth. If you are really a ruler, then put the candle in your mouth and let it burn until it has melted completely in your mouth'. Handing over other candles to the Company gentlemen, Bau Sonba'i said: 'Then you must also do it'. Bau Sonba'i opened his mouth, and there was no candle to be seen; it had melted. He gave another one to the gentleman so that they [the VOC staff] could also burn the candles like him, but the gentleman could not do it.

Upon that he was ordered: 'If you are really a ruler, then we shall take the large iron weight and weigh you with that weight'. Bau Sonba'i hung in the scale at one end, and they put the large iron weight in the other scale. 'If you are really a ruler, you will outweigh this weight. If you are not a ruler, then the iron will outweigh you'. Well, they put him in the scale and he lifted the

iron weight, he hung in balance but then suddenly became hea-
vier and outweighed everything.

Then Sonba'i in turn said: 'Knead the earth into a ball and
weigh me with that. If I am just as heavy as this earth, then this
is my land; then I am its ruler, the earth having the same weight
as me'.

At that the Company said: 'Sonba'i has numerous lands. His
tricks overcome mine. We should exile him to another land'. He
had three children; only the father was exiled. His two daughters
remained in Kupang, and the young boy who was still quite
small, remained with his sisters. The two sisters wept and wept
and thought about their father, and their tears became a spring
at Oè Pula [close to Kupang]. They cried and cried; then water
came streaming from the ground in the middle of the house.
The main pillar still stands in the midst of the present spring.
The two sisters then gave birth to the rajas of Kupang.[31]

The account goes on to relate the fate of the later Greater Sonba'i rulers. The son of the exiled Sonba'i, Tafin Sonba'i (reigned 1760-1768 in
Dutch records) was in due time approached by the four main chiefs of
the domain. They smuggled him out of Kupang in a mat and established his residence in a place called Tèlom Talmanu, although they
did not break completely with the Dutch in Kupang who still received
tribute in kind. Tafin Sonba'i's son in turn, Ais Le'u (that is, Kau Sonba'i, 1768-1819), moved further into the interior highlands upon the in-
stigation of the two principal lords, Kono and Oematan (Middelkoop
1938: 442-443). The story is followed to comparatively modern times,
when the power of the Dutch is being felt; the last royal prince mentioned by the account passes away in Dutch-dominated Kupang.

8   Differing perspectives

There is a basic similarity between the colonial and indigenous versions of the story. The Sonba'i ruler Baob Sonba'i arrives in Kupang
after being attacked by the Portuguese in his homeland. He is given a
place to stay in the vicinity, but after a while, a non-warlike confrontation occurs with the Company. The ruler is apprehended by the ner-
vous Dutch and exiled to Batavia. The Dutch resident himself is depicted as a mean and dishonest type. The son of Baob remains behind
in Kupang; he later succeeds to his father's royal prerogatives and continues the line of the Sonba'is.

What is most apparent here, however, are the differences in the versions. That Sonba'i was plotting against the Company is at the most va-

guely alluded to in the Middelkoop version ('he searched for lands to put him on equal terms with the Company'). Nor does tradition mention the Portuguese effort to secure the renewed allegiance of Sonba'i, or the collusion with Amarasi.[32] The VOC records, of course, do not mention anything about a personal contest between the ruler and the resident, let alone any supernatural properties attributed to Sonba'i. Finally, the dynastic situation has been very much simplified in the latter version; it omits all of the ruler's sons except Tafin who perpetuated the dynastic line and, furthermore, erroneously presents Tafin as a minor at the time his father was exiled.[33]

For our purposes, these similarities and differences are only part of the picture. We must also inquire about how the indigenous account was constructed, against a background of the values of prestige and governance that are epitomised in the figure of Baob Sonba'i. The image of a Dutch-Timorese contest, which establishes Baob Sonba'i's magical powers, is historically implausible but this does not detract from its interest as a historiographic construct; on the contrary, its inclusion demands a contextualisation of the process of history-telling in the Timorese world view.

In the traditional system, the position of an individual Timorese was basically determined at birth. Although there was no literal noble class, the *amaf*, *usif*, *liurai*, etc., all maintained their positions based on heredity, and established a political system with a relatively limited degree of social mobility or input from the outside. The system was accentuated by a large number of ritualistic opposites, often in terms of 'male' versus 'female' components. According to H.G. Schulte Nordholt, the West Timorese Atoni society 'can best be characterized as a political system which is based on ritual relationships which are laid down in rites and myths, consolidated by a network of affinal relationships, maintained by a system of tribute consisting of agricultural products, and both strengthened and weakened by repeated, almost regularly recurring wars' (Schulte Nordholt 1971: 403). In this society, the Liurai-Sonba'i were at the ritual apex, and were associated with great supernatural forces. Even storytellers who were hostile to Sonba'i did not question his centrality.

Then, what happens when this ritually significant figure is confronted with an external force, which does not share the Timorese culture? Several instances indicate that the Timorese tended to incorporate these external entities into their own myths and origin stories. In Timor Leste, the Mambai people have incorporated the Portuguese colonisers into their mythical genealogy, which represents the latter as returning Mambai relatives (Traube 1986: 52-54). Similarly, the *mestiço* leaders of Oecusse are included in legends that fix the relationship between the *mestiços* and the local Timorese to particular (but unhistorical) events upon the arrival of the first Portuguese ships on the island (Müller 1857 II: 189; Fobia n.d.).

In the same way, the confrontation between Baob and the Company is the first Sonba'i-Dutch meeting mentioned in these oral stories.[34] In a way, it determines the future relationship between the two realms, which will always be marred by suspicions and incidents. The account does not question the Company's might, however. It was all too clear for the twentieth-century storytellers that the small Timorese prince-doms had no chance to defeat the colonial forces. None of the versions suggest that the arrest and exile of the *liurai* took place after an armed clash; like in the contemporary VOC records, the Sonba'i subjects of the VOC in the oral story are understood to have silently acknowledged the deed without a show of resistance.

As for the contest itself, it consisted of three parts: the crawling through a blowpipe, the wax candle in the mouth, and the weighing. This is found in both the Middelkoop and Fobia versions; Spillett omits the wax candle but adds two other parts (making trees change place, walking on a string). This threefold contest is significant, since it touches three important aspects of princely power. By changing into a snake and crawling through the hole of the blowpipe, the *liurai* were referring to the totemist aspects of the dynasty. Princely lines on Timor were often associated with particular animals in the origin myths. In the case of Sonba'i, he is portrayed as a python.

The second part, the burning of the wax candle in the mouth, al-ludes to the beeswax and honey that was collected in the local prince-doms and delivered to the Dutch and Portuguese along the coast. While the sandalwood trade had its ups and downs, the frequent occur-rence of bee swarms in the woods made these two items, and particu-larly beeswax, important export products (Ormeling 1956: 115-116). Tri-butes handed over to the colonial masters often consisted largely of beeswax, which made the collection of the wax a princely concern. This is made more explicit in Fobia's version, which has the Dutch com-mander saying: 'If you are the king of all the honey and beeswax pro-duction on the Island of Timor, then try to put the burning end of the wax candle that I lit in your mouth. If you are the ruler, then surely the wax candle will burn down but your mouth will not be burnt by the flame.'[35]

The third part of the contest involves the scales and refers to the san-dalwood. The valuable wood used to be brought down to the coast by the subjects of the various Timorese princes, and was there weighed by the Europeans or *mestiços* on a large scale. The high prices for sandal-wood in India and South China made it a strategically vital product, which was actually a prime reason why the Europeans colonised Timor (Ormeling 1956: 94-103). Again, this is more clear-cut in the Fobia ver-

sion, where the contest is preceded by a conversation. The Dutch commander asked: 'If I wish to fetch sandalwood, honey and beeswax, to
whom shall I make the request?' The *liurai* answered: 'You must seek
approval from me, since I rule the Island of Timor.' The Dutchman
then challenged the *liurai* to weigh more than the assembled sandalwood on the other end of the large scale, which he easily did.[36]

In this way, the three-part contest represents a discourse of kingship,
where the Dutch are each time subdued in terms of ritual/supernatural
prestige/power. The turning point in the Middelkoop version is when
the ruler threatens to prove his rights to the land by being of equal
weight as a ball made of earth. No longer daring to challenge him directly, the Company resolves to get rid of the dangerous prince by 'un-
just' means. A reformulation of this basically historical event proves,
one may say, the existence of the various levels of power the two protagonists have: the indigenous ritual and the external executive. An interesting view of colonialism emerges, where the white foreigners are portrayed as somewhat ridiculous and despicable, although, at the same
time they are shown to be superior arbiters of physical power.

It is almost unfeasible to accurately reconstruct Timor's historical
events up to the nineteenth century from oral materials. A comparison
between various versions and with European documentary records demonstrates the difficulties of such an undertaking.[37] However, a careful
comparison between various categories of materials may enrich our
understanding of how history is made and remade by posterity. Historical consciousness is closely tied to the emotional and ideological features in a given society, and the purported continuity of history will legitimate the institutions of such a society (Karlsson 1999). In spite of
widely differing significations of 'history', this is likely to also apply to
materially advanced literate societies, as well as low-technologically illiterate societies. In our case, the exile of the *liurai* was a calamitous
event from the perspective of subsequent generations; still, the *liurai*
himself was never seriously criticised. Posterity needed to see the event
in terms of ritualistic relations and transcendental power rather than
Realpolitik. A man considered by the colonialists to be a despicable trai-
tor was seen by the Timorese as an upright figure of superior supernatural skills, who could only be vanquished by evil forces. The historiographical tables had been turned.

Notes

1   Research for the present study was made possible with funding from the Swedish
     Research Council (Vetenskapsrådet), and an affiliated fellowship at the International
     Institute for Asian Studies (IIAS), Leiden.

2   Vansina 1961. One should note that Vansina later significantly reassessed his views on oral traditions; a comparison with his more recent work *Oral Tradition as History* (1985) is illustrative.

3   The problem of the transmission of oral materials is highlighted by the academic controversy surrounding the Islamic *hadith*, which are often seen by Western scholars as highly unreliable sources of the Prophet's words and deeds, while scholars in Muslim countries tend to emphasise the faithfulness of the transmission of religiously significant stories. Within Scandinavian studies, the use of thirteenth- and fourteenth-century saga literature for the reconstruction of the history of the Viking Age (c. 790-1066) has been increasingly discarded (cf. Christiansen 2006: 238-240, 301-314).

4   The story of the early colonial partition of Timor is presented in great detail in De Roever 2002.

5   The principal work on the political system of West Timor is Schulte Nordholt 1971. See also McWilliam 2002; Parera 1994. For Timor Leste, some materials on traditional politics are found in Ospina & Hohe 2002.

6   Castro 1867: 457-458, mentions 49 *reinos* ('kingdoms') in the Portuguese sphere.

7   Schulte Nordholt 1971: 262-306, discusses the significance of Sonba'i in Timorese legends and society.

8   The methodological problems of using oral tradition are discussed in Finnegan 1996: 126-134.

9   A brief but classical study of the Topasses is found in Boxer 1947.

10 See briefly Hägerdal 2007: 18.

11 The term *usif*, often loosely translated as prince, is used in a variety of contexts. Sometimes the central ruler himself was known as an *usif*. There are also examples of royal consorts who held this title.

12 VOC 1252, f. 679, 1211, in NA, 1.04.02; Matos 1974: 251.

13 Later traditions suggest that two other grandee families, Taiboko-Ebenoni, held regent positions under Kono-Oematan, so that the structurally important quadrupartition of the realm was achieved (2 + 2); see Fobia 1984: 87. The *fettor* (regent) Ebenoni was the assistant of the Greater Sonba'i ruler in 1798; see letter from Alphonsus Adrianus (alias Kau Sonba'i) and Fettor Ebenoni to the Dutch authorities, in LOr 2238.

14 ANRI Timor: 36.

15 VOC 2741, f. 143, 167. A letter from the five traditional VOC allies to Batavia (VOC 2741, f. 163-8, received 1 Oct. 1749) refers to the Sonba'i ruler as Nabi Bahoe. A later list of subservient Timorese rulers from September 1751 calls him Bau Leu Tomenu (VOC 2780, f. 128). He seems to have been the son of Dom Pedro Sonba'i alias Tomenu, mentioned as the Greater Sonba'i ruler in 1704-1726, and a brother of the Lesser Sonba'i rulers Bernardus Leu (1717-1726), Corneo Leu (1728-1748) and Daniel Taffij Leu (1748-1760). It is, at any rate, certain that there were close dynastic ties between the two Sonba'i domains, where Greater Sonba'i princes were sent to the Dutch enclave to be enthroned as VOC-allied rajas without the Portuguese being able or willing to prevent it. In that sense, the ground was prepared for the coming of the Greater Sonba'i.

16 Fobia 1984: 75-78. Weidner 1932 quotes a similar tradition: that Baob Sonba'i fled to Kupang Kuatae due to an issue (*perkara*) with the Portuguese. The meaning of *Kuatae* is not known to the present writer; it is possibly related to *Kotae*, the name of the princely residence of the Lesser Sonba'i group in Bakunase, close to Kupang.

17 Heijmering 1847 and Roo van Alderwerelt 1904 briefly relate these events, although in rather cryptic terms. It seems highly unlikely that the illiterate *adat* experts of the interior were aware of this historiography.

18   Such 'topogeny' – the recitation of an ordered sequence of place names – occurs fre-
      quently in Austronesian societies; an anthropological discussion of the phenomenon
      is found in Fox 1997: 8-15.

19   VOC 2941, f. 113-4. These witnesses, who included five princes and three Portuguese,
      asserted that Da Costa's army consisted of more than 20,000 men. This is still a re-
      markably high number, since the population of the entire island, judging from later
      censuses, was no more than approximately half a million people, and probably sub-
      stantially less.

20   The Dutch report on the battle of Penfui has been printed in Haga 1882: 390-402.
      See also Boxer 1947: 14-15.

21   VOC 2763, f. 594; VOC 2799, f. 99-100; VOC 2941, f. 61.

22   VOC 2780, f. 108.

23   VOC 2799, f. 11-28.

24   VOC 3779, f. 5707. The rumour is mentioned by the Portuguese governor on Timor
      in a letter to the Dutch authorities in Kupang, on 25 February 1787.

25   VOC 2941, f. 644. The Sonba'i elite requested the VOC commissioner J.A. Paravicini
      to hand back the gold, estimated value 5,000 Rijksdaalders. The request, however,
      was turned down.

26   VOC 2799, f. 87.

27   His Portuguese name, Dom Alfonso Salema, indicates that he was at least nominally
      a Catholic. Whatever his personal piety, Portuguese symbols were quite important for
      the Timorese elites until fairly recent times.

28   Middelkoop 1938: 441-442; Fobia 1984: 78-81; Spillett 1999: 85-86. Finnegan (1996:
      129) has emphasised the need to consider how formalised the recorded accounts
      might be; there were non-literate kingdoms in Africa where rulers kept close control
      over centralised and authoritative versions of the past. The three versions discussed
      here were recorded long after the demise of Sonba'i, but nevertheless appear to ren-
      der a central tradition. The informers used by Middelkoop and Spillett were close to
      the Sonba'i dynasty. The same goes for some informers of Fobia, himself the son of
      the *mafefa* of the raja Tua Sonba'i of Mollo (d. 1959).

29   Roo van Alderwerelt 1904: 199 very briefly mentioned that the ruler of Amakono
      (i.e., Greater Sonba'i) was exiled with his son and some grandees in 1752, however
      with no further details.

30   Thus, similar to the two ladies Bi Sulat Sonba'i and Bi Aolasi Sonba'i, who are men-
      tioned by F.H. Fobia as sisters of the *liurai*. A third version that deals with the iden-
      tity of Bi Sulat and Bi Aolasi can be found in Heijmering 1847: 38, 44, where they
      are mentioned as sisters of Nai Utang (alias Baki Nisnoni), the Sonba'i prince who al-
      legedly fled to Kupang and founded the Lesser Sonba'i princedom, thus in the seven-
      teenth century. They evidently enjoyed an important dynastic role since their names
      are included in an alternative appellation for the Lesser Sonba'i people: *Bi Sulat'm Bi
      Aobeis, Soes Lasi'm Bi Patbesi* (Parera 1969: 48). All the variants illustrate the hazards
      of reconstructing a concrete historical sequence from the oral materials.

31   Middelkoop 1938: 441-442. My translation via the Dutch; the punctuation has been
      modified. The Fobia version adds that Baob Sonba'i was sent to Batavia, and that he
      was accompanied in exile by his brother-in-law Ta'eko Mella and his retainer Aba
      Tnone. The Spillett version does not explicitly say that the ruler was exiled.

32   The violent end of the Amarasi ruler in 1752, on the other hand, is mentioned in the
      historical traditions of this princedom, as published by Middelkoop 1939: 77-79. Con-
      versely, the Amarasi tradition does not mention the role of Sonba'i.

33   In Fobia's version, Baob is succeeded by a son called Sobe Kase (later, the father of
      Tafin) who stays in Kupang and adopts European fashions, hence his name (*Sobe
      Kase*, foreign hat). Alternative genealogies recorded by Middelkoop (1938: 509) and

Weidner (1932) omit Tafin altogether, and make Kau the son rather than grandson of Baob. In spite of all these variations, one must admit that the Timorese storytellers have been able to preserve a roughly correct princely pedigree going back hundreds of years. For the methodological problems of using oral genealogies as historical sources, see Finnegan 1996: 130-131.

34 There is not one reference in the extant traditions to the earlier contacts recorded by the Dutch and Portuguese sources: the concluding of a VOC-Sonba'i contract in 1655, the flight of a Sonba'i ruler to Kupang in 1711-1713, etc.

35 Fobia 1984: 79. In this version, the *liurai* tricks the Dutch by keeping betel in his mouth, so that the flame does not burn the inside of his mouth.

36 Fobia 1984: 78-79. The idea that the Sonba'i lord governed the entire island is, of course, a great hyperbole even in terms of traditional Timorese hierarchy, though he was indeed the most prestigious ruler among the Timorese proper, i.e., the Atoni population.

37 Yeager and Jacobson (2002) endeavour to trace the history of the various West Timorese domains from mainly oral materials. In spite of the many merits of the book, its problems are obvious.

Africans in Asia: The Discourse of 'Negritos' in Early Nineteenth-century Southeast Asia

Sandra Khor Manickam

Introduction

After having spent nearly ten years in Southeast Asia, John Crawfurd wrote in 1820 of 'so unusual a phenomenon' that there were two indigenous races in Southeast Asia,[1] the 'brown' thought to be the original race of the region, and the 'negro' who was assumed to be indigenous only to the African continent. The other labels he used in reference to African or African-like people in the region were 'dwarf African negro', 'woolly haired race' or 'Papua' (18-23). Earlier in 1817, Stamford Raffles spoke of a 'race of blacks entirely distinct from the rest of the population' found in the mountain regions of the Malay Archipelago and who formed the majority of people in the island of New Guinea. He did not label this group of people 'Negrito', which would have called attention to their small stature. He did, however, highlight the 'black' colour of their skin and the 'woolly' texture of their hair (ccxxxv). Both authors were building on previous speculation by European travellers on the subject. The terms 'Negrito' or 'Negrillo' were first applied by Spanish missionaries who came to the Philippines to apparently small(er) statured and dark(er) peoples on those islands in the seventeenth century (Leyden 1811: 218; Blair and Robertson 1973: vol. 38, 27). These terms were copied and used by other European travellers and colonial officers in Southeast Asia to label various peoples considered to be small(er) and dark(er) compared to other people thought to be more widespread on the islands of Southeast Asia such as the Malays.

Locating Africans both literally (in terms of Negritos[2] being seen as remnants of prehistoric or more recent migrants from Africa) and figuratively (in being compared to Africans though not necessarily identified as African) in Southeast Asia was propped up using the 'hard science' of racial typecasting and migration theories. Physical attributes given to so-called Negritos by Europeans formed the basis for the assumptions about connections to Africans. The authors above listed the ways in which both groups 'looked the same' with their similar skin tones, hair types and bodily proportions. Migration theories posited a few scenarios, such as Negritos being the descendants of slaves whose ship was wrecked somewhere in Southeast Asia, or Negritos as the first

wave of peoples populating Southeast Asia from Africa during a prehistoric time (Crawfurd 1820: 27-30; Raffles 1817: ccxxv). However, other
migration theories were formulated to explain the simplistic notion
that those who looked 'African' were incongruously found in Asia.

There are several problems with these underlying tenets of the Negrito label. Purporting that someone looks like another makes the act
of looking as objective, monolithic and comparable from one person to
the next. It places the act of looking outside of cultural influences and
changes across time and space. Listing the ways in which people are similar to other people by virtue of physical attributes camouflages the
cultural and scientific meaning of those attributes in the eyes of the ob-
server. These were not the only elements that supported the Africanness of certain people in Southeast Asia. British authors saw similarities between the degraded states of both groups of people in the general scheme of races. This pervasive attitude influenced how Negritos
were portrayed in texts and images in the early nineteenth century. Visual technologies, such as engravings and drawings with text, were
used to naturalise character similarities already perceived between Negritos and Africans.

This article questions the very notion of Negrito as a category and investigates the ways in which the term was problematically used and
perpetuated in the context of an emerging field of anthropological
study following closely at the heels of, or growing concurrently with,
British colonial expansion in parts of Southeast Asia. Instead of describing these scholars' actions as 'identifying' Negritos, they were instead actively constructing the category and fitting various peoples into
it. A person was only classified Negrito when he was compared to another type, either similar to stereotypes of Africans, for instance, or dis-
similar from stereotypes of a more widespread group on the islands of
Southeast Asia, namely, the catch-all 'Malay' racial group. The encapsu-
lation of various groups under a single heading was a scientific endeavour, one that entailed describing people through words and images.
As noted by Peter Hanns Reill in reference to another early subject of
natural history, plants,

> the illustrator has to use conventions of representation and in
> doing so, no matter what the medium, enter into a world that
> encompasses far more than the desire to render as faithfully as
> possible a true, 'objective', view ... (Reill 1996: 293-304).

These modes of representation, as applied to Negritos, are examined as
they appeared in the primary writings of Raffles (1781-1826) and Crawfurd (1783-1868), two well-known British administrators and authors of
books on the Malay Archipelago. Raffles' *A History of Java*, published

in 1817, and Crawfurd's *History of the Indian Archipelago, containing an account of the manners, arts, languages, religions, institutions, and commerce of its inhabitants* published in 1820 are of particular interest here. Besides writing on people later called Negrito and being early proponents of categorising some people in the Archipelago under a similar heading, they also present the reader with early instances of drawings of Negritos. The combination of the text and drawings brings to the fore the stereotypes surrounding Negritos and illustrates how they were aligned with Africans.

Early studies on Negritos could come under the heading of colonial anthropology or merely European anthropology depending on the emphasis put on colonial endeavours during this time. Together, the two authors served in the British administrations of Penang, Melaka and Batavia in the period before writing their books. Extrapolating from these circumstances, these authors' writings could be approached from the perspective of colonial knowledge based on colonial conditions in Southeast Asia. Yet, if knowledge can never be separated from the conditions of its making, colonial anthropology is repetitive, since colonial relations characterised much of European anthropology in the region. As Talal Asad writes, while anthropology did not necessarily push forth colonialism in a remarkable way, colonialism was an important, if not the determining, mindset of the anthropologist at this time (1991: 315). Furthermore, though colonial inroads were just being formed in the region, the contact between Europeans and Africans had been taking place for hundreds of years and an unequal relationship was consolidated in the fifteenth century with the subjugation of Africans in the trans-Atlantic slave trade (Curtin 1964: 30). This relationship between Europeans and Africans is central to this study of Negritos in Southeast Asia due to the parallels drawn by these authors between Negritos and Africans.

John Crawfurd and Stamford Raffles as early anthropologists

The works of Crawfurd and Raffles have been positioned under many fields of study, history and the literature of Southeast Asia being the most common two. Not many, however, would consider them relevant to the field of anthropology or see them as anthropologists, though their work clearly comes under the rubric of early anthropological data gathering and theorising on the region.[3] In the early nineteenth century, the study of anthropology relied heavily on travel accounts and reports from overseas as information for their studies. It also utilised the study of language and investigated the relationship between languages to determine connections between groups of people and their civilisational status. Raffles and Crawfurd stayed and travelled extensively in the Malay Archipelago, placing them outside the category of 'armchair anthropologists', those Europeans who wrote about peoples and places far away from Europe without ever having left their chairs. However, these authors do have some of the stereotypical characteristics of that group, because, although they reported on their personal experiences of meeting various people, they often repeated reports from other travellers especially when it came to a theorisation of Negritos who were in general difficult to meet because they lived in inaccessible areas or in locations beyond the sphere of influence of the European powers (Stocking 1987: 50).

The analysis of the representations of Negritos will start with Crawfurd's *History of the Indian Archipelago*. Crawfurd was one of the early scholars of Southeast Asia who, along with Raffles, produced works on the region still utilised by scholars today. His *History of the Indian Archipelago*, as the Malay Archipelago or the island portion of Southeast Asia was then called, is an ambitious work written in three volumes. Contained therein are accounts on the 'manners, arts, languages, religions, institutions, and commerce of its inhabitants', as well as maps and engravings of scenes and people in the region. It was based on nine years' experience in the Archipelago, as the advertisement assured the reader, from the time he was appointed as medical staff member in Penang in 1808, to his stay in Java from 1811 until it was returned to the Dutch. The testimony on his background was important to readers of the time as a way of determining the veracity of his account. His own experiences were supplemented with, and compared to, anthropological knowledge from other individual authors. This emphasis on the personal account was one of the ways in which claims may be supported or refuted; based on the type of description offered, whether 'accurate' and 'interesting' or 'vague and general', and the reputation of the author, further inferences can be made by the anthropologist who otherwise was not present and could not speak from 'experience' (Crawfurd 1820: advertisement, v, vi, 25-7; Crawfurd 1856: v).

There are features of a text of this sort that were expected of the writings of British authors in the tropics. C.A. Bayly notes a 'sharpening of racial attitudes' in general among Britons of the eighteenth and nineteenth centuries, and indeed, racial attitudes abounded in Crawfurd's book (1989: 147). Stating judgements on culture and civilisation in terms of 'inferior' and 'superior', assuming hierarchies among peoples and civilisations and within the region were features of Crawfurd's work. These judgements, however, influenced how Crawfurd thought about the development of peoples in the region. The topographical differences from one place to another and the varied species of animals and vegetation all had an impact on the type of people and civilisation perceived in the archipelago. Thus, well before Alfred Russel Wallace's book, *The Malay Archipelago*, was published in 1869, Crawfurd divided the region into five 'natural and well-grounded divisions or classes' making the generalisation that the level of civilisation of the people there decreased from West to East, in conjunction with the change in geographical features and food production of those countries. While he found this to be true in general, he noted the presence of inferior Negrito races in the western portion of the archipelago, although they were usually more commonly found in the east (1, 3, 6-16).[4]

Crawfurd's writing on Negritos was based in part on material already presented by Raffles in his *A History of Java*. Crawfurd, in fact, had served under Raffles and was well acquainted with his work, though he had a low opinion of the book (Raffles 1817: xviii; Smithies 1983: 366). Raffles' earlier discussion on a 'race of blacks' relied on his encounter with an individual from New Guinea. While discussing the background of slave-raiding practices in the archipelago, he recounted how a young boy named Dick came to be in his service after having been kidnapped from New Guinea and brought to Bali. Dick was considered to be an 'Oriental Negro' and was brought to England and examined by the medical officer Sir Everard Home, where Dick was compared to an African.[5] That Dick should and could be compared to someone from Africa seemed natural. Earlier in the passage, Raffles had already mentioned the theories regarding Oriental Negros. He posited that they were either migrants from Africa or indigenous to the area, theories reproduced in Crawfurd's *History* (Smithies 1983: 366). Dick was compared on the basis of the colour of his skin, his type of hair, the angle of his forehead, the shape of his lips and his buttocks among other things. Based on Home's initial examination, he reported that the boy, and Papuans in general, were different from 'the African negro', thereby shifting the analysis from an individual specimen to the general type. This examination was also reproduced in Crawfurd's *History* but applied to a discussion on 'dwarf African negroes'. Crawfurd then added that only 'in [a] mere exterior stamp that the puny Negro of the Indian islands bears any resemblance to the African' (Raffles 1817: 23-24; Crawfurd 1820: 24).

If the only physical examination made by Home did not support the comparison between Dick and Africans, and this was reaffirmed by both Raffles and Crawfurd, how was such a link maintained and reinforced with the on-going labelling of some groups as 'Oriental Negros'/ 'race of blacks' by Raffles and 'dwarf African negros' by Crawfurd? The physical examination was but one pillar that supported the façade of those labels. The inclusion of certain groups in an African-like race went beyond how similar they supposedly looked to Africans. Instead, the reader was led by the authors to see similarities based on the

authors' presentation of the groups as being primitive. As mentioned
by Jan Nederveen Pieterse in reference to the science of race, 'beyond
their grounding in biology or skin colour, is a pathos of inequality'
(Pieterse 1992: 51). The connections between impressions of Africans
and African-like people seen in Southeast Asia by Europeans were
fraught with assumptions concerning the hierarchy of and relationship
between races. Raffles and Crawfurd painted impressions of certain
groups as Negrito in a number of different ways, but three main associations will be analysed: Negritos as slaves, Negritos as Africans, and
Negritos as exotic miniature people.

Seeing Negritos as slaves

Slavery as practiced in Southeast Asia was different from slavery as it
was practiced in the trans-Atlantic slave trade from the fifteenth to the
nineteenth centuries. Resulting from the huge volume of the latter
trade and its particular practices, slavery now is understood to mean
chattel slavery whereby a slave is property that can be owned, sold or
purchased wholly by a master (Pieterse 1992: 52-53). In Southeast Asia,
the terms slave and slavery used by Europeans to describe the various
forms of servitude they encountered may encompass such a definition
but not necessarily.[6] There were other forms of institutionalised servitude that did not consider slaves property. Slaves sometimes retained
certain rights and could even purchase their freedom after a certain
period of time, depending on the societies in which they were found.
As such, some scholars have preferred the term debt-servitude/debt-
slavery/debt-bondage rather than, or in addition to, slavery (Endicott
1983: 216; Valentijn 1994: 82).

Slavery was made into a visible issue for Raffles during his time as
Lieutenant Governor of Java. In 1807, the slave trade was outlawed under English law, but it was only in 1811 that this was understood to apply to Asia as well (Wright 1960: 185). Raffles arrived in Java in 1811
during the British invasion of the island. He held his post until 1815,
when Java was returned to the Netherlands based on agreements made
as a result of the Napoleonic Wars. In 1817, the *History of Java* was published with accompanying illustrations. In it, he frequently alluded to
the ills of slavery and to his successful attempts at eradicating forms of
slavery. However, H.R.C. Wright points out that Raffles' commotion
over slavery was lip service paid to his and, in general, the British administration in the archipelago. It was an attempt to draw attention to
the shortcomings of foreign and native people who were involved in
the slave trade, in particular the Dutch, for not doing enough to stamp
out slavery, and Arabs and Chinese for continuing the practise. Slavery

was a pawn in the public relations campaign in which the British were poised as the responsible caretaker of the region to those in the British Isles who were against slavery. Wright further argues, however, that this did not have much impact on the way the British and Raffles were viewed by people back home or the locals (Wright 1960: 185). Nevertheless, the ways in which slavery was discussed, and the descriptions of people who were enslaved, tell us much about the act of classifying people as 'a race of blacks' and subsequently 'dwarf African negros'.

Raffles was aware of the connotations of 'slave' and 'slavery' and the feelings that these words would evoke in a British parliament and public that had in the late eighteenth century begun to outlaw slavery in its possessions. In the lead, until the British invasion of Java, Raffles compared the Dutch government in Java to those European countries who sold people in their possessions in West Africa to the Americas (Wright 1960: 184). He used the term slavery despite evidence that he understood that conditions in Java may have been different from conditions of the West Africans in the Americas.[7] Using 'slavery' in *History of Java* could also be seen as strategic on the part of Raffles. He wanted to draw comparisons between the trans-Atlantic slave trade of Africans to the Americas, and what he depicted as a similar trade transpiring in Southeast Asia, and, further, to highlight his role in abolishing slavery.

According to Raffles and other sources, those who were brought into servitude consisted of a variety of different people. François Valentijn (1666-1727), who was in the Spice Islands while the Dutch East Indies Company were in ascendancy in the archipelago, wrote about the slave trade and the conditions of people under debt-servitude in Bali. He also provided an engraving of a Balinese slave woman and mentioned Makassar slaves in his account (78-88). Owen Rutter, publishing in 1930 but referring to the mid-nineteenth century, highlighted a slave trade on the island Nias off Sumatra, slavery in Borneo and Sarangani off Mindanao. Papuan (or Papua, according to Raffles), Spanish and Filipino slaves were apparently commonplace (49). Raffles mentioned that 'the pagan tribes in the vicinity of the Mahometans, such as those on Bali and some of the tribes of Celebes, the Harafuras, the black Papuas or oriental negros, the original inhabitants of Halamahira, Goram, and other easterly nations' were often kidnapped and turned into slaves (1817: 234). Despite the scepticism that should accompany these accounts of rampant enslavement based on the aforementioned reasons, we can deduce that forms of servitude, whether a trade in chattel slaves or societies producing debt-bonded people, formed parts of many different societies in Southeast Asia at this time such that there may not have been one single group of people targeted and known as slaves per se.

Despite this, one group was more closely linked to slavery by Raffles, a group he considered to be 'black'. The few places Raffles discussed

'black Papuas or oriental negros' were in tandem with slavery. Oriental
Negroes were often victims of slave raiding by Arab, Bugis and Chinese
traders. In his one personification of Papuans, in retelling the story of
Dick and the examination he underwent, Raffles presented him in the
context of his enslavement and emancipation. David Smithies hypothe-
sises that Raffles may have purchased Dick in a slave market in Bali,
which was how Dick came into the service of Raffles (1960: 366). In
Raffles' stereotyping of Oriental Negroes as slaves, he associated slavery
with perceived blackness, as many Europeans before him had done.
Pieterse and Curtin write that the association of the curse of Canaan
with slavery and eventually black skin colour became commonplace in
the seventeenth century and was used up until the nineteenth century
as a justification for slavery (Curtin 1964: 30; Pieterse 1992: 44). In
Raffles' attempts to portray the depravity of slavery and to argue for
emancipation, he saw blackness in the Papuans and thereby reinforced
and transferred the associations of blackness and slavery in European
literature to Southeast Asians whom he saw as 'black'.[8] The association
between Papuans and enslavement in Southeast Asia was parallel to
the association between Africans and the well-known Atlantic slave
trade. Both groups were enslaved and both groups were stereotypically
regarded as being less than human: the former group due to European
racial theories surrounding the inferiority of 'blackness' and people
coming from Africa which supported practices of slavery, while the latter due to practices of slavery within the archipelago.

Crawfurd repeated this connection made by Raffles between Papuans and slavery and blackness. Crawfurd further provided a context
for new information subsequently collected on them. The association
between Oriental Negros and slavery was left intact and supported with
new evidence. He cited subjects brought from the mountains of Kedah
and from New Guinea whom he had seen as slaves and whom he said
were Negritos, adding yet another aspect to this grouping, that of their
diminutive stature. Though he did not explicitly make enslavement a
determining feature of this group, he was sweeping in his assumptions
of the relationship between the 'fairer', lank-haired or brown-complex-
ioned race and the Papua woolly-haired, dwarf African Negro race. He
said that 'whenever the lank and the woolly-haired races meet, there is
a marked and wonderful inferiority in the latter.' Furthermore, 'whenever negritos are encountered by the fairer races, they are hunted down
like the wild animals of the forest, and driven to the mountains or fast-
nesses incapable of resistance' suggesting that Negritos were frequently
brought into a condition of servitude by 'brown' races due to their inherent inferiority (Crawfurd 1820: 25-26). His confidence in stating
such a relationship draws from his observation of this truism in the
Western world as well.

The brown and negro races of the Archipelago may be considered to present in their physical and moral character a complete parallel with the white and negro races of the western world. The first have always displayed as eminent a relative superiority over the second as the race of white men have done over the negroes of the west (Crawfurd 1820: 18).

In a much later article by Crawfurd entitled 'On the Physical and Mental Characteristics of the Negro', he reiterated that Africans had always been considered slaves by the Egyptians, Jews, Arabs and Persians (Crawfurd 1866: 212-239). Thus, while Raffles alluded to the relationship between Asiatic blacks and servitude, Crawfurd brought the connection into sharper relief and made it into a stereotypical role of 'negros' in general, and Asian Negritos in particular.

This discussion has focused on the ways in which Raffles and Crawfurd saw slaves in Southeast Asia. To Raffles, slaves were an important point in his tenure as administrator in Java. He attempted to show that slavery was inherent in Southeast Asian societies and that it was encouraged by the former Dutch colonists. He presented himself as the saviour of the slaves whom he said were numerous and encompassed several groups including Papuans. However, of all the groups known to have been enslaved the only group that was represented pictorially and personified in the form of a personal encounter was Dick, the Papuan. In the course of the book, this special attention paid to Dick tied him inextricably to slavery and Raffles' civilising mission. Crawfurd continued to write in this line of thought. He linked Oriental Negroes and the condition of being enslaved even closer together and at the same time introduced comparisons from the West between the white races of Europe and the black races of Africa. Whereas in Raffles' book, the report of the physical examination by Home refuted any links to Africa and Africans, Crawfurd reinforced these links in a variety of ways. The parallels between the black races of Africa and of Southeast Asia in their perceived inferiority to, and enslavement by, white and brown races, were meant to highlight the Africanness of the Asiatic Negroes. The construction of the Negrito revolved around the perception of blackness, which was related to Africans, which was then linked to slavery. In the next section, I will discuss how blackness and Africanness were shown to exist among the Oriental Negros.

Portraying Negritos as African

Depictions of Africans in European travel and exploratory literature abound. Africa had been known to Europeans for hundreds of years

and the depiction of Africans throughout history is by no means uniform. David Brion Davis writes that the association between black skin
colour and demeaning characteristics was present in Arab literature in
the eighth and ninth centuries. This viewpoint was subsequently also
professed by European Christians (1984: 42). Gustav Jahoda argues
that while Africans were not portrayed negatively in pre-medieval literature, a change came during the thirteenth through the fifteenth centuries due to the animosity between Christians and Muslims (1999: 28).
However, these associations emerged and spread prior to the eighteenth and nineteenth centuries, with the advent of scientific studies on
the origins of humans, on the demarcations between apes and humans, and on the origins and nature of particular races, particular
tropes about Africans emerged. In the early nineteenth century, stereotypes of Africans as savages, child-like or sub-human or ape were commonplace in scientific and travel literature. The facial angle, used initially as an aesthetic device but later as a marker of racial difference, was
one way of rationalising the perceived differences between Europeans,
Africans and other people. The impact of this theory can be seen from
the depictions of Africans during the eighteenth through twentieth
centuries (Smith 2006: 182, 186, 200-202; Stafford 1996: 254; Pieterse 1992: 46-49, 58).

We can discern some overlap in Raffles' and Crawfurd's depictions
of Negritos with the tropes used in the discourses of Africans. With
Africanness 'seen' in their analogous state of slavery, it was also 'shown'
through the mere presence of an aquatint of Dick (Figure 1). As mentioned previously, the discussion of slavery in Raffles' book was not
limited to Papuans. They formed only one of a number of groups that
were enslaved. Yet, despite the pervasiveness of enslavement, the only
representative of slavery referred here is Dick who belonged to 'the
black Papuas or oriental negroes', even though he might not be the
most common of slaves (1817: 234). Thus we have the distinction between the drawing of a slave, and the text which discusses slavery in
various parts of the book. Raffles typified the drawing of black Papuans
as slaves, even though the text mentioned more diversity among the
population of slaves. This reinforced the link between slavery, blackness and Africanness.

These three elements are drawn closer together in the details noted
in the text relating to Dick and the image of him. Before focusing on
the aquatint itself, it is useful to consider the artist who created the image and his experience in depicting people and scenes in Southeast
Asia. William Daniell was employed to produce coloured aquatints representing figures in Raffles' *History of Java*. William and his uncle,
Thomas, had been travelling in India since 1785 and Thomas had begun painting watercolours and engraving plates of scenery in India

Figure 2   *Dick, a Papuan from New Guinea, illustration taken from Thomas Stamford Raffles,* History of Java.

A Papuan oNative of New Guinea. 10 years old.

shortly after. Both Thomas and William learned the engraving technique of aquatinting while they were in Calcutta, where their skill in producing aquatints was admired and their prints popular (Archer 1980: 13-16). They travelled from India to China, passing through the Strait of Melaka and drawing and producing aquatints of various people and scenery along the way (Sutton 1954: 161). John Bastin, in his introduction to the *History of Java*, suggested that Daniell was approached by Raffles in 1816 to produce the aquatints based on drawings by Captain Godfrey P. Baker, based on surveys done in Java (1988: vii). Raffles himself, in the preface to the book, states that 'many of the designs [were] from the pencil of Mr. William Daniell, who has devoted his undivided attention in forming a proper conception of this subject, and spared neither time nor exertion in the execution' (x). The aquatint of Dick, however, may have come about via a variety of means. He may have been drawn by Baker and aquatints were produced based on those by Daniell, or Daniell himself may have drawn and made aquatints of

Dick. Michael Smithies asserts that Dick was drawn by Daniell himself sometime during Dick's stay in London with Raffles, instead of having been painted from a sketch by Captain Baker, and instead of being drawn in Java or Bali (366-367).

The depiction of Dick has to be read in tandem with the other depictions in the *History of Java*. The plates that accompanied the *History of Java* encompassed a large variety of subjects. There were drawings of scenery, architecture including religious temples, carvings of deities, musical instruments, weapons and even alphabets. Of these, only a handful were drawings and paintings of particular people. There were paintings of several members of Javanese society, from court officials to ordinary people, as well as sketches of Balinese society. What is apparent in comparing these drawings and sketches to the drawing of Dick is the starkness of the latter drawing. For instance, the drawing of a lower-class Javanese woman was depicted in front of *kampong* scenery, with a bullock cart and a device to pound rice. These objects were placed there to indicate the subject's place in society and to give meaning to the drawing. Much attention was paid to the subjects' dress based on a variety of roles and occasions, as was evidenced by the separate depictions of a Javanese in wardress, ordinary dress and court dress.[9] Whereas the previous drawings presented the subject in ornate costumes with implements and background, Dick was shown in a loincloth with few other objects in the background to indicate his place in society. In the drawing, Dick is standing on a cliff looking out to sea. There are rocks and grass on the cliff, with a handful of palm trees. There are the outlines of far off islands or mountains and two ships, and the sky is overcast. If attention to clothing can be taken as an indicator of civilisation, Dick's lack of ornate clothing may be taken as an indication of a lack of civilisation.[10] The lack of accompanying objects in the background could also indicate that the painter was not sure how to rationalise Dick's position and present it in the scheme of his painting, or perhaps that Dick was not to have any position other than a person close to his natural surroundings, in other words, 'primitive'.

Dick's body was presented in profile, looking up into the sky with his hands crossed across his chest, with his weight on one leg and the other bent. The side view allowed the viewer to deduce the facial angle of the subject. In fact, this was one of only three times in the book where the profile view was used to depict anyone in Java. There are several questions that should be asked about the use of the profile. To what extent did the ideas of facial angles influence Daniell's or Baker's depiction of Dick? Theories surrounding the face were still circulating and the influence of these theories can be seen in many artworks, especially subjects presented in profile (Staum 2003: 23-35, 105-108). In Daniell's depiction of the head, a profile angle was used whereby one can

presumably calculate Dick's facial angle. The facial angles of the other
two subjects could also have been calculated from their portraits and
the conclusion can be made that their angles indicate a measure of civilisation. They were also depicted in ornate costumes and captions
that read that they were important figures in their societies, whereas
Dick has no such accompanying objects and the caption merely reads
'A Papuan or native of New Guinea. 10 years old.'

In Crawfurd's *History*, the same drawing was used and the context
surrounding Dick was expanded to make him into a specimen of 'negro' and 'woolly-haired races' found throughout the archipelago, including the Semang in the Malay Peninsula. Crawfurd made an engraving
of the same person, but with a few crucial additions. He combined it
with another engraving and together they were to be in contrast with
one another and serve as types (Figure 2). Dick was a type from the
'negro race', as the caption 'A Papua or Negro of the Indian Islands' in-

Figure 3   *The Papuan Dick and Katut, native of Bali, illustration from John Crawfurd*, History of the Indian Archipelago.

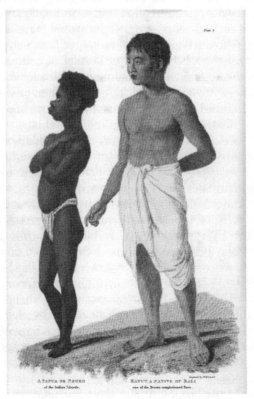

dicated, and the other was a type of the 'brown race', as the caption
'Katut A Native of Bali, one of the Brown complexioned Race' read.[11]
The contrast operates on a number of different levels. Going back to
clothing, the drawing of Katut showed him wearing a sarong or *dhoti*,
which covered most of the body from his waist down, while Dick was
still in a scanty loincloth. The difference in skin tone, or the darkness
of Dick's skin, was emphasised by also presenting a drawing of a light-
er-skinned person. Hair types were distinguished in the drawing, from
Katut's 'lank' hair to Dick's 'woolly' hair. These aspects of the drawing
equated Dick with all 'woolly haired races' and to other groups considered darker and different from the 'brown race'.

Seeing miniature people

Besides showing the African-like qualities of Dick, another characteristic was attributed to Dick, which was associated mainly with Africans:
that of being miniature or pygmy. In re-presenting Raffles' drawing,
Crawfurd added a crucial trait, that of Dick being dwarf-like compared
to Africans from Africa and to other Asians in Southeast Asia. Though
Home referred to Dick as a 'puny Negro' in his examination and this
comment was reproduced in Raffles' *History of Java*, nowhere else were
Papuans referred to as being small or smaller in comparison to other
Southeast Asians or Africans. No mention was made when recounting
the circumstances surrounding Dick's emancipation or when slavery in
general was discussed. Even when Papuans were mentioned in an earlier travelogue that Raffles inserted into the *History*, they were described as 'a race as black as negroes', and not additionally as small
(ccxxxv). It appears that Raffles did not think the stature of Papuans
worthy of mentioning, or that he did not consider them to be any smaller on average than Southeast Asians or Africans.

The same cannot be said of Crawfurd, who said that 'the Papua, or
woolly-haired race, of the Indian islands, is a dwarf African negro.'
This was shown by a 'specimen' of a 'full-grown male' brought from
Kedah in the Malay Peninsula, and slaves from New Guinea and neighbouring islands where he said he saw them firsthand, who were no tal-
ler than five feet. They also had 'spare and puny frames'. Dick was
brought into this interpretation of small-ness when testimony of
Home's examination was included as part of the description of a dwarf
negro and when the same drawing of Dick, which appeared in Raffles'
History was included in Crawfurd's book with a few additions and dele-
tions (23-25). What had been a specific drawing of a ten-year-old Papuan boy had now been expanded and generalised into a typical specimen of a puny Asian 'negro'. Dick's original engraving was combined

with another engraving in the same frame, highlighting the contrast in height. The fact that the original drawing was of a child who may still be growing was omitted from the caption and in Home's description of the examination. The drawings were presented as examples of two adult members of their respective racialised groups, reinforcing Crawfurd's interpretation of minuteness.[12]

Interestingly, the term 'Negrito' was not employed by Raffles. The term *negrito del monte* (little negro of the mountain) had been used earlier by John Leyden in 1811 in an article published in the *Asiatic Researches*. Leyden was aware of its initial application by the Spanish to the Igolote (Illongot?), which he applied to the Papuans as well. However, other than this initial mention of the name, there was no further mention of the diminutive stature of the groups called Papuas, which included Andaman islanders and Semang Bila. Leyden, who was in ill health during his time in India, came to know Raffles when he took a leave of absence to go to Penang to recover. Leyden became close to Raffles and his wife, and it was likely that the two men shared notes on their academic activities and writings, making it all the more striking that both men did not draw more attention to the height of their subjects. While it could be that Leyden did not encounter many of the people he wrote about, Raffles, however, professed to having personal knowledge of Dick.

Another explanation for the sudden interest in the height, or lack thereof, of Papuans by Crawfurd, is the mythology of pygmies in studies of people in newly explored regions. Chris Ballard traces the European fascination for people smaller than themselves in the classical writings of Homer, Aristotle and Ovid. The pygmy, a Greek term referring to the distance between the elbow and knuckles, reappeared in mediaeval literature of the late sixteenth to early seventeenth centuries (Ballard 2006: 133-151). Spanish missionaries in the Philippines, for instance, drew from this mythology when they met with and tried converting what they saw as a group of diminutive blacks they termed 'negrillos' in the late sixteenth century on the island of Panai. It is noteworthy that while some groups in the Philippines were described by missionaries as black with curly/woolly black hair, and were compared to Africans, missionaries did not always see them as Negritos or Negrillos although Blair, Robertson and Rahmann presented just such an interpretation.[13] Such discrepancies are typical, as were the discrepancies between Leyden and Crawfurd, on the one hand, and Raffles on the other, whereby earlier information was reinterpreted under the heading of Negrito.

Positioning Dick as a dwarf or pygmy was yet another way of emphasising his inferiority and tying him more closely to the negative connotations of blackness and being African. The mythology of the pygmy was the assertion of the 'lack' in those peoples in terms of civilisation, in comparison to either colonising powers or other native groups. 'Their puny stature, and feeble frames' were compared to the 'vigorous constitutions' of the archipelago's brown race. The diminutive aspect of their stature was translated into deficiencies in other areas of civilisation. So reluctant was Crawfurd to discard this category that he discredited testimony that there were people from New Guinea who were 'robust' (25-26). He preferred to stick to the idea that there were pygmies, which allowed him to draw from the stereotype of pygmies as being African, as Jahoda argues was the general understanding (35). The miniature person was also an assertion of childhood, and represented stunted growth, someone trapped at a particular point in the history of human development.

The perpetuation of Negritos

The desire to explain African-looking people in Southeast Asia as exemplified by Crawfurd and Raffles has not diminished over time. Numerous articles are still written today, particularly in the field of biological anthropology, seeking to place Negritos within the scheme of peoples in Asia and taking their outward appearance as a starting point.[14] In an article published in 1999, David Bulbeck writes that 'the distinctiveness of the Negritos' distinguishing traits in a Southeast Asian context is clear enough. Coiled or woolly hair... exceeds 90% in its frequency among Luzon, West Malaysian and Andaman Negritos... [A]necdotal evidence [of Negrito skin colour] suggests darker shades than the medium brown tones which dominate between Indochina and Sulawesi' (Bulbeck 1999: 15). He goes on to talk about these characteristics in relation to migration theories, much like Crawfurd and Raffles did, though minus the remarks concerning their inferiority. Others, however, refute that there is any obvious distinction between Negritos and the neighbouring populations. Geoffrey Benjamin writes not of the Negritos but of the Semang, indicating a tribal grouping distinguished by a foraging lifestyle and an egalitarian social system among other things. This emphasis on lifestyle, rather than physical features, is supported by R.K. Dentan, who points out that entire tribes are called Negrito even though members may not fit the stereotypical outward appearance of what the term implies (Benjamin 2002: 10; Dentan 1981: 422). Regardless of who has 'got the facts right', in the present or in the past, the main concern of this paper has been to provide some critical background to the early uses of this term. The issue at stake is not so much whether there was a difference between groups called Negrito and those not, but that scholars such as Crawfurd and

Raffles perceived differences and sought to quantify, enunciate and explain these differences using whatever vocabularies of inferiority were available at that time. In the writings of Crawfurd and Raffles, the Negritos' 'difference' was explained by using the negative tropes of slavery, Africanness and miniatureness. Interest in Negritos continued with expanding colonial and anthropological activity in Southeast Asia, which had lasting effects on racial categories of people in the region.

Notes

1   The area referred to by Crawfurd and in this article is slightly different from present-day Southeast Asia. It sometimes includes the Andaman and Nicobar Islands in the western extreme and part of New Guinea in the eastern extreme. This area was often called the Indian Archipelago in nineteenth-century texts. Throughout this article, the terms Southeast Asia will be used in reference to this region, with the Malay Archipelago used to indicate the island portions only.

2   For the remainder of the article, 'Negrito' will be written without single quotes and with initial capitalised 'N'. Following Chris Ballard, this choice is based on the assumption that Negrito is a potentially flawed category and that the term refers to stereotypes of people labelled as Negrito (Ballard 2006).

3   Crawfurd's later ascendancy to the Presidency of the Ethnological Society of London notwithstanding, most scholars of Southeast Asia know him for his work on Southeast Asian history and literature, and not for his later anthropological writings and his term as president. See, for instance, Merle Ricklefs' introduction to John Crawfurd's A Descriptive Dictionary of the Indian Islands and Adjacent Countries.

4   Wallace would also divide the archipelago into five groups of islands with a main distinction being between islands on either side of his Wallace line which ran from the east of the Philippine islands, between Borneo and Sulawesi down to between Bali and Lombok. While the distinction was based mainly on his collection of species and observations of the natural environment, civilisational attributes of the peoples found on those islands also played a part. The distinction between Malays (Indo-Malayan) and Papuans (Austro-Malayan) was partially based on physical attributes and on their supposed intellectual and moral characteristics, with the Papuans found to be lacking (Wallace 1869; 2000: physical map, 8, 450-453).

5   The reader is not told what the 'standard' was for an African 'negro' used in this comparison. It was taken for granted.

6   Southeast Asian languages have a broad range of terms that describe conditions of servitude. See, for instance, the terms in Malay (Matheson & Hooker 1983).

7   Wright described Raffles as being uninformed regarding the concept of slavery when Raffles withdrew from his earlier definition of slavery as chattel in order to justify his lack of action in completely eradicating slavery from Java in 1812. It is equally possible that Raffles was well informed regarding the meaning of slavery as chattel. Instead, he altered his understanding of slavery in Java in order to justify his actions (Wright 1960: 185).

8   Various Southeast Asian groups such as Malays in the Malay Peninsula have also remarked on the blackness of non-Muslim and non-Christian tribes, which were called Negrito by Europeans, suggesting a more complex relationship in the construction of Negrito that takes into account the viewpoints of locals (Leyden 1811: 218).

9   See Plates two through six of Raffle's History of Java.

10 If Daniell indeed drew Dick while they were both in London, it is certainly curious
    that Dick was depicted in a loincloth where presumably he would have been wearing
    something quite different in the London climate. However, this choice of clothing in
    the drawing may also point to Daniell's knowledge of the way slave attendants
    dressed in the period of Dutch power in Batavia. Jean Gelman Taylor writes that a
    slave's non-Muslim status was indicated by sparse clothing, a loincloth in the case of
    men (Taylor 2007).
11 Raffles' original caption read 'A Papuan of Native New Guinea, 10 years old'.
12 Raffles himself, in a critique of Crawfurd, pointed out this blatant disregard for the
    context of his original drawings and writing (Barrow 1822: 114).
13 Though Rahmann uses sections of Blair and Robertson's translations as though they
    pertained to Negritos, some of those references did not seem to mention Negritos,
    but simply "blacks" who were sometimes even considered "strong and robust". See,
    for instance, Vol. 16: 75, and Vol. 37: 170-171.
14 See, for instance, articles by Peter Bellwood, David Bulbeck and Keiichi Omoto.

Women's Education and Empowerment in Colonial Bengal

Rachana Chakraborty

Summary

The basic aim of this essay is to trace the genesis and development of women's education in colonial Bengal until the country's independence in 1947. My investigation begins in the nineteenth century, when the women's question became a part of the greater discourse of progress and modernity, and a movement for female education started as part of the 'colonised males' search for the 'new woman'. At the outset, the missionaries took up the cause of educating women, as a way of enlightening the poor, heathen women. However, indigenous forces represented by the educated Indian male reformers later on took up the cause of women's education and worked towards its proliferation. The British government also responded by setting up a host of new schools and institutes of higher learning for the women of Bengal; but it primarily corresponded to the gendered construction of womanhood and the dicta of traditional prescriptions, i.e., the 'good mother', 'good wife' models. As in colonial Bengal, socio-cultural and socio-political responses to colonialism were not unrelated, but facets of the same phenomenon, i.e., the growth of nationalism. But as political awareness was also intimately connected with social awareness, women's entry into the public 'male' space of politics undermined the socially constructed artificial dichotomisation of the 'male' sphere of the public and the 'female' sphere of the domestic domains. This inevitably meant that alterations at many levels would have to follow. Women became aware of the existing gender inequalities in Indian society as they became educated, and generated an urge to free themselves from the grip of prescribed belief systems and roles that had historically operated against their interests. The cue for the women's uplift came initially from men. This set an implicit limit to the aspirations of women. For the more sensitive women, however, participation in the freedom movement meant a protracted struggle against two different badges of servility: colonialism and patriarchy. While education empowered women, to play a historic role in eradicating British colonial domination as co-partners of men, their struggle against patriarchal domination remains an unresolved issue.

Women's education: the nineteenth century backdrop

In the nineteenth century, the 'woman's question' loomed large. This was not so much a question of what women wanted, but rather how they could be modernised. It became the central question in nineteenth-century British India, because the foreign rulers had focused their attention on this particular aspect of society. Enamoured with their civilising mission, 'influential British writers condemned Indian religion, culture and society for their rules and customs regarding women'.[1] The women's question figured prominently in these discourses as Western observers, like James Mill, used it to construct a 'civilisational critique of India.' The degraded condition of Indian women was taken as an indicator of India's inferior status in the hierarchy of civilisations.[2] It is therefore no wonder that the status of women became the main focus of the reforming agenda of the modernising Indian intellectuals of the nineteenth century. In their response to the damning critique of the West, they imagined a golden past, where women were treated with dignity and honour; they urged reforms of those customs that they considered to be distortions or aberrations. Thus female infanticide was banned, *Sati* abolished; and widow remarriage legalised. Female education received special encouragement. In the new age construction of womanhood, it was the conventional image of woman as wife and mother, simply garnished by education and some Victorian womanly ideals borrowed from the West, that was projected as 'ideal' for the 'good' Indian woman. Even the *Bamabodhini Patrika*, the journal for women's enlightenment, published in Bengal by the enlightened and educated Brahmos, propagated such a model.[3] The *Bamabodhini Patrika* in (1311 B.S.) 1904 AD wrote, 'The wife, who like Goddess Lakshmi worships her husband as if he is a God Hari, will go to heaven after her death and will taste every happiness along with her husband just as God and Goddess, Hari and Lakshmi, enjoy eternal happiness.' In their resolution of the 'woman question', as shown by Partha Chatterjee,[4] the home was projected as the inner spiritualised space of the nationalist male, where women preserved the age-old Indian *dharma*. The material world might have been lost to the colonial rulers, but the home remained the site of the nationalist victory. That is why the idea of the modern, educated housewife was always tied to the older patriarchal imagination of the mythical divine figure of Lakshmi. Lakshmi as a model Hindu wife combined submission with loyalty. This new concept of womanhood was a fine blending of the self-sacrificing Hindu wife and the Victorian helpmate. Far from having an emancipating effect, education therefore reinforced the confinement of women to idealised domestic roles as good wives and better mothers.[5] Although there were some differences, the Muslim *bhadra-*

mahila also shared significant common grounds with their Hindu counterparts. The goal of the Muslim educators of women, as Gail Minault argues was 'to create women who would be better wives, better mothers and better Muslims.'[6]

In the nineteenth century, the women's question became a part of the greater discourse of progress and modernity, and a movement for female education started as a part of the 'colonised males' search for the 'new woman'. The agency for the spread of education lay with three groups of people, as Geraldine Forbes has classified them: the British, Indian male reformers and educated Indian women.[7] The initiative was taken in Calcutta by men like Radhakanta Deb and the School Book Society and later on by Keshub Chandra Sen and the Brahmo Samaj, in Western India by Madhav Govind Ranade and Prarthana Samaj, in North India by Dayanand and his Arya Samaj and in Madras by Annie Besant and the Theosophical Society. So far as the issue of Indian educated women was concerned, we should mention the endeavours of Pandita Ramabai in Western India, Sister Subbalakshmi in Madras and Begum Rokeya Sakhawat Hossain among the Muslim women in Bengal.[8]

Official agenda on women's education

During its early years, the English East India Company, with its preoccupations in trade, had remained somewhat indifferent to the problems of Indian society. It is therefore not surprising, that the official surveys on the state of indigenous education undertaken by the governments of Bombay, Madras and Bengal Presidencies in the 1820s and 1830s revealed almost a total absence of female students in the village schools as well as in the higher institutes of learning, both Hindu and Muslim.[9]

Though the majority of girls had not yet acquired the opportunity of entering the portals of schools, not all of them were illiterates. Women from 'respectable' families often studied at home. Adam found in Bengal, wives and daughters of *zamindars*, courtesans and the *Vaishnavis*; i.e., women followers of the sixteenth-century saint Shri Chaitanya, as literates. Gauri Vaisnavi, for example, taught the women in Dwaranath Tagore's family. Raja Radhakanta Deb too engaged a Vaisnavi to instruct the women in his household. The Vaishnavis could read the Ramayana, Mahabharata and stories of the Purans. Pearychand Mitra, a great literary giant of nineteenth-century Bengal, wrote in the preface of his autobiographical work *Adhyatmika* that his grandmother, mother and aunts could read books, write in Bengali, and keep accounts even though there were no female schools in those days. Debendranath Tagore's mother-in-law could read difficult religious texts. Similarly, upper-class Muslims employed Uttanis, who were often wives or widows of *maulavis*, to teach women the Quran and other religious teachings at home. Sir Syed Ahmed Khan's mother, Azizunnisa Begum (1780-1857), a woman in strict *purdah*, knew Arabic and Persian.[10]

While Christian missionaries and social reformers had been active, the East India Company still remained passive in its efforts to provide steps for the education of girls of Bengal. In 1853, Col. Jacob had told the Select Committee of the Parliament, that he did not think that a single female had been educated by the government education system of that time.[11] In none of the Dispatches relating to education submitted or received from the Court of Directors during the first half of the nineteenth century was there any mention of female education.

A significant change in the official attitude came with the advent of John Drinkwater Bethune, the Law Member in the Governor General's Council and President of the Council of Education. Convinced of the need to educate girls in Bengal, Bethune opened a school for the sake of female education in Calcutta in 1849. Though originally known as the Hindu Female School, it maintained a secular approach. Instruction was imparted in Bengali and there were no fees. For girls who lived far away, and were unable to afford transport, a carriage was provided. On the carriage was emblazoned a Sanskrit verse declaring that a daughter's education was her father's religious duty. The first two pupils of this school were the daughters of the orthodox Pandit Madan Mohan Tarkalankar.

In addition to the donation of his personal library collections, including books worth Rs. 5,000 for the school, Dakshinaranjan Mukherjee also presented a plot of land in the Mirzapur area, in favour of the construction of a building for this school. The wealthy merchant, Ram Gopal Ghose also provided help. The citizens of Calcutta also lent a helping hand to the cause of female education in Bengal, when Bethune died an untimely death in 1851. Lord Dalhousie, the then Governor General of India, between 1848-1856, decided to support the school and renamed it he Bethune School, after its primary benefactor.

It was in the Wood's Dispatch of 1854 that the first positive interests towards female education were expressed. In his famous Dispatch, Sir Charles Wood noted, 'The importance of female education in India cannot be overrated; and we have observed with pleasure the evidence which is now afforded of an increased desire on the part of many of the natives to give a good education to their daughters. By this means a far greater proportional impulse is imparted to the educational and moral tone of the people than by the education of men.'[12] Dalhousie hailed it as 'the beginning of a great revolution in Indian habits.'[13]

Bethune had led the way; Indian social reformers furthered the cause of women's education in Bengal. The Brahmo Samaj led the movement for female education in Bengal. Keshab Chandra Sen organised in 1862 the Bamabodhini Sabha to facilitate women's education. In the same year, Umesh Chandra Dutt started publishing the *Bamabodhini Patrika* that not only carried articles on women's issues, but also organised a correspondence course for girls through its columns known as *antahpur shiksha* or education in the seclusion of the home.[14]

In Bengal, as elsewhere, a debate on the content and purpose of women's education was unleashed at the end of the nineteenth century. A wide cross-section of the people ranging from social reformers, to conservatives, housewives and even women who were receiving education actively participated in this on-going debate. The *Bamabodhini Patrika*, for example, published a number of articles under the title *Strisangini* (wife as companion), which were basically vignettes from the lives of women who helped their husbands in their careers by providing them with a caring and understanding home ambience.

Upon his return from England in 1871, Keshab Chandra Sen had started a Native Ladies' Normal School under the auspices of the Indian Reform Association. But Sen's views on women's education did not satisfy the radical exponents of the Brahmo Samaj. By 1874, the radicals – Dwarkanath Ganguly, Shibnath Sastri, Durgamohan Das and others – broke away from Keshab Chandra Sen to set up the Hindu Mahila Vidyalaya with the help of the visiting Unitarian, Annette Akroyd. They believed that women also had the right to receive a higher education and study subjects such as mathematics, philosophy and sciences – a claim that was denied by Keshab Chandra Sen. Miss Akroyd, however, did not stay long with the reformers. Undaunted by her desertion, the eminent Brahmos like Durgamohan Das sent his own daughters, Sarala (who later on married PK Ray and started the Gokhale Memorial Girls' School) and Abala (who later married the eminent scientist Sir Jagadish Chandra Bose and founded the Brahmo Girls' School.) Jagadish Chandra Bose's sister, Swarna Prabha, Manmohan Ghosh's sister, Binodmani as well as Kadambini Basu (a cousin of Manmohan Ghosh and later Dwarkanath Ganguly's wife) all joined the new school. In 1878, this school merged with the Bethune school to give birth to Bethune College.[15]

The Indian Education (Hunter) Commission instituted in 1882 to review the progress of education in India had exclaimed that primary education among the girls had registered some progress, since the opening up of the Bethune school in 1849, but the state of education at the secondary and higher levels were yet to record any advancement. The Hunter Commission thus recommended that 'female education be treated as a legitimate charge alike on local, municipal and on provincial Funds, and receive special encouragement.' It demanded that all females' schools should be regarded as eligible for receiving government aid and that the conditions for receiving the same should be made somewhat easier than that imposed on the boys' schools. The standards of instruction in the girls' schools were to be made accordingly, undemanding and simpler than that what the boys received. Special attention was to be paid to the requirements of household life in the case of girls' schools. It further recommended that liberal aid be offered to girls' schools that taught English in addition to the vernacular languages. Similarly, it suggested that provisions be made for special prizes and scholarships for the girls to motivate and encourage them.[16]

With the gradual increase of girls' schools both in numbers and enrolment, the necessity of starting up something like a normal school to train female teachers in Calcutta was strongly felt. In tune with the call of the day, a normal school had already been instituted for the Christian female teachers of Calcutta. With the arrival of Miss Mary Carpenter, a philanthropic English lady and a friend of the Women's welfare movement, in Calcutta on the 20 November 1866 new endeavours were made in this direction. With the help of some of the ardent advocates of the cause of women's education in Bengal, such as Pandit Iswar Chandra Vidyasagar, Keshub Chunder Sen, Manomohan Ghose and Dwijendra Nath Tagore, she suggested the necessity of opening up a non-denominational normal school in the metropolis.[17] She insisted that the greatest obstacle to the improvement of females' schools and to the expansion of female education was indeed a dearth of female teachers. In 1868, the Secretary of State approved her proposal and the Government of India's scheme for the establishment of females' normal schools in the Presidencies of Bengal, Madras and Bombay was well under way. A sum of Rs. 12,000 was designated for this purpose over a five-year period. The Female Normal School survived for only three years. In the latter half of this period, Dwaranath Ganguly, editor of *Abala bandhab*, a Bengali monthly, worked earnestly to make the school a success. He even collected a number of adult pupils for the school, but his efforts proved in vain. The Government, too, could no longer be satisfied with the state of things and the opinion of Vidyasagar with regard to the fate of such an institution proved prophetic. The result was that official orders were given for the abolition of the Normal school on 24 January 1872.[18]

The abolition of the Female Normal School brought the Bethune School back to its former prominence. It remained under the direct supervision of the Government for some time. The Report on the Public Instruction of Bengal, for 1876-1877, observed that the amalgamation of the Bethune School with the Ballygunj Banga Mahila Vidyalaya in 1876, would lend it a new dimension.[19]

The years of transition: From Bethune School to College

Hitherto, no girl student of either school had ever taken the entrance examination of Calcutta University. Miss Chandramukhi Bose, daughter of Bhuban Mohan Bose, a native Christian of Dehra Dun had already prepared herself for the entrance examination and wanted to take the exam in 1876 from the Dehra Dun school. Although the Junior Board of Examiners had granted her permission, the authorities of the Ballygunj Banga Mahila Vidyalaya forced the Vice-Chancellor of the Calcutta University, Sir Arthur Hobhouse, to arrange for a test examination for two of its students, namely Kadambini Bose and Sarala Das as a precondition for their qualifying for the entrance examination. The University Senate, in its meeting of 27 April 1878, accordingly agreed to allow the two female candidates to take the entrance examination, subject to certain rules pertaining to the conduct of the examination. Miss Bose was successful in obtaining a second division, missing the first division by only a slender margin of one mark.[20]

A new era was ushered in for the Bethune School,[21] and women's education received a fresh impetus in India, because of Kadambini's success, as well as her desire to further her studies in the same institution, the Lieutenant Governor decided to appoint a lecturer qualified to teach the first arts course and consented to raise the status of the school. Baboo Sasi Bhusan Dutt, who had transferred from the Cuttak College was asked to serve the Bethune School on a full-time basis.

With the initiation of College classes at the Bethune School, in 1879, both Chandramukhi and Kadambini could attend these classes and take their B.A. examinations from this institution. In January 1883, they became the very first women graduates in the British Empire.[22] Chandramukhi Bose preferred to continue her studies to receive her M.A., while Kadambini Bose, who had by then married the Brahmo leader Dwarkanath Ganguly, forsook the beaten track and applied for admission to the Calcutta Medical College, as a regular student. During the previous year, other women such as Miss D'Abreu and Miss Abala Das had applied for similar reasons but were denied entry from the Council of the Medical College in Calcutta. Not baffled by the opposition at home, these two ladies joined the Madras Medical College, where there was a provision for the instruction of women in Medicine.[23] The Brahmo leaders led by Dwarkanath Ganguly now started agitating for opening the admissions at the Medical College to women. But before the movement could gather momentum, the Lieutenant Governor of Bengal, Sir Rivers Thompson intervened, and Kadambini was admitted into Calcutta Medical College. The medical profession had thus been opened up to women in Bengal.[24] When the Government in 1884 announced a scholarship of 20 rupees a month for wo-

men medical students, Kadambini took advantage of this assistance
and in 1886 was awarded the GBMC (Graduate of Bengal Medical College). Kadambini immediately began a private practice and found her
services much in demand. By 1888, she was appointed to the Lady Duf-
ferin Women's Hospital, earning a monthly salary of 300 rupees.[25]

Women's education under diarchy

Diarchy is the name of power sharing outlined in the Government of
India Act of 1919 (Montaigue Chelmsford Reforms), which had placed
the nation-building portfolios in the hands of Indian legislators. Transferred subjects at this time included local self-government, education,
health public works, agriculture and industry, while revenue and law
and order departments remained in the hands of the Governor. This
was at a time when the Indian population became increasingly agi-
tated, the trade balance had shifted against India, and agricultural pro-
ductivity was on the decline. At this very difficult juncture of history,
the Indian middle class with its limited franchise (considering the very
small numbers of Indians who actually had the right to vote) had become partners in the 'civilising mission'. They too were now engaged
in answering the awkward questions regarding the health, education
and welfare of the Indian population.[26]

While inaugurating the Bethune School on the 7 May 1849, J.E.D.
Bethune had expressed his hope that the day would soon arrive when a
new call by the young men of Bengal to extend the benefits of education, from which they themselves had so largely benefited to the other
half of the population. He had also emphasised that the happiness of
domestic life would be enhanced 'by the graceful virtues and elegant
accomplishments of well-educated women'.[27] Issues and the debates relating to girl's education continued to dominate the leading educational
surveys and reports in the first two decades of the twentieth century.
By 1916-1917, there were already three girls' colleges in Calcutta: the
Diocesan College, Bethune College and the collegiate department of
the Loreto House. But the contributions to the Bethune College could
not be compared to the other two. *The Fifth Quinquennial Review of the
Progress of Education in Bengal* (1912-1913 to 1916-1917) noted that 'The
Bethune College is the oldest Government institution for the education
of girls in India'.[28]

The issue of women's education once again became a compelling issue when India's Secretary of State, H. Sharp, received an important
announcement on 5 November 1915.[29] This announcement highlighted
some of the major impediments that stood in the way of progress regarding female education in the country. It pointed out the insignifi-

cant number of girls being educated, and the utter lopsided ratio of male to female students, it further expressed its deep apprehension that if this problem were to go unresolved, it might endanger the well being of the Indian community. It recommended the formation of representative committees to enquire into the matter. The Government of India's response was to invite local governments to poll the opinions of competent people, local governing bodies, committees and other authorities in order to draw up a uniform policy on the matter.

In the meantime, the Calcutta University Commission had been constituted under the stewardship of Sir Michael Sadler (1917-1919). The Commission raised two pertinent issues regarding women's education. The first one was, to what extent and in which areas were additional and special facilities required for the higher education of women? The second question was related to the more thorny issue of identifying the particular needs and difficulties that affected the higher educational options of women in India.[30] The Commission identified some of the key factors preventing progress in women's education in Bengal such as early marriages, the custom of *purdah* and, of course, a general distrust of Western education. All of these factors were inextricably related to the very fabric of Indian society, and so, only a radical change in the life, customs and ideals of the country could usher in the desired changes. Numerically speaking, however, within a decade (1907-1917), the number of girls in school had already doubled.[31]

The Calcutta University Commission explained the drawbacks of the system of educational progress, in terms of a paucity of private enterprise engagement as distinct from Governmental and missionary efforts in matters of post-elementary training of female students in Bengal.

Turning to the characteristics that were hindering the development of female education in Bengal, the Commission pointed out the difficulty of providing sufficient numbers of competent teachers as an important factor. As very few Hindu or Muslim women adopted the teaching profession, the employment of foreigners or members of the domiciled community, became imperative, which was expensive, however. Christian teachers, or the employment of male teachers in girls' schools were generally not considered the best options. Secondly, the unsuitability of the curricula was partly responsible for this. Finally, it was also the dominance of the examination system that added to the problems. Sir Michael Sadler had observed in the report,

> Secondary education for girls, labours under exceptional difficulties in Bengal; it is surrounded by prejudices; it is distorted, even more unnaturally than the education of boys, by the malign influence of the examination fetish ... The Commission feels that the schools must be saved from the desolating domi-

nation of the examination system which now mischievously influences all their work.[32]

Though the report of the Calcutta University Commission had struck a
sombre note regarding the question of women's education in Bengal,
the subsequent period (1918-1927) saw an overall expansion of female
education in the province. By 1918, the Bethune College had already
earned considerable praise from the Indians. The steady increase in enrolment, no doubt put increased pressure on the available accommoda-
tions at the College. But the College undertook new initiatives to establish a company of 'girl guides' and to revive its magazine *Usha* in
1918.[33] *The Sixth Quinquennial Review of Progress of Education in Bengal*
(1917-1918 to 1921-1922) also remarked that a redeeming feature of the
College during the period under review was that there had been a remarkable increase in the demand for science education among the
girls.

The question of women's education was also mentioned on the floor
of the Bengal Legislative Assembly. In reply to a question (Question
No. 23) on the issue, Dr. Brajendranath Seal confirmed the judgment
of Dr. Adityanath Mukherjee who had written from his personal experiences as a long-time faculty member at a women's College. He regarded the intellectual capacities of the Bengali girls to be equal to that
of the boys. Dr. B.N. Seal added that from his personal examinations of
matriculation figures and other examination scripts of the Calcutta
University, he was convinced that the quality of work done by the girls
were of a high order, while, in the case of written English, the writing
style as well as the power of expression of the girls, was often better
than that of the boys; and was marked by a greater degree of independence of opinion.[34]

By the early decades of the twentieth century, the educated woman
of Bengal had already developed a voice of her own. This discernible
change becomes nowhere more pronounced than in the response of
the young woman, Ashabati Sarkar, a third-year student at Bethune
College. She wrote an article entitled 'Message of the Age to Girls', that
was published in the college's magazine and was included in the Calcutta University Commission's Report of 1919. In it she wrote,

> The girls of Bengal have been receiving education for about forty
> years. The time has come when we shall have to choose one or
> other of the ways. What way are we going to choose? The first
> glamour of awakening has passed. It is time some of the unplea-
> sant features of the emancipation of women should pass also,
> and make room for reason and clear thought which will make
> every girl of Bengal a true woman ... It is the spirit in which life

is led that matters. The power of self-control is another name
for liberty. Liberty consists in the right of choosing according to
conscience and reason. This control was forced upon women by
men before, but now has to come from within ourselves. To this,
love must be added. Reason is supreme only by the side of love.

She further reiterates,

Received and given in this spirit, education may impart the
power alike of self realization and self restraint. The woman is
[the] true guardian of the early education of the children of the
race, and she herself must have that which she alone can impart
in turn to them. The way to much of what is best in education
lies through the education of girls and women.[35]

The late 1920s and early 1930s saw the growth of a rich and highly
complex spectrum of political experience in Bengal, including a resur-
gence of the Congress-led nationalist movement from 1928, revival of
revolutionary terrorism and a wide variety of peasant and working-class
actions. With the launching of the first Non-Cooperation movement by
Mahatma Gandhi in 1921, and his appeal to women to join *satyagraha*,
women emerged out of their homes in large numbers to picket shops
selling foreign cloth and liquor, march in processions in the streets,
hold public meetings and risk imprisonment, all of which helped
weaken the traditional bondages.[36] In the towns of Comilla and Noa-
khali in Eastern Bengal, women from upper-class conservative Muslim
families played a similar role. Bose managed to get Nari Satyagraha Samiti in Burrabazar, the business heart of Calcutta, involved and she
also organised special wings for girl students within the Bengal Provincial Student's Association.[37] In fact, the use of women in certain types
of demonstrations seemed to have been a deliberate Congress strategy,
as this was expected to reduce the intensity of police repression, especially in the case of respectable middle-class, urban women.

The apparently smooth, painless politicisation of women belonging
to a certain milieu that had traditionally restricted their role within
well-defined domestic confines was a process that met with applause
rather than resistance from their male guardians. This was for most
women the first time they had been allowed to participate in activities
outside the household. There can be no denying that this step must
have been preceded by an acute, indeed revolutionary, struggle with
their own sensibilities and inhibitions that they could overcome with
education and awareness.[38]

Women's associations had started to emerge all over India by the
late-nineteenth and early-twentieth centuries. Although their activities

were limited to the holding of discussions on women's issues such as education, child marriages, the observance of the *purdah* and women's status in the family, nevertheless, they shared the common goal of bringing women together to discuss their own problems. In Calcutta for example, Swarna Kumari Debi, sister of poet Rabindranath Tagore, founded Sakhi Samiti (Society of Friends). Her daughter, Sarala Debi Chaudhurani, started the first all-India women's association, the Bharat Stree Mandal in 1910, which unfortunately was short lived. Three major national women's organisations emerged in the post First World War period: the Women's Indian Association (WIA), the National Council of Women (NCW) and the All India Women's Conference (AIWC). The main objective of the AIWC was the promotion of women's education. True, the AIWC did not advocate mass education for all women, but the majority of delegates wanted the education system to produce better wives and mothers in addition to women teachers, doctors, professors and lawyers. The AIWC collected donations for an All India Women's Education Fund, which, in turn, led to the establishment of Lady Irwin College in Delhi.[39]

Conclusion

As education was a necessary pre-condition of women's social empowerment, it was meant to contribute positively towards women's agency, and to free her from her passive victimhood that colonial society had imposed upon her. At the onset of colonial times, the missionaries often took up the issue of educating women as a way of enlightening the poor, heathen women. However, the indigenous forces soon took up the cause of women's education and worked towards its spread.

In colonial Bengal, socio-cultural and political responses to colonialism were not unrelated but were facets of the same phenomenon, i.e., the growth of nationalism. Women's entry into the public 'male' space of politics undermined the socially constructed artificial dichotomisation of the 'male' sphere of the public and the 'female' sphere of the domestic domains. This inevitably meant that alterations at many levels would follow. Women became aware of the existing gender inequalities in Indian society and generated an urge to free themselves from the grip of prescribed belief – systems and roles that had historically operated against their interests.[40]

When the enlightened *bhadralok* of nineteenth-century Bengal supported the reform movement, their aim was not to attack the prevalent patriarchal system in any way, or to challenge the power and position enjoyed by men, still lesser to make women the equal partners of men in the societal or economic roles outside the family. Their purpose was to improve the position of women within the patriarchal framework, so as to make them into good wives and mothers within the family. That is why the paradigm of a model woman was imported from Victorian England with the traditional qualities of Indian women embedded in it.[41] The reform movement was the upshot of the struggle between the two ideologies – the colonial and the indigenous. The challenges envisaged and faced were attempts to challenge 'the pretended supremacy of the culture of the coloniser' as well as 'to reassert the cultural identity of the colonised'. The result of this double pull in two opposite directions was the evolution of a Western model and the Indian ideal, where the Indian women were expected to combine the womanly qualities prized both in the 'modern' West and the 'ancient' East.

While nineteenth-century contradictions were not resolved in the twentieth century, new forces and influences were released to shape the contours of women's consciousness. British feminists like Annie Besant, who had been an active suffragette in England and had played a key role in forming the Women's Indian Association (1917) in India or Margaret Cousins who had also been a Theosophist and a suffragist from Ireland and a promoter of the All India Women's Conference (1927) brought Indian women under the influence of Western feminist ideologies, and the spread of education generated new ideas.[42]

In Bengal, the chief women's organisation to fight for women's franchise was the *Bangiya Nari Samaj*, guided by Kumudini Bose, Kamini Roy, Mrinalini Sen and Jyotirmoyee Ganguly. Though the initial resolution to permit women to vote was defeated in Bengal Legislative Council in 1921, by 1925, the Bengal Legislature had approved a limited female suffrage, which the women exercised for the first time in 1926. It symbolised for them formal entry into the hitherto exclusive male public world of political decision-making.[43]

The cue for women's uplift came initially from men. This set an implicit limit to the aspirations of women. For the more sensitive women, however, participation in the freedom movement meant a protracted struggle against two different badges of servility: colonialism and patriarchy.[44] Involvement in the freedom struggle had taught women the basics of activist politics, and the breaking of the carapace of traditional domestic life had widened their horizon. It had whetted their appetite; but it did not satisfy them.

According to the Baconian engineering model, 'knowledge was power' implying that knowledge was an instrument for gaining power, although the two could exist quite independently. Foucault on the other hand, argued that the goals of power and that of knowledge were inseparable for in knowing we control and in controlling we know. For example, the system of examination in any educational institution combined hierarchical observation with normative judgment. It was a prime example of what Foucault called power/knowledge, since it combined into a unified whole 'the deployment of force and the establishment of truth'. It was thus an instance, whereby the truth about those who underwent the examination could be elicited, informing us what they actually knew, and at the same time controlling their behaviour by forcing them to study.[45]

The fact that women were latecomers in the newly organised educational space the issue was fraught with the entire baggage of the power/knowledge syndrome, to a degree unimagined by Michel Foucault, the author of this hypothesis. Thus education was constantly intertwined in the caste-class ethnicity divide that was even more fortified by gender discrimination. Thus during the colonial period education not only emancipated women but also brought them into the vortex of yet another struggle, the struggle for empowerment that remains as yet an unfinished agenda.

Notes

1   Forbes, G. (1998), *The New Cambridge History of India, vol. iv. 2: Women in Modern India*. Cambridge University Press, p. 12.
2   Chakraborty, D. (1994), '*The difference – deferrals of a colonial modernity: Public debates on domesticity in British India*', in Arnold, David and Hardiman, David (eds.), *Subaltern Studies: Essays in Honour of Ranajit Guha*, vol. 8, Delhi: Oxford University Press, p. 54.
3   Ray, B. & A. Basu (eds.), *From Independence Towards Freedom, Indian Women since 1947*. New Delhi: Oxford University Press, p. 6.
4   Ibid., p. 7.
5   Borthwick, M. (1984), *The Changing Role of Women in Bengal, 1849-1905*, Princeton: Princeton University Press; and see also G. Murshid (1983), *Reluctant Debutante: Response of Bengali Women to Modernisation 1849-1905*. Rajshahi, Sahitya Samsad, passim.
6   Minault, G. (1998), *Secluded Scholars: Women's Education and Muslim Social Reform in Colonial India*. Delhi: Oxford University Press, p. 215.
7   Forbes, G. (1998), *Women in Modern India: The New Cambridge History of India*, vol. 4, p. 60.
8   Bandyopadhyay, S. (2004), *From Plassey to Partition – A History of Modern India*. New Delhi: Orient Longman Ltd., p. 383.
9   Ray, B. (ed.) (2005), *Women of India: Colonial and Post-colonial periods*. New Delhi: Sage Publications Ltd., p. 184.
10 Minault, G. (1998), *Secluded Scholars: Women's Education and Muslim Social Reform in Colonial India*. Delhi: Oxford University Press, p. 18.
11 Richey J.A. (1922), *Selections from Educational Records, Pt. II 1849-1919*. Calcutta, p. 34.
12 Richey J.A. (1922), *Selections from Educational Records, Pt. II 1849-1919*, Calcutta, p. 388.
13 Ibid., p. 62.
14 Ray, B. (ed.) (2005), *Women of India*. p. 188.
15 Ibid., p. 189. See also K. Nag (ed.), *History of the Bethune School* op. cit.

16 Richey, J.A. (1922), *Selections from Educational Records*, pt. II, 1849-1919. Calcutta, pp. 155-157.

17 Nag, Dr. K. (ed.) (1950), *Bethune School and College Centenary Volume. 1849-1949*. Calcutta, p. 27.

18 Ibid., pp. 30-31.

19 Ibid.

20 Ibid., pp. 37-39.

21 Ibid., pp. 39.

22 Ray, B. (ed.) (2005), *Women of India*, p. 191.

23 Nag, Dr. K. (ed.) (1950), *Bethune College and School Centenary Volume*, p. 41.

24 Ray, B. (ed.) (2005), *Women of India*, p. 191. See also M. Karlekar, *Kadambini and the Bhadralok: early debates over women's education in Bengal*, EPW 21:17 (26 April 1986) ws25-ws31.

25 Forbes, G. (2005), *Women in Colonial India*, p. 89.

26 Ibid., p. 91.

27 Nag, Dr. K. (ed.) (1950), *Bethune College and School Centenary Volume*, p. 107.

28 Ibid., p. 68.

29 Government of India \ Department of Education Edu-A Oct 1919, file no. 27 (National Archives of India, New Delhi).

30 *Bharatvarsa, Paus to Jaistha 1324-1325 B.S.* (1917-18), p. 631.

31 Government of India \ Department of Education Edu-A Oct 1919, File No. 27, p. 2.

32 Government of India \ Department of Education Edu-A Oct 1919, File No. 27 (National Archives of India, New Delhi), p. 3.

33 Nag, Dr. K. (ed.) (1950), *Bethune College and School Centenary Volume*, pp. 69-71.

34 *The Report of the Calcutta University Commission 1917-1919* vol. I, Part I (1919.) Published by Supt. Govt. Printing, India Calcutta, pp. 132-133. (Bethune College Archives Collection).

35 *The Report of the Calcutta University Commission 1917-1919*, pp. 141-142.

36 Ray, B. (ed.) (2005), *Women of India: Colonial and Postcolonial periods*, p. 194.

37 Ananda, Bazar Patrika, op cit.; see also Home Confidential, GOB, Poll599 (Sl. no. 1-14) of 1930. Letter 387 C of 24.5. 1930 from District Magistrate, Comilla: GOB Home Confidential, Poll441 (Sl. no. 1) of 1929 – Lowman's Note on Youth Association in Bengal.

38 Krishnamurty, J. (ed.) (1999), *Women in Colonial India: Essays on Survival, Work and the State Delhi*. Oxford University Press, p. 237.

39 Ray, B. (ed.] (2005), *Women of India: Colonial and Postcolonial periods*, pp. 194-195.

40 Ray, B., 'Beyond the Domestic/Public Dichotomy: Women's History in Bengal, 1905-1947' in S.P. Sen and N.R. Ray (eds.) (1988), *Modern Bengal: A Socio-Economic Survey*. Calcutta, pp. 240-256.

41 Ray, B., 'The Freedom Movement and Feminist Consciousness in Bengal, 1905-1929' in B. Ray, (ed.) (1995), *From the Seams of History; Essays on Indian Women*. New Delhi: Oxford University Press, p. 179.

42 Ibid., pp. 181-182.

43 Ray, B., 'The Freedom Movement and Feminist Consciousness in Bengal, 1905-1929', in B. Ray (ed.) (1995), *From the Seams of History: Essays on Indian Women*. New Delhi: Oxford University Press, pp. 192-193.

44 Ibid., p. 216.

45 Rabinow, P. (ed.) (1997-1999), *Essential Works of Foucault, 1954-1984*, 3 volumes. New York: New Press.

Her Old *Ayah*: The Transcolonial Significance of the Indian Domestic Worker in India and Australia[1]

Victoria Haskins

The historical representation of white women in India and Australia bears a striking similarity: on the one hand, we find the *'memsahib'* and, on the other, the *'missus'*, with both of them designated by their role not only of wife and mother to white men, but as mistress to native workers. In the case of the former, this designation as mistress is paramount, for, in the nostalgic construction of the British Raj, perhaps no one figure looms quite so large as the cherished *ayah* or lady's maid. This paper is a rumination on the significance of this image of the Indian domestic worker in imagined women's relationships of (Anglophone) colonialism. Sparked by the recollections of my Australian-born great-grandmother, Joan Kingsley-Strack, reflecting on the life of her Anglo-Indian grandmother, Maggie Hobbes (and in her case the term 'Anglo-Indian' is fittingly ambiguous), my discussion tentatively traces the constitution of an ideology of white colonial womanhood, through the systems of circulation of cultural ideas and attitudes that emerged in Anglophone colonialism. In a transcolonial culture, the figure of the *ayah* was significant, in a way that the very banality of the women's work she performed tends to obscure.

The domestic frontier in Australia

In the settler-colonial nation of Australia, domestic service, as a site of colonialism – a frontier of colonisation – became an arena for state intervention and manipulation in the twentieth century. Relationships between indigenous and white women were created in this crucible in interwar Australia, as the state (literally, state governments of the former colonies) forcibly and systematically removed young Aboriginal women from their families and communities and indentured them as household servants. They were almost always placed in the homes of married white women with young children, and many of those homes were in the newly emerging suburbs of Australian cities (Haskins 2005).

Such policies were carried out with the aim of breaking up persistent Aboriginal communities in south-eastern Australia, while in areas where white settlement was sparse, the policies targeted mixed-descent girls especially, there being a concern that unless they did so a danger-ous 'hybrid race' in the centre and northern regions would eventually emerge. The participation of white women as employers was crucial to the success of this project, providing their homes as the locale for a policy of dispersal (Haskins 2004). While there was a persistent ser-vant shortage in urban areas (Walden 1995: 196),[2] the decision of a pri-vileged white urban woman to engage an unknown Aboriginal girl as a servant, most commonly as a nursemaid, was indeed remarkable, con-sidering not only the racism of the times, but the Board's public justifi-cation of its policy on the grounds that the girls came from 'contami-nating' and 'vicious' communities, and were inherently immoral.

That a number of such women (admittedly a small number) could and did take Aboriginal girls into their homes reflects the ubiquity of what art historian Madeline McGuire has called the 'good fella missus legend' (1990: 135-139). This 'dominant historical myth about the rela-tion between white women and Aborigines [that] portrays the former as kind mistresses and the latter as objects of their maternal care' (McGuire 1990: 124) was an integral strand of a popular mythologising of pioneer and frontier life that held sway in middle-class urban Aus-tralian culture throughout the Board's regime. Its classic expression was found in the immensely popular writings of Mrs Aeneas Gunn, who described her relationship with the Aboriginal women workers of Elsey Station in the Northern Territory thus:

> They knew as well as I did that, as long as the work was well done, I would let them play over it as much as they liked. You see, I was what white people would call a 'bad mistress;' but the blacks called me 'goodfellow missus,' and would do anything I wanted without a murmur (Gunn 1924: 40).

An index of class status ascribing an honourable, indeed, virtuous role to white women who utilised the cheap labour of those whose land they had appropriated, a desire to cast themselves in such a light un-derpinned the willingness of women like my great-grandmother Joan Kingsley-Strack to engage Aboriginal apprentices through the Protec-tion Board. Studies of the imagined relationships between white wo-men and Aboriginal people have tended to focus inwards, mirroring the nationalistic thrust of such constructions (see, in addition to McGuire 1990: Godden 1979; Grimshaw & Evans 1996; Vivers 2002). However, with a reorientation of Australian studies of colonialism di-recting our attention toward transnational influences (for instance,

Woollacott 2003; Grimshaw & Standish 2007) it might be suggested that the fashionable image of the white mistress was in fact a wider, transcolonial construction, created in the Raj and reworked in other colonial contexts – including Australia.

'Mrs Anglomaniac': transporting the Raj

By the late nineteenth century, the relationship between the *'memsahib'* and the Indian servant who was her foil was recognised throughout the Anglophone world as a symbol of British rule. A telling 'joke' was published in an 1888 newspaper produced by and for the Native American students of Carlisle School in Pennsylvania, Massachusetts. This school was originally established to cater to prisoners-of-war during the western plains wars, and subsequently started up the so-called Outing System under which young American 'Indian' girls were placed in domestic service indentures. The gag runs so:

> *Must be English.* Mrs Anglomaniac – I see you advertise to furnish servants of any nationality.
> Employment agent – Yes: madam, no matter what. If we haven't 'em on hand we'll get 'em.
> Mrs Anglomaniac – Very well. I see by the *Court Journal* that Queen Victoria is using Indian servants, and I want some nice, tidy squaws, right away.[3]

Offering an illustration of Tony Ballantyne's point in his study of Orientalism in the British Empire, notwithstanding the emphasis on the metropole, the joke reminds us of the need to 'foreground the relational quality of the imperial past', focusing on imperial networks and cultural exchange patterns to elucidate the integrative power of empire and the indigenising forces that worked to adapt introduced ideas to local imperatives (Ballantyne 2002: 2-3, 14-15).

We might note, indeed, that the Australian impulse to support aggressive intervention by the state over Aboriginal lives in the 1920s and 1930s was directly connected to what contemporary Australians conceived to be the British way in India. When the NSW Aborigines Protection Board presented its 1925 report to Parliament newspaper coverage reported that the 'problem' was the 'future of the half-caste race':

> The same difficulty is encountered in other countries under British rule. In India, despite every effort, the half-caste remains as an unassimilable section of the community. It has to be remem-

bered that the Indian half-caste is for the most part a higher type
than the Australian. Many of the half-caste women of Hindustan
have exhibited talent of an advanced order to which they add a
certain personal charm, which is not always noticeable in other
half-caste races. In Australia, the half-castes are the product of
an aboriginal mother, wholly untutored, and but little removed
from barbaric races (Maynard 2007: 80).[4]

Let us not forget that the British first introduced the very term 'half-
caste' in India, back in 1789. A derogatory term for mixed-race children
of European and Indian unions designed to begin the long process of
social exclusion of such hybrid people (Edwards 2003), it was to have a
longstanding and poisonous impact in Australia.

From the turn of the twentieth century mixed-descent people in Australia were a source of great and increasing anxiety to the authorities;
while there was no place imagined for Aboriginal people in 'White
Australia' (it being assumed their extinction was inevitable) the vitality
of Aboriginal communities was attributed to the 'white blood' within
them but they remained 'unassimilable'. 'It is a danger to us' one NSW
Board member and parliamentarian warned in 1915, 'to have a people
like that among us, looking upon our institutions with eyes different
from ours'. Such fears drove the impulse to go into Aboriginal communities and take out the girls and women of child-bearing age, to be
placed in service.[5]

Today, the live-in, indentured or bonded domestic worker is typically
a 'foreign worker' rather than a 'native'. Nevertheless a pattern set in
the colonial period persists. Native female domestic workers were almost always in some sense 'colonial hybrids' themselves, individuals
who both culturally and racially straddled the divide between coloniser
and colonised, often drastically and even violently displaced from their
native communities of origin, and occupying a vulnerable yet danger-
ous liminal status in the colonial world. Nupur Chaudhuri's study of
white women's attitudes toward Indian servants found that 'many' preferred Christian *ayahs*. However, they also considered 'converts' un-
trustworthy, and that these Christian servants were descendants of the
Portuguese, Indians and Catholics meant that they were also viewed
with distrust by the predominantly Protestant British (1994: 552). The
classic example from the colonial period is the 1860s *ayah* Anna de
Souza, a Goan Christian from Calcutta, who in giving us one of the
few recorded voices of an *ayah*, reveals that she was keenly aware that
she had no family of her own (Prasad 2003: 12, 18). Then as now, however, the workers' role was more than just the performance of repro-
ductive labour. As the symbol of domesticated otherness they served to
define racial, cultural and class borders and to indeed, affirm the integ-

rity of their employers as individuals and representatives of their collectivities as being unquestionably of the ruling race and class.

She was born in India: creating Maggie Hobbes

So, by the early twentieth century, the figure of the native nursemaid was a crucial signifier of status in a transcolonial world, where identities that might be traced to colonial origins were often unstable, fractured, and subject to sudden reversals. Margaret Ann Hobbes *nee* Goldie, the grandmother of my great-grandmother Joan Strack, would serve as a model 'little Missus' for her granddaughter Joan Strack in Joan's relations with Aboriginal people in the 1920s and 1930s. Joan Kingsley-Strack employed a series of young Aboriginal women as servants through the Aborigines Protection Board in the 1920s and 1930s and in her doing so, she consciously modelled her behaviour on her own great-grandmother, who had used the domestic labour of women from the Aboriginal camp adjacent to her selection on the Far South Coast of NSW in the nineteenth century. Maggie Hobbs 'mothered nursed and cared for the Aboriginal men women and babes ... she fed and clothed them until they came to look upon her as their own "little Missus"' wrote my great-grandmother, as Maggie lay on her deathbed in 1934.[6] This was the panegyric of obituary, but in a letter written around the same time, reflecting on her grandmother's life, Joan Strack touched on her exotic colonial origins:

> Gran was a very beautiful and proud Scotch girl (her father was ... Commodore of the Brit. East India Clipper fleet). She was born in India and sent at an early age back to Scotland with her Ayah. She had never 'worked' in her life, but did most exquisite embroidery and artistic work of all kinds...[7]

In this account, the native *ayah* functions as a potent signifier of Maggie's class and race (and, by extension, her descendants'), the link between the two clauses, 'she was sent back with her *Ayah*' and 'she never worked in her life' makes this even more clear. And importantly, the *ayah* also functioned as a link between Maggie's 'imperial' position in India and her colonial role in Australia, as the loving mistress of servants, and again, by extension, the position of her granddaughter Joan. Thus, in a manuscript Joan crafted, which she hoped (in vain, as it turned out) to have published as a series of Aboriginal legends for children, Joan wrote that her grandmother had a 'a carved Indian box' that 'had been given to her by her old *Ayah* for she was born in India many years ago'. This box became a rhetorical device to launch into a recollection both of her own childhood relationships with the Aboriginal people on her grandparents' property, as she and a few Aboriginal friends pored through the box for treasures on a rainy day, and her relationship with her grandmother's Aboriginal maid, the 'Queen' of the local tribe, who brought them 'hot scones, Brownie, sweets and glasses of milk all round'.[8]

Joan's wistful evocations of her grandmother's Indian childhood do not, however, totally agree with Maggie's own account. For Maggie asserted she was brought from her Scottish birthplace to India by her mother, at four months of age, leaving behind an older brother and rather incredibly, surviving a shipwreck and several days in a small boat at sea, to meet her father. Her earliest memories, moreover, were of Singapore, where her maternal grandfather was harbour master, and where two younger sisters were born in quick succession. At about the age of four, according to Maggie, she was returned to her mother's family in Scotland and soon left orphaned, her father having died of cholera (en route to Russia) and her mother of longstanding childbirth complications. As her mother's family was not 'kind', at the age of seventeen, Maggie and her next youngest sister 'ran away' on an assisted passage to the Australian colonies, where more maternal relatives lived. Having listed their occupations as 'nursery governess', Maggie found work as a governess in Sydney, in the process meeting and fairly quickly – as was the way in the colonies – marrying an English widower. She raised his children, and another eight of her own, on land selected by her husband and sons on the far southern coast of NSW.[9]

Though Maggie had been in India only briefly, potent mythologies of empire suffused Joan's depiction of her return to her ancestral home with a loving *ayah*. Maggie's position as a young, poor and unattached Highlander woman looking for work was precarious. Upper-class English emigrant Amy Henning in her seaboard journal written onboard the *Calcutta* from England to Australia in 1854 described meeting a 'Mrs MacDonald', 'quite a lady,' who had 'been in India a great part of her life' and knew various friends of the Hennings, thus cementing her equivalent status. She was going to Australia to meet her husband who had had to give up his Indian appointment 'from bad health' and had been seeking his fortune in Australia for the past two years. However, Hennings' editor writes that 'the unfortunate' Mrs MacDonald had, in fact, been abandoned by her husband, and 'As a result of his rejection of her, on her arrival in Sydney she was reduced to taking a position as a governess ...' (Thomas 1984: 82, 88). Mrs MacDonald's predicament reveals the dangers that awaited Maggie Hobbs. Arriving in 1858, Maggie came just at the start of an influx of some 90,000 single British women to the Australian colonies in the second half of the nineteenth century (Gothard 2001: 2). Single women emigrating on as-

sisted passages to Australia in the 1850s primarily to supply the need
for domestic workers (these included women brought from the Scottish Highlands to alleviate poverty there) were treated with a discernible anxiety by the authorities and respectable society in general who
subjected them to rigorous moral scrutiny (see Gothard 1991; also
Gothard 2001: 3). In fact, not long before Maggie's arrival, some of the
women sent out to colonies 'under the auspices of the Highland and
Island Emigration Society had been rejected by the colonists because of
the extreme poverty of their background and their total inexperience in
domestic service' (Gothard 2001: 45). Cautionary tales advising single
emigrant women of the need for appropriate behaviour circulated, such
as ex-Indian army officer Charles Mundy's account, published in 1852,
of the downfall of 'two young orphan girls, little more than children,
daughter of a respectable professional man, [who] came out from England' with the 'ostensible object [of] procure[ing] situations as nursery
governesses' but the real aim of finding marriage, 'soon began to show
such levity of manner as to forfeit the protection of [their] kind patrons'
and their downfall was 'predictable'. '... And these were emigrants at
the cost of the territorial revenue of the colony!' (Baker 2006: 180-181).
A socially ambiguous position for an unmarried woman in British society (Gathorne-Hardy 1972: 71) it was even more so in the colonies
(Higman 2002: 9). Would-be governesses dominated the female job
seekers in Sydney between the 1850s and the 1870s, and they could
not easily resist the pressures to take on a wider range of more menial
domestic duties (Higman 2002: 149, 150; Daniels & Murnane 1980:
237-238): Maggie could well have ended up as a servant herself. In this
situation, emphasising her Raj origins was a way of identifying her inclusion in the colonial elite.

The *ayah* played an important role as a foil not only of class, but of
race – and for Maggie, arriving in the Australian colonies not twelve
months after the Indian Mutiny of 1857 (as it was then called by the
British), perhaps more significantly. It had not been uncommon in the
earlier colonial period for British men in India to call upon their British wives or female relatives to take on responsibility for their children
born to Indian women, and even later into the nineteenth century
when attitudes to mixed-descent children were less hostile in England
than in India. Rosemary Raza, for instance, writes of the acceptance of
'the Eurasian children who arrived [from India] in the Highlands' in
the late 1700s, where 'illegitimacy was prevalent at all levels of society',
but noted the 'deepening prejudice' in India since the 1820s against
'half-castes' (2006: 78; see also Brendon 2006: 41-67; Ghosh 2006:
100-105, 125). Whether or not orphaned Maggie and her sister had Indian ancestry, in the gossip-ridden and prejudiced colonial society of
NSW we may be sure that many would have thought so. (As Kirsten

McKenzie [2004] shows, while colonial societies offered opportunities to British settlers for re-invention that they exploited with a vengeance, scandal was never far behind.) A faded photographic portrait of a pensive young Maggie reveals, above a tartan neck bow and stiff Victorian bodice, her olive skin and dark hair and eyes. In 1866, Maggie's husband in his diary recorded that his 'dear wife' had been 'most grossly insulted and treated most cruelly' by one of his sisters:

> I was very sorry and greatly grieved for her sake, she, who does her duty so nobly and works so hard for the children, to be treated by people so much inferior to her in every thing, except perhaps, in having a greater share of money in their pockets. There is much need for me to be very kind indeed to her, more so indeed than I am, to make amends for the cruel deficiency exhibited by the rest of my family may they be forgiven, I cannot do it.[10]

While her husband did not reveal the nature of the insult, such was her sisters-in-law's hostility that they would not even offer their condolences when the couple's first-born child died in an accident as a baby.[11] It may well be that for Maggie herself as well as her own female relatives in the colony playing up her position as a blue-blooded Scottish daughter of the Raj was strategic. Considering the numbers of women migrants coming to Australia with similar fragments of colonial experience, we might hazard a guess that the class and race-defining role served in the figure of the native nurse was more generally more prominent than actual experience warranted.

Chaudhuri quotes a white mistress who wrote, when Maggie was one year old and by her account had just arrived in India, that 'If my child were to stay long in this country, it would be worthwhile to send for an English nurse, but as it is, I hope to bring her home before it becomes of any consequence and meanwhile I keep her as much as possible with me' (1994: 552). British wives were expected to send their children away or leave their husbands in India when the children came of an age to require education 'back Home'. Thus we might – conceivably – justify the decision of Maggie's mother to leave her young son in Scotland but bring her newborn daughter with her to India to join her husband, and again, her decision to go back when Maggie was about four or five years old in 1844. According to a recent historian of Bengali domestic service, Swapna Banerjee, during the British colonial period, Indian domestics were sometimes taken back to Britain but she suggests that this was not typical: 'Some of [the British] even took back to England their 'faithful' Indian domestics' (2004: 53-64). Perhaps, Maggie's mother was indeed very attached to her children's caretaker.

However, it is intriguing that, despite Maggie later telling her descendants she was born in Scotland, she had actually given her birthplace
as Singapore on her Australian shipping record. Had Maggie's ostensible mother *collected* Maggie (and perhaps her sisters too) upon voya-
ging to South-East Asia to join her husband? Could Maggie's *ayah* have
been, indeed, her biological mother?

Maggie never mentions the *ayah* in her own few surviving written
accounts; and after Maggie's prodigal return to Scotland the woman
fades from the scene altogether in Joan's stories. I suspect that,
whether she was Maggie's nurse or mother, the *ayah* did not, in fact,
return to Scotland, but this was an embellishment that Maggie's granddaughter could not resist.

Changing attitudes: Native nursemaids in India and Australia

By the 1930s the image of a cherished *ayah* had been enshrined in the
nostalgia of the Raj that was generated at the close of the nineteenth
century. As that image took on a life of its own, individual recollections
of British colonials were compressed and compelled into the one abid-
ing memory, as Margaret MacMillan put it, of 'a much-loved *ayah*,
usually a small, plump woman with gleaming, oiled hair, dressed in a
white sari, who had sung to them, comforted them, and told them
wonderful Indian stories' (1998: 137).

The *ayah*, the lady's maid, was very likely the only female servant in
a British home, but her presence had become ubiquitous in the nineteenth century, with even lower-class British women in India (i.e., soldier's wives) likely to have had an *ayah* to assist them (Procida 2003:
127-128, 146). In 1828, a doctor dispensing advice to young British
mothers arriving in India declared 'native nurses' to be a great danger.
He was at pains to explain that their object was to make money and
make 'ingratitude' their invariable stance: 'I have known ladies to be-
stow on them repeated presents of clothes and money, to induce them
to be kind to their infants, but without avail; kindness, in fact, seemed
to induce, in many of them, impudence and threats, for the purpose of
exaction', he warned (Fildes 1988: 204-205). The appearance of an
etching showing an 'Ayah stealing a child'[12] at this time suggests a
complex of fears about the dependence of white women on Indian
childcare. At this time, the native female servant was in fact destabilis-
ing social boundaries. By the twentieth century, however, the *ayah's*
function had fundamentally shifted, from necessary evil to status symbol for a beloved white wife. Now the *memsahib* was explicitly exhorted
to take on an *ayah*, even if she had no young children. 'Chota Mem' –

linguistically the Raj equivalent of the 'Little Missus' – told her readers in 1909:

> [I] was always very glad my husband insisted that I should have one. The ayah is a most useful servant and if she is willing and clever will be a tremendous help to you, and you must own it is nice to have one woman in the house. It is such a comfort when you come in hot and tired... (Blunt 1999: 432).

The *ayah's* significance as a female at this time had become heightened in a way unlike that of earlier generations. Steel and Gardiner, those custodians of correct female behaviour in India, advised their readers to treat the *ayah* 'with consideration and respect', being 'the only wo-man-servant in the house'; both they and a writer in the early 1920s advised that the *memsahib* should demonstrate she held her ayah 'equal' to the other servants 'whether she be a sweeper or not' (Blunt 1999: 432).

As ideas about uplifting downtrodden Indian women infiltrated the domestic service relationship, the paranoia expressed about native wet-nurses in the 1820s gave way to the admonitions against 'race preju-dice' evident in the now apparently 'universal horror of wet-nurses' in India. '[If] the Western woman is unable to fulfil her first duty to her child, let her thank Heaven for the gift of any one able to do that duty for her', Steel and Gardiner stated (Blunt 1999: 433).

The *ayah's* role as caretaker of the older children was still hazardous, however. Steel and Gardiner themselves argued that an *ayah* should help care for infants but young children were better cared for by an English nurse, whose superiority in 'upbringing and nice ways, knowl-edge, and trustworthiness' was assumed. 'The Indian *ayah* has many good points; she surrounds her charges with an atmosphere of love and devotion and has infinite patience,' another writer conceded in 1923:

> They make a charming picture – the fair-haired English child and the swarthy-faced ayah with her voluminous white drap-eries, tinkling silver bangles, and gay scarlet coat, as she sits soothing him with magnetic touch, crooning an old-world lulla-by...

But, she warned, 'children left to the care and companionship of native servants run a serious risk of acquiring bad habits, of becoming un-mannerly, and of developing in undesirable ways'. Interestingly, the same writer was also critical of the practice of engaging orphanage girls as nursemaids, underlining their unsuitability whether mixed-descent or of 'pure English extraction', because of their 'infectious' Eurasian accent. A 'judicious English nurse or governess' was needed to train the older children of the British elite (Blunt 1999: 433-435). The *ayah* becomes essentially a picturesque foil to the young white child, underlining, not threatening, the inviolability of her mistress's race and class.

Meanwhile, in Australia, white women were being called upon to 'uplift' Aboriginal girls by taking them into their homes, where they tended to the care of pre-school aged children and babies. As in India, there had been a significant shift in the way that relationships were imagined between white and Aboriginal women. In the 1850s, one Emma McPherson published her account of a Lady's travels in the colonies in which she stated she 'been told, that the native women make kind and careful nurses to European children' but she did not have the confidence to trust them out of sight. She did archly admit to 'get[ting] one of the young girls to carry [the baby] for me when I went out for a stroll, or to walk up and down the veranda with him awhile I sat at work, and very glad I was of such assistance, for nursing in hot weather is a somewhat fatiguing business'. The girl had to first 'bathe in the river' and put on 'a frock' she kept for such occasions, before she 'allowed her to touch my wee one' (1860: 230-231). Emma McPherson and her husband both had Indian backgrounds; their son, also, would join the Indian civil service in the late nineteenth century.[13] Throughout the nineteenth century the requirements of white feminine gentility was transported to the colonies by such women (Russell 1994), which meant there was a noticeable preference for mixed-descent, fairer-skinned women to work as servants. Mrs Gunn's young live-in worker Bett-Bett, for instance, was the daughter of a white man (Ellinghaus 1997: 85). Atlanta Bradshaw relied on the assistance of another abandoned daughter of a white man for the care of her children in late-nineteenth-century central Australia, insisting that her other 'housegirls' left their specially made white uniforms back at the house when they went back to their camp and 'slept with their beloved dogs' (De Vries 2005: 119-120, 123). In the twentieth century, however, the striking yet familiar depiction of the picturesque *ayah* would be echoed in a series of portraits of demure dark-skinned Aboriginal women in white aprons, produced by government administrative 'Protection' boards to circulate amongst prospective white employers, and to promote the policy of indenturing Aboriginal girls and women.

Her old *ayah*: colonialist nostalgia and identity

In my book *One Bright Spot* I have written about Joan Strack's story
and touched upon her grandmother, but did not elaborate on the significance Joan invested in the stories of her grandmother's Indian
childhood and an *ayah* who accompanied her young mistress back to
Scotland before fading from the scene altogether. But there, amongst
Joan's many photographs of her beloved Aboriginal servant, Mary (ap-
prenticed to her between the years 1920 and 1926 under the terms
and conditions established by the Aborigines Protection Board), is a
creased and unidentified sepia shot of a small nineteenth-century white
child – sex indeterminate – with a sari-clad *ayah*. I have no idea who
the child or woman are, nor when the little photograph was taken, but
I can be sure that this anonymous image was treasured as a memento
of colonialist nostalgia that helped Ming to identify and locate her own
experience in a familial web of empire.

There is a well-established, even classic tri-generational genesis of
the 'good fella missus' ideal: from the 'sterling mother' (the British
emigrant) to the 'Australia's daughter' (born in the bush), and then finally, the 'modern urban woman' (McGuire 1990: 143). In this persua-
sive paradigm, my great-grandmother Joan Strack can be depicted as
the third generation and her grandmother Maggie as the first. But the
elusive and provocative wisps of story that point to the Indian connection suggest that the imagined relationships between white women
and 'natives' in Australia were constructions of a larger transcolonial
network of women's lives. Maya Jasanoff (2005) writes of the plethora
of exotic items, transported around the world by colonial travellers before 1850, that helped to fashion a collective mythology of empire. Just
as I suspect that in reality no *ayah* actually accompanied young Maggie
back to Scotland, I am rather sceptical of my grandmother's story about
a carved Indian box of treasures, given to Maggie by her 'old *Ayah*'
many years ago. Yet, if it did exist, it surely was an instance of the imperial mania for collecting. Certainly as a metaphor for an imaginary
idea of colonialism transported from colony to colony, the carved Indian box signifying a gift of native devotion certainly evokes the way
that cultural ideas were transported around the webs of Empire. In the
travels of women like Maggie Hobbes, the image of the loving *ayah*
they carried with them fundamentally shaped our understandings of
white womanhood in colonialism.

Notes

1   This essay was originally presented as a conference paper at the ICAS5, Kuala Lum-
     pur, under the title, 'Memsahib and Missus: transcolonial constructions of the white
     mistress in India and Australia'. A version of this paper, under the same title, appears
     in the *Journal of the Oriental Society of Australia* (forthcoming, 2009).
2   Walden elaborates on this point in her unpublished 1991 BA Honors thesis, 'Aborigi-
     nal Women in Domestic Service in New South Wales, 1850 to 1969', University of
     New South Wales, Sydney.
3   *The Red Man* vol. VIII, October 1888, no. 11, 6.
4   Abbreviated version. See *The Newcastle Morning Herald* 10 February 1926, quoted in
     full in John Maynard's 2003 Ph.D. (Aboriginal Studies) thesis, 'Fred Maynard and
     the Awakening of Aboriginal Political Consciousness and Activism in Twentieth-Cen-
     tury Australia', Ph.D. (Aboriginal studies), University of Newcastle, Callaghan.
5   Robert Scobie, *NSW Parliamentary Debates*, 27 January 1915, vol. 57, p. 1965. It
     should be noted, however, that Scobie himself argued against instituting the tactic of
     child removal.
6   Joan Kingsley-Strack, diary entry 5 May 1934: Series 2 (6), Joan Kingsley-Strack Pa-
     pers MS 9551, National Library of Australia.
7   Joan Kingsley-Strack to [Brian Penton], undated, c. 1934: series 1 (11), Joan Kingsley-
     Strack Papers MS 9551, National Library of Australia.
8   Joan Kingsley-Strack, unpublished manuscript, 'Nareen and Gooli': series 6 (5), Joan
     Kingsley-Srack Papers MS 9551.
9   From a letter by Margaret Hobbes (*nee* Goldie), n.d., to one of her children (original
     in possession of Joan Strack's cousin Jenny Carter), transcribed by Joan Kingsley-
     Strack, Sydney 1957: Series 9 (1), Joan Kingsley-Srack Papers MS 9551.
10 John Thomas Hobbes diary, 22 May 1866, personal possession of Peter Haskins.
11 John Thomas Hobbes diary, 22 May 1866, personal possession of Peter Haskins.
12 'Rape of the infant', c. 1825, T. Little [ed.], *Confessions of an Oxonian in Three Vo-
     lumes. Vol. II.* London: J.J. Stockdale 1826 (front plate).
13 I am indebted to Stephen Foster for this information.

The Chinese, the Indians and the French Exchange Control during the French Indochinese War or How to Endure, Fight and Mock the Colonial Power (1945-1954)

Daniel Leplat

Introduction

'The piastre is not a currency, it is an object of traffic.' A government official, in the French Ministry of Finance, summed up the whole monetary history of Indochina from 1945 to 1954 in this way.[1]

Whereas the exchange rate of the piastre had been set at FF 17 on 25 December 1945, piastres could soon be found on the Asian markets for the equivalent of FF 3 or FF 10 (FF = French francs). This phenomenon led to multiple arbitrages and caused a stir in France where this 'ordinary' Asian speculation became a scandal, because it was through this trafficking, that the French Treasury resources were prodigally spent.

The French and Indochinese press soon started to depict the suspect, frightening circle of Asian financiers. The journalist-cum-novelist L. Bodard wrote:

> They are the souls of the markets, speculations, exchanges, and trafficking. Each of them has a fortune of his own which often amounts to dozens of millions of piastres. Each of them is at the head of an organisation of his own, namely his own men of straw, touts and even 'killers'. His family is a tribe.[2]

This paper does not aim to present a full account of the Asian networks of money trafficking or draw up an exhaustive list of the wrong ideas that have circulated on this subject.[3] The police archives and military archives are unfortunately seldom or never used, especially since access to them is restricted. My study is essentially based on the French public civil archives (mostly from the Ministry of Finance and the Ministry of Justice) and belongs to the study of the diasporas and colonialism, notably in the economic field. Lastly, it aims to provide a historical approach to the current studies by the international financial organisations on the Alternative Remittance Systems.

The Chinese and Indian diasporas were the main Asian diasporas in French Indochina in the period 1945-1954. These two groups were severely hit by the troubles in Asia after World War II: the independence of India in 1947, the victory of the Communists in China in 1949, and the presence of the Chinese nationalist armies in Southeast Asia. In addition to all of these major events, there was also a troublesome colonial war in Indochina. Because of all this, the diasporas had to change their organisations.

However, a strict exchange rate aiming at protecting the piastre was established in Indochina at the very same time and it was the source of particular difficulties for the groups in question: not only were the usual financial practices suddenly prohibited, but this prohibition took place at the worst possible moment, when they had to change their positions.

By what means did international communities in Indochina succeed in circumventing the French exchange controls? How can we account for these dealings, which, even if illegal, are far from being totally inspired by the rapacious thirst for profit?[4]

After presenting the rules that were imposed on the two diasporas, I shall study the practices of money transfers among the Chinese, and then the Indian, diasporas.

I.   The game and its rules

A.   Indochina as a 'golden cage'

On 25 December 1945, the French government set the exchange rate of the piastre at FF 17. This rate was to remain unchanged until 11 May 1953 when it was reduced to FF 10. The reasons for this choice and for its confirmation were the cause of much debate. It was mainly the result of French politicians' desire to stimulate a quick return to prosperity in Indochina and to win the support of the local populations. Later, however, the ongoing negotiations between France and the Associated States prevented any alteration in the exchange rate.

It proved a costly choice, however, for the overvaluation of the piastre triggered inflation and the monetary difficulties that hit France at the time.[5] The French Treasury consequently tried to lower the value of the piastre: it tried to limit the circulation of the piastre to Indochina exclusively. In the Indochinese colonies, imports were still facilitated by the parity of the franc and the piastre. Yet the official import plans tried, without much success, to limit the purchases.

The Indochinese Exchange Office (IEO), a branch of the Exchange Office of the French Ministry of Finance in Paris, was responsible for controlling the circulation of the piastre. Year after year, the Treasury attempted to reduce the cost of the prolonged Indochinese war, and the IEO thus became the all-governing body of Indochina's financial world.

What were the relationships between the IEO and the diasporas being studied?

In commercial matters, Chinese or Indian distinctions should not be overstated. The Chinese and Indians both sought to protect themselves against the risk of a sudden devaluation of the piastre, and similarly to what the French and Vietnamese merchants did, they also imported and stocked goods, especially non-perishable ones.[6] Like the Indochinese, the Indians and Chinese got lost in the intricacies of the IEO's regulations and unwittingly committed fraud, but most of these innocent traffickers were Chinese people.

Why? We will now turn to an analysis of these two communities.

B.   The Chinese in Indochina and the French Exchange Control

The presence of the Chinese in Indochina is fairly long-standing and multifaceted (the first mention of Chinese merchants in Vietnam dates back to the fourteenth century, moreover a large number of political refugees arrived in the seventeenth century). This presence has had a great influence on the history (i.e., the case of the eighteenth-century sub-kingdom of Ha Tien in southern Vietnam), demography, and economy of Vietnam, and it has accordingly been thoroughly studied. During colonial times, the activities of Chinese people as essential mediators between the colonisers and the colonised have been abundantly described, with most of these studies stressing the ambiguity of this role: the Chinese being exploited by but also exploiting the colonial power.

However, all these studies have not been able to resolve the many issues raised by the Chinese diaspora in Vietnam. The precise delimitation of the group that should be considered is an unsolved, probably unsolvable, problem. Consequently, estimates of the economic or demographic place of the Chinese community diverges widely: in 1955, the estimates of the Chinese population living in South Vietnam varied from between 620,858 to more than one million. According to the Statistical Yearbook of South Vietnam, Chinese companies received 31 per cent of the delivered trading licences, but some specialists believed that their influence probably accounted for 50 per cent of the South Vietnamese economy.[7] Thus, the Chinese were the largest diaspora on the peninsula, and the French had to set up exchange controls accordingly.

Moreover, the international context forced the French to adopt an apparently benevolent position towards the Chinese. In 1945-1946, Chiang Kai-shek had the upper hand and the French had to concede a great many privileges in order to gain a peaceful evacuation of Chinese troops from Northern Indochina. Later, the fall of the Nanjing regime restored the balance of power, but soon after, the silent threat of a Communist invasion from the Beijing Republic and the wish to negotiate the preservation of the French position in China itself convinced the French to maintain their benevolent attitude.

Yet this benevolence was very ambiguous. Admittedly, some decisions show that the French wanted to establish peaceful relations with the Chinese. The Bank of China received an agreement for the carrying out of international operations at the very same time as two prominent British banks did so.[8] Besides the French took into account the specific needs of the Chinese consumers and granted them licences to import tea, spices and other products. Lastly, when Indochinese 500-dollar bills were devaluated, the authorities in Nanjing obtained the conversion of the funds of piastres held in the Yunnan Province. These favours, however, are typical of the complicated game that was then being played in Indochina. If France authorised the repurchase of the piastres held in Yunnan, it was because some of these bills had a compromising origin. In other words, because they lacked currencies, the French troops in North Indochina had sold their stocks of devaluated bills in early 1946! In spite of instructions requiring discretion, Chinese authorities discovered this manoeuvre, and France was thus forced to repurchase the piastres![9] The episode of the special import licences is perhaps of the same nature. Indeed, if the French administration gracefully authorised the imports, it forgot to provide the corresponding currencies, and the Chinese thus had to buy them on black market.[10] The Chinese Embassy diplomatically asked France to correct this mistake. However, it is possible that the French authorities had taken this problem into account, but that, by forcing the Chinese to buy currencies on the black markets, France hoped to spare itself the chore of having to provide currencies. The French benevolence was thus very diplomatic and though seemingly peaceful, Franco-Chinese relations were plagued with difficulties.

Another difficulty was that the Chinese were still using gold as a common currency, but trading with gold was tightly regulated by the exchange control. While gold could generally be openly transported within Indochina, exporting or importing it required special permits. Eventually, the French legal system gave in and a few convictions were overturned, in consideration of these traditional Chinese uses for gold. More often, however, the Chinese were still being portrayed as vulgar traffickers.

As for the currencies, the exchange office required some documents to allow financial transfers but most of the Chinese were not accustomed to these administrative procedures. In order to get around them, they preferred to use simpler, yet illegal, ways.[11]

Even for the merchants' group, which was acquainted with the official regulations and operations regarding money, these transactions were not that easy. The Indians could rely on the structures if not on the support of the powerful English banks established in Indochina (HSBC, Chartered). The Chinese, on the other hand, sometimes suffered from weaknesses in their own banking structures. Admittedly, powerful Chinese banks were established in Indochina (Bank of China, Bank of Communication, etc.) but at the beginning of 1950, these institutions were affected by the revolution in China and their transfer capacities were limited.

The role of the Chinese in the trafficking should also be cautiously interpreted because to some extent, it reflects the difficulty, not to say the impossibility, of the latter to adapt to French exchange controls.

However, in spite of the attested activity of the Chinese networks and the daily difficulties raised by and with the 'Celestial', the question of the exchange controls in Indochina never contributed to the tensions existing between France and China. This contrasts greatly with the Franco-Indians relations.

C.   The Indians in Indochina and French Exchange Controls.

The Indian communities in Indochina have been far less studied than the Chinese diaspora.[12] The Indians, however, had an important influence on the history of the countries that constituted the former Indochina (like Kampuchea, South Vietnam and the kingdoms of Champa and Founan) – but the rather small size, the diversity of the cultures, and the situations or the legal statutes that characterised the Indian community in colonial Indochina makes any study difficult.

Some studies estimate the number of Indians living in Indochina in 1930 as follows. 5,000 came from the British Empire, especially from Tamil Nadu in the south although there were groups of Indians from the north as well, coming from Sind or Gujarat. There were also 1,000 Indians coming from the French Indian Settlements, primarily from Pondicherry and Karikal. However, these estimates are quite unreliable since only males were counted. The community originating from French India was surely the more important.

We can basically distinguish three groups, according to their statutes:

1. the renonçants came from the French territories and were mainly employed in the administration or the army.
2. the non-renonçants from the French territories[13] lived sparingly from employments in private companies, especially manual labour.
3. the merchants, comprised mostly of British subjects. There were Moslems and Hindus, as well. Among the Moslems, the Sindi mer-

chants should be mentioned, because they were important in the textile trade, particularly the silk trade. Among the Hindus, there are 300 *chettys* (or bankers) listed in 1930.

It was primarily due to the latter category that the Indian diasporas, although of smaller size, played a significant role in the economy of Indochina: a 1929-1930 report estimated that the *chettys'* resources amounted to 12 billion francs, including 500 million invested in Indochina (approximately € 230,000 in 2000 terms).[14] We know that the upheavals of the 1930s and the war drove some Indians out of Indochina. The economic importance of this diaspora remained considerable: in June 1946, the assets of 117 *chettys* near the Saigon branch of the Chartered Bank increased to 4.9 millions piastres,[15] and we know that the assets of one Sindi merchant from Hanoi were worth several millions.

The introduction of an exchange control in Indochina produced various problems for the Indians. The *renonçants* could easily transfer their salaries to the French Settlements. The financial networks and the domestic finances of the non-*renonçants*, and especially the merchants from the former British Indies, were stretched to the limit. The majority of these Indians had left their families in India and they needed to regularly transfer sums to provide for the needs of their relatives and finance their own return to India (a *chetty* returned to India every 2 or 3 years).

Did France take the Indians' need for a certain freedom in handling their funds into account?

I did not find any examples of hostility or racism in the documents I reviewed and, given the small size of the Indian community (and thus the limited financial consequences of their requests), the French authorities would no doubt have been well disposed towards their requests. The question of Indochina's Indians, however, is part of the history of the whole region.

The French Treasury at first feared that if they granted favours to the Indians in Indochina, then the Chinese community would ask for similar favours – which, because of the size of the Chinese community, would have exceeded the financial capacities of France. The requests for the transfer of non-French Indian inheritances of those who had died in Indochina were thus rejected.[16]

However, the crucial question of the French Indian Settlements and, in general, of French goods in India, remained. Since the end of World War II, the Indian Custodian of Enemy Property retained 4 to 10 million rupees worth of French possessions.[17] These goods were mostly concentrated in the French Indian Settlements and, as early as 1947, the problem of Pondicherry was raised. The government of independent India tried through commercial, political and financial pressure to retrieve these lost pieces of Indian territory, pointing out its hostility to the French policy to come back to Asia as a colonial power.[18] In financial matters, the tensions were further fed by the fact that Pondicherry was the centre of the diamond and gold trafficking trade – and these two items were not allowed to be imported into India.[19]

The problems of freeing the French Indian Settlements were never really solved during these years and they have helped to give a very special tone to the Franco-Indian negotiations that contrasts greatly with the threatening yet tactful tone used by both the Chinese and the French. Although the Indians could have hoped for more flexible treatment, their capacity to engage in transfers was basically dependent upon the progress in the negotiations between the two governments and thus some transfers were blocked or limited.

The French authorities did not persecute the Indian communities, however, particularly because a significant part of these Indians were by then French citizens. Besides the dozens of refusals already mentioned, the Indians enjoyed rather favourable, if not privileged, conditions when engaging in transfers. They were allowed to promptly transport currencies for them to take along on their journeys. The transfer formalities involving families were also made easier.[20] This is undoubtedly one of the reasons for their apparently insignificant part in the trafficking of piastres. To carry out their daily transfers, they did not need, as the Chinese did, to use illegal means – and if they wanted to speculate, they had more discreet means (i.e., dummy entries between Pondicherian and French companies, trafficking via the Stock Exchange, etc.). In this way, they easily evaded the authorities.

II.   'The International Celestial Corporation Ltd.': Chinese commercial practices and fraudulent methods in Indochina

The problem of the exchange control system was very different for the Chinese, because the Chinese communities did not have the same needs and they had a different set of rules to observe. How did the diasporas react to these constraints?

Because of the lack of resources, we cannot truly study how the Chinese and Indians complied with the exchange controls put into place and thus we have to limit our study to the infringements on the system committed by the diasporas. This aspect has real historical implications because it concerns the criminal behaviour of some of the Chinese (the gang of 'le Grand Monde', etc.) who came to the attention of French public opinion. Use of the various sources is made more difficult, however, by the inaccuracies that are discerned among the writings of various protagonists.

First, with the Chinese community I will first try to specify the types of fraudulent financial practices that the Chinese preferred, before studying in greater detail how their networks operated. Finally, I will deal with the existence or the non-existence of definitely criminal or politically influenced networks.

A.   Trade and fraud: a statistical study of some Chinese financial practices

The police files have some characteristics which make their statistical use difficult: the services performed are often cyclical, qualifications vary, etc. In the Ministry of Justice archives relating to piastre trafficking, the files of various jurisdictions within the Marseilles-Aix area are thus fairly equal in percentages compared to France in general. No doubt, this partly reflects reality: as Marseilles was then the principal port for ships heading to Indochina, most traffickers had to go through Marseilles. This development is however largely contingent on the fact that in 1948-1952, the national administration turned its attention to trafficking that took place through the postal service but lacked the means to successfully deal with these crimes. Thus the authorities could only examine the problem locally at the Marseilles post office. The statistics drawn from a simple census of the files preserved in the Ministry of Justice archives can thus not be used to study piastre trafficking (inter)nationally.

Our study is based on a census of all those mentioned in the piastre trafficking files kept by the Ministry of Justice, the Ministry of Finance and the Ministry of Relations with the Associated States (i.e., the old colonies). Two lists have thus been produced. The first one includes 3,008 individual names, listed by country of origin (Europeans, Indians, Chinese, Vietnamese, etc.), by the types of fraud perpetrated, and the total amounts involved. The second list presents the groups of traffickers, using the same categories.

We should not be impressed by these figures because they are not particularly reliable: the majority of the files are still being investigated, thus the list includes people who will later be found innocent; also, there are other files that we know exist, that are not mentioned here. In particular, those who were tried in Indochina are barely mentioned because the Indochinese Exchange Office, as well as the local police force and Indochinese courts, supplied very little data. What is really notable, however, is that this list only mentions the cases prosecuted in urban areas, which is a severe limitation when one is studying colonial history and the colonised people!

Table 1 Number of fraudulent activities committed by people of the same origin group group / Type of fraud

	French name	Indian name	Arabic name	Chinese name	% of this fraud for all frauds committed by the Chinese	Vietnamese name	Other	Unknown	Total	% of this kind of fraud for all frauds
Unknown or not related to the exchange control regulation	599	7	10	35	19.6 %	144	21	66	882	0.26 %
Postal	760	2	7	25	0.14 %	59	11	8	872	25.7 %
Probably by post	50	0	0	2	1.1 %	2	0	1	55	1.6 %
Financial transfer trafficking	200	4	0	24	13.5 %	63	5	4	300	8.8 %
Probably financial transfer trafficking	240	10	6	21	11.8 %	64	3	19	363	10.7 %
Private transactions	36	1	1	9	0.05 %	25	4	1	77	2.3 %
Probably private transactions	8	1	0	0	0 %	1	0	0	9	0.3 %
Commercial transaction trafficking	85	1	0	5	2.8 %	35	3	2	131	3.8 %
Probably commercial transaction trafficking	24	10	3	5	0.03 %	10	1	2	55	1.6 %
Illegal transport of currencies	303	4	11	34	19.1 %	62	4	18	436	12.8 %
Probably illegal transport of currencies	14	0	0	1	0.6 %	2	1	1	19	0.5 %
Illegal transport of gold	108	5	2	12	6.7 %	26	5	8	166	4.9 %
Probably illegal transport of gold	16	7	0	5	2.8 %	3	0	0	31	0.9 %
Total	2,443	52	40	178	10.7 %	496	58	130	3,396	99.9 %
World-wide trafficking	38	2	0	19		14	1	3	77	2.3 %
Probably world-wide trafficking	49	10	0	2	0.01 %	1	2	0	64	1.9 %

Table 2   *Composition of the group of traffickers described in the files of the French Ministry of Justice*

	Number of people in...	Per cent
Group with only French names	343	42.5
Group with only Vietnamese names	122	15.1
Group with only Chinese names	29	3.5
Total for groups with only one kind of names	494	61.1
Group with French and Vietnamese names	118	14.6
Group with French and Chinese names	16	2
Group with Chinese and Vietnamese names	12	1.5
Group with three kinds of names or more	166	20.6
TOTAL	806	100

Source: CARAN, BB 18 7092 sq.

Despite these limitations, these lists do provide some valuable information. Table 3 synthesises the information that focuses on the Chinese networks.

First, we will notice the very small number of Sino-Vietnamese networks comprising a dozen people out of a total of 900. The number is far fewer than we expected. This small sample may mean that there was a certain distance between Chinese and Vietnamese economic circles, but it also reflects the particular *modus operandi* of the Asian financial networks. Indeed, we generally know only the central aspects of these circles; the incoming (supply of the funds) and the outgoing (final destination) details of the trafficking remain unknown. I will reconsider this problem later.

Second, the Chinese often resorted to a system of 'private compensation' (in one-third of the cases, as opposed to less than three per cent among the French networks). This technique simply consists of making a sum in one currency available to a client in one place, while the equivalent of this sum is paid out somewhere else in another currency. For example, M. Dupont gives 10 piastres to M. San in Saigon and, upon his arrival in Paris, M. Dupont withdraws 170 francs from M. Si, cousin of M. San. This very simple system is almost impossible to detect by the authorities: If the French authorities managed to discover three Chinese cases, it means that the Chinese were very actively involved in this type of transaction, which largely went undetected.

Thirdly, we note the importance of the Chinese in the business of world-wide traffic (WWT). By WWT we mean the return of a sum originating from Indochina back to Asia. The exchange rates made this operation far more beneficial than the simple conversion of overestimated piastres into francs. Of the 141 people suspected of having taken part in world-wide trafficking, 46 per cent were French, while only 10 per cent were Vietnamese and 15 per cent Chinese. These data show that the Chinese often did resort to world-wide trafficking: 11.8 per cent of the Chinese traffickers took part in WWT, versus less than 4 per cent of the French traffickers and 3 per cent of Vietnamese traffickers. The diagram below represents one WWT system developed by a network known as TCC and its allies, according to statements by two of its members.[21]

Figure 4   *World-wide traffic: TCC's network*

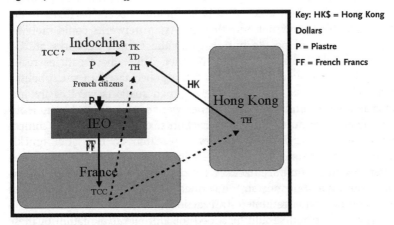

The two framed initials are those of two brothers. The unbroken arrows represent currency transfers and broken arrows represent the transmission of information.

And finally, we must deal with the immense transport capacity of the Chinese networks. The data, however, remains dubious, as is also the case for business data. In other words, the number of funds involved changes during the various stages of the procedures. A list based only on the files of the Ministry of Justice shows that, whereas a fraudulent transaction committed by a French person involved 9.8 million francs on average (2.91 million per person), a fraudulent transaction committed solely by Vietnamese suspects involved 21.1 million (6.52 million per person) and those committed by Chinese people averaged 28.45 million (9.95 million per person).

Table 3 *Comparison between networks involving individuals of only one nationality*

criteria / group	Metropolitan French	Vietnamese people	Chinese people
Number of files	70 files	21 files	9 files
= Involved Money	= 685.59 million FF	= 443.16 million FF	= 256.13 million FF
Average involved money per file	9.8 million	21.1 million	28.45 million
Average number of people per file	3.36	3.2	2.8

However, while the first three points are fairly certain, provided our re-marks are taken into account, this last point appears particularly du-bious. The files show not only that the Asian networks could mobilise a great number of people but also that the French networks are de-scribed in an abnormally precise manner. These discrepancies result largely from the working conditions the police faced in metropolitan areas. The networks involving solely French suspects were easily ana-lysed as a whole and individual names were often put in charge. How-ever, when it came to the Asian networks, only their French compo-nents could be scrutinised, and even research on the latter quickly butted against the silence or the pretended ignorance of the convicts. A better statistical analysis (factor analysis) carried out on all of the re-cords, does not show any strong connections between nationalities and the amounts of the fraudulent transactions.

A further method should be added for a proper exploitation of these data. We know that a regrouping along patronymic bases is a dubious method but some aspects that do not concern criminology and involve the study of the diasporas in Asia, however, appear to be established here. Without the development of any culturalist model and by means of a comparison imposed by two facts, namely (1) the actual existence of the Chinese networks; and (2) the attestation of relations of confi-dence which hold a significant place (cf. use of the private compensa-tion), it matters very little what name (*guanxi, xinyong*) one gives to this spirit of 'confidence'.[22] It is the effectiveness of these networks that made it possible for some Chinese people not only to adapt to but also benefit from the hardening of the monetary sector, which characterised the post-Second World War period. 'The Chinese are born exchangers', acknowledged J. Maxime-Robert, a director at the very influential Bank of Indochina.

B.   Operation of the Chinese networks: case studies

The above quotation by one of the most important French bankers in Indochina is not that original, however, because all visitors to Indochina soon recognised the talents of the Chinese moneychangers and their networks. It is necessary to recall a cliché about both the framework and the context of activities involved in exchange trafficking among the Chinese, which were known to everybody.

The collapse of China after the war, the difficulties of the French 'Reconstruction' period, the war in Indochina, and the installation of the Bretton Woods system, all occurred within a few years. They could not have taken place without being first phased in to acclimatise the various actors involved. The Chinese had to engage in their money changing activities in various grey zones, just below the radar of the authorities.

Because of French regulations, Chinese exchange activities had to be practised discreetly (underground) but it was far from being totally clandestine. In December 1950, for instance, a Chinese travel agency as a natural thing recommended that the Indochinese Exchange Office should feed the French financial reserves with Hong Kong Dollars by means of its clients' money.[23] When, in January 1953, the French Ministry of Finances came up with the idea of buying piastres for itself on the black market, Chinese businessmen naturally came to the IEO to offer their services.[24] Of course, none of these moneychangers were ever prosecuted.

Actually, the discrepancies between the official and black quotation of the piastre was so big that the trafficking was integrated in the economy of Indochina. The Chinese took the lead in exploiting this parallel economy without meeting much resistance, because the French generally feared being prosecuted in the metropolitan areas. Large, world-famous companies, such the rubber companies[25] and various import-export businesses[26] thus turned to the Chinese community to engage in speculation but also simply survive the times. They used trafficking to limit the increase in their selling prices, which resulted from the parity of the piastre.

How was this grey economy organised? In the multi-cultural networks, in particular, we constantly find the figure of the single intermediary, who exclusively ensures transactions between various parties. These individuals, who may have had a specific title or not, clearly acted as compradors, or go-betweens, for various economic groups; they also provided lists of names and raised capital.

Thus, if the piastre trade was declared illegal, it was these grey zone networks that were used to foster money exchange traffic. This recourse to the old system of the 'instituted passor' reinforces some scientific notions that the compradors were not specifically part of a colonial structure.

However, is this similarity with the comprador relevant? The recourse to an intermediary is found in most networks that introduce

people of the same culture, and is easily turned to by those working in
a hostile or foreign environment. The use of the delegate system had
numerous advantages: it covered or repudiated the intermediary if
caught by the police but, most of all, this system was very mobile and
made contacts easier and, thus, facilitated the exploitation of all the options. Asian people contacted French citizens who then sold their big
transfer options to them,[27] and the Chinese sometimes even profited
from the Vietnamese diaspora to France[28] – these Vietnamese were
contacted through the efforts of this 'grey comprador'.

In fact, this similarity seems relevant because of the social position
of most of the known intermediaries. Indeed, it was just simple students who were implicated in some of these cases, but the Chinese involved in the most documented cases were influential people in the Indochinese commercial world. For example, at least one President and
one Vice-president of the Chinese Chamber of Commerce,[29] one member of 'Le Grand Monde',[30] and one comprador,[31] are mentioned in
these files – not to mention one more dubious case.

Did all this go on secretly, right in the middle of the war in Indochina? Chinese networks were in fact put to a severe trial and, while
the structures remained more or less stable, individuals had to overcome the shock of the upheavals. General G. Buis tells how, when he
was the head of the 'Sécurité Générale de Saigon', the head of a Chinese congregation asked him to hold on to his money or transfer it
back to his widow, because he feared for his own life. Mr. Buis refused,
thinking he was trying to bribe him. And yet, two days later and despite extra police protection, this notable Chinese person was mur-
dered and his fortune disappeared.[32] Thus we need to study the black
zones after we have looked at the grey zones.

C.   Asian gangsters?

The illegal activities of the Chinese gave birth to fantasies and various
French writers in Saigon spoke of the 'Chinese Al Capone',[33] who was
the 'suave and always smiling yellow billionaire.'[34] Some supposedly
informed authors wrote about 'the Chinese communist network' that
was speculated in the piastre, with worldwide networks going from Saigon through Paris, Zurich, New York, and returned to Asia, via Manila,
Hong Kong or Bangkok.

TCC's business dealings, along with some other cases, reveal that
there was some truth in these descriptions. Geneva, New York, etc.,
were all interested in the piastre business – but imagination and xeno-
phobia were to play a large part in these descriptions. What was the actual importance of these global speculation networks led by the Chi-

nese? Was it for their own benefit or that of specific interest groups (i.e., the Communist Party, criminal organisations)?

The French intelligence services were already trying in 1949 to come up with an assessment. A very secret report dated 25 August 1950 from the Technical Office of Connection and Coordination (*Bureau Technique de Liaison et de Coordination*), which was in charge of intelligence in Indochina, pictures a Chinese group related to a group in Macao. It was 'the richest and most powerful group, [which reportedly accounted for] 70% of the Chinese traffic', and quickly imposed itself upon an older, local Chinese group. These two groups were known as 'Le Groupe du Grand Monde'.

Some developments are well-known like the surge of a new group in collaboration with the great centres of international currency trafficking. The information was, however, very unreliable. In fact, a report from August 1950 gives a C/3 value to the intelligence, which means the lowest level of intelligence reliability.

The French did not manage to get more information and in 1956, all piastre exchanges were re-examined in order to better detect the trafficking that could have been directly used to benefit the Viet Minh. A senior police officer, after having card-indexed nearly 900 people, could only conclude that 'it is materially impossible... to bring the least solid proof [that the piastre traffic had benefited to the Viet Minh].'[35]

By comparing information found in the archives, a historian can only draw conclusions about the activities of some individuals such as the Lau brothers – one was the President of the Chinese Chamber of Commerce in Saigon and had contact with the Viet Minh as well as Binh Xuyen in 1952.[36] However, these cases only point to the obvious, that is, that it was impossible for the Chinese to remain neutral regarding all of the political turbulence on the peninsula. The Chinese, who had to pay tithes and put their sales networks at the service of the belligerents, could obviously not avoid having to offer their exchange network services.

The movements of gold during this period in Hong Kong and bound for Indochina were probably used to support the Viet Minh via international exchange revenues, but to what extent has not been fully established.

III.   The Indians of Indochina and piastre trafficking

A.   There are as many ways to traffic as there are Indians

We do not have as much on the Indians as we do on the Chinese, and no instructive statistical study can thus be carried out. However, the files that have survived show that the Indians used every existing trick to outfox the French: via the postal service,[37] via the commercial world,[38] or via financial transactions,[39] the Indians in Indochina attempted to evade the French authorities.

We might characterise the fraudulent practices of the Indians. They had a liking for gold,[40] which at that time certainly had a connection with the Pondicherry trafficking. They seemed to practice speculative traffic in a fairly important proportion. Resorting to 'daily' frauds was spared them thanks to the generous legislation which has already been described. Moreover, the people associated with the Indians came from a wide variety of different groups: the French, Lebanese, the Vietnamese, etc.[41]

However, as we noted earlier, all of these observations were based on very few cases; therefore they remain uncertain and only two points seem to have been verified on any level.

B.   The Indians' diplomatic traffic

First, the groups that made up the Indian diaspora were aware early on of the political aspects of the situation, and they did their best to pursue their interests during the Franco-Indian negotiations. It is therefore possible that, among the transfers requested by the authorities, some were used for speculative trafficking.

There were no illegal operations that could be pinpointed, but the French government was indeed impressed by the philanthropic generosity of the Indians in January 1951, when India requested authorisation to send 193,000 rupees to Sind. Then in July, the Indian Consulate transferred 75,000 piastres for various Indian social organisations, while a second donation by an Indian merchant went to the construction of a maternity hospital in his village. In 1951, people donated money to India because of a major earthquake in Sind, not to mention that 1951 was the worst economic year of the entire 1950s-1960s period.[42] However this generosity also came at the time of France's major defeats in Tonkin, and it was also the same year that French businesses began leaving Indochina.

While the Vietnamese and French may have profited from political transfers, the Indian people tried to do so via diplomatic transfers.

C.   Mister L.'s story: mocking the colonisers[43]

My other observations are based on a single case. The documents of this case are more numerous than for all of the other cases, since the guilty party was living in France at the time.

Mr. L. was born in Hyderabad in 1921. He was an English citizen but he established a successful textile business in Lyons. His success, however, attracted the attention of the French police who discovered that Mr. L., besides having established a vast European exchange system (France – Switzerland – Italy), had organised a system of over-invoicing in an Indochinese context. Buying kilos of textile from the 'Plymouth company', L. invoiced the same produce but replaced the kilos with meters, thus quintupling the price of the goods (according to customs estimates). This kind of fraud, which consists of replacing the unit of measure, is the first point which distinguishes L. from the usual traffickers because it is the only known example of this practice.

The second point relates to the relations between L. and the French justice system. The behaviour of the accused is seldom mentioned in the police files but that of L. is condemned as disdainful – which was all the more intolerable for the French policemen since the person of L. was unassailable. Indeed, whereas abusing transfers was an offence in Indochina, the over-invoicing that had allowed these transfers was not punishable in France. Consequently, L. only went back to India, thus escaping French legal proceedings.

The case of L. does not readily lead to generalisations, but this example of a citizen from a French colony cunningly manipulating the colonisers, remains an interesting case because it points out the well-known defects of French legislation which could be exploited by this young man. One has to wonder whether the practice of faking the measurement units was not the idea of someone with a British connection, who knew the difficulties of people used to the metric system in handling Anglo-Saxon measurements.

Conclusion

The unique nature of the Indochinese situation and the French political will to maintain a strong sense of parity to the then still unstable piastre, lent the entire piastre trafficking case its distinction. This episode, however, occurred in a broader history of the entire international monetary system. By imposing a system of fixed parities on a troubled world, the system of Bretton Woods provided numerous occasions for exchange trafficking to emerge and the piastre affair is only one example of this larger issue.

However, the Indians and the Chinese of Indochina both felt the ill effects of the exchange control system because they had specific needs regarding the mobility of capital. However we need to insist on giving attention to the human cost of this exchange control, especially for the diasporas. But that falls outside of our limited scope and time restraints, and thus I can only further present the singular case of the Kouo Tsing couple. Mrs. Kouo had come to France looking for a cure

for her tuberculosis and was soon immobilised by her disease. However, she eventually had to return to Asia in order to evade the Ministry
of Finance's investigations of her. There is no doubt that this Chinese
woman, who was confined to bed and under treatment, did not survive
long after her return to her war-torn homeland. The Kouo couple, it is
true, did resort to various illegal practices, misleading the Foreign Exchange Office and tax officials – but how could this Asian couple have
successfully abused an exchange control legislation that frightened
even French citizens?

In order to evade the French government, the diasporas used their
community's Alternative Remittance Systems (ARS). To some extent
they therefore managed not only to free themselves from the constraints imposed on them by the colonial power, but also – for some of
them and to some extent – to make profit from them, selling their assistance to the colonisers, who had become the captives of the Indochinese 'golden cage'.

Many details remain unclear, however. It would have been interesting to specify the particular behaviour of the sub-groups that constituted each of the diasporas; whereas the South Chinese Tch'aoutchéou
group seems to have had a very active role in the traffic, the Indian
chettys do not appear anywhere. It could have also been interesting to
study the repressive activities of the French authorities in Indochina
vis-à-vis the traffickers. A thorough study of the expulsion laws enacted
against the Indians and Chinese could perhaps offer some new data.[44]
Lastly, we would have liked to have been able to specify the characteristics of each network such as whether the typologies established by the
contemporary experts of ARS stand up to historical proof.

If money circulates, it does not circulate everywhere in the same way
– and in order for it to circulate well, the protagonists must agree and
a precondition to any agreement is that they truly understand each
other. The study of the Alternative Remittance Systems has blossomed
during the past 5 to 6 years, but almost exclusively in Pacific Asia:
from the Tokyo meeting of the Asia Pacific Group on Money Laundering in March 1999[45] up to the latest (at the time of this article) Interpol report from May 2005.[46]

The management of traditional remittance systems is an old problem. Only a truly general reflexion which has other objectives than
the particular, will enable us to understand them better.

« Un ami fidèle est une tour forte et
qui l'a trouvé a trouvé un trésor. »
: dix mille merci à Anne Tassin
pour l'aide indispensable
apportée dans la traduction de cet article.

Notes

1　Interview with André Valls, Archives Orales du Ministère des Finances, tape 2.
2　Bodard, 1997.
3　This article is the updated version of an article presented in Shanghai in 2005. I have altered the statistical data, which now offer a more comprehensive overview. For an even more up-to-date and complete presentation, please see my coming thesis.
4　*Important methodological note:* These issues, the documents used and the complications of the laws regarding nationalities in the colonies forced me to adopt a special definition of the studied groups. Allowing for exceptions (quotations of other works or administrative sources) or those mentioned in the documents of the nationalities of the groups here under scrutiny, we regard as 'Chinese' the people who have a Chinese sounding name and as 'Indians', those with Hindi sounding names. This patronymic regrouping is extremely approximate and leads us to classify as 'Indians' people who were French citizens from a legal point of view (*Renonçants* of the French Indies) and, on the contrary, to exclude those from the Indian group who have Arabic sounding names. In the same way, it is possible that some Chinese who have 'Vietnamised' their names were misclassified (but a Vietnamese teacher has helped us in sorting this out).
5　From 1945 to 1954, the average yearly inflation rate (which is not very significant) was 25.9%.
6　Cf. Centre des Archives d'Outre Mer (CAOM), *Fonds Conseiller Politique, c. 99* – *Bulletin de renseignements*, 20 avril 1946.
7　Tsai Maw Kuey 1968: 70, 136-137.
8　CAOM, 1 Affeco 366.
9　CAOM, HCI, 254/742 & 741.
10　Cf. Archives du Ministère des Affaires Etrangères (MAE), Chine, c. 294, note du 11 septembre 1947.
11　Cf. the story of Mr.V.B., Centre des Archives Nationales (CARAN), BB18 7093, dr. 109.
12　Mani, A. & Ks. Sandu, 1993; Simon, P.J. 1981; Brun, Ch., Maitrise d'histoire sur *La communauté indienne à Saigon: les chettys, prêteurs d'argent indines* – Aix, 2002-2003 ; and a still unpublished study by Natasha Paraideau.
13　The *renonçants* were people who were born in the settlements who had renounced their customary laws and chose to live under the jurisdiction of French law. The conditions required to obtain this status have varied over the course of the history of these settlements. On this matter, see the studies of N. Paraideau.
14　Estimates of the Banking Committee in Burma, quoted in *la République, 5 septembre 1935.*
15　Cf. Chartered Bank Archives, Guildhall Library, London.
16　MAE, Inde, c.109 and AEF, B6626, lettre du 27 octobre 1950.
17　CAOM, Fonds Office des Changes, c.45.
18　Neogy Ajit 1997.
19　MAE, Indes françaises, c.63.
20　Avis 26,96,159 de l'OIC and AEF, B 6626, lettre du 13 février 1951.
21　CARAN, BB18 7093, dr.95.
22　This answers the very critical approach of Ruppert Hodder (1996) to the studies of history and economic sociology of the Chinese worlds.
23　AEF, B 6626, lettre du 12 décembre 1950 du Directeur de l'Office des Changes aux Finances Extérieures, 2ème Bureau.
24　AEF, B 48872, notes sur les relations économiques et financières de la France avec les Etats Associés, 31 janvier 1953.

25 AEF, B 43917, lettre manuscrite du 2 avril 1953.
26 AEF, B 6626.
27 CARAN, BB18 7093, dr.87.
28 CARAN, BB18 7093, dr.119.
29 AEF, B 6626 and B 6627 – Archives de Paris, 1577W541.
30 CARAN, BB 18 7093, dr.87.
31 AEF, B 6626.
32 *Leclerc et l'Indochine* 1992: 133.
33 Armorin, J. F., 1951: § – Saigon.
34 Bodard, L., 1997.
35 For all these remarks, cf. Bibliothèques d'Information Contemporaine (BDIC), Fonds Delarue, Trafic des piastres.
36 AEF, B 6626 and B 6627 and Service Historique de l'Armée de Terre (SHAT), c.10H532, Note sur les activités chinoises au Sud Vietnam (avril 1952) – quoted in Goscha, Ch., *Le contexte asiatique de la guerre franco vietnamienne*, Thèse EHESS 2000, § – Les réseaux chinois à l'intérieur du Vietnam.
37 AEF, B 6626, lettre du 24 aout 1950.
38 CARAN, BB18 7093, dr.106.
39 AEF, B 6626, lettre du 13 octobre 1951.
40 AEF, B 6626, lettre du 24 aout 1950 & CARAN, BB18 7093, dr. 74 and 105.
41 CARAN, BB18 7093, dr. 88 and 105.
42 Tomlinson 1993: 200.
43 CARAN, BB18 7095, dr. L.
44 Yet, the archives that were easily accessible show that people were expelled mainly for political reasons. See CAOM, HCI, 168/508.
45 Asia Pacific Group on Money Laundering, Money Laundering methods and typologies workshop "*Underground banking and alternative remittance systems*", Tokyo, 2-3 March 1999.
46 Lisa C. Carroll, *Alternative remittance systems distinguishing sub-systems of ethnic money laundering in Interpol member countries on the Asian continent*, Interpol 26 May 2005.
    – See also Christine Howlett, *Investigation & Control of Money Laundering via Alternative Remittance and Undergroung Banking Systems*, 2000 Churchill Fellowship, (4) 2001.
    – Note of Informal Value Transfer Systems of the US Treasury – Financial Crimes Enforcement Network, (3) 2003.
    – Asia Pacific Group, *Annual Meetting 2003 – Consideration and adoption of the APG Alternative Remittance Regulation Implementation Package*.
    – GAFI / FATF, *Combating the abuse of alternative remittance systems*, 20 June 2003.

Living the Colonial Lifestyle: Australian Women and Domestic Labour in Occupied Japan 1945-1952[1]

Christine de Matos

Introduction and background

The United States may have dominated control of the Allied Occupation of Japan (1945-1952), but Australia also contributed to the occupation force and occupation control machinery. The aims of the Occupation were to demilitarise and democratise Japan. Australian male military personnel began to arrive in Kure, a city in the Hiroshima prefecture southeast of Hiroshima city, as part of the British Commonwealth Occupation Force (BCOF) in February and March 1946, where they retained a presence until 1952.[2] About 45,000[3] Australians served overall with BCOF, the most provided by any of the participating Commonwealth nations. The Australian base was in Hiro, while the BCOF headquarters was located in nearby Kure. BCOF was comprised of Australian, New Zealand, British and British-Indian troops, but always had an Australian Commander-in-Chief. At the height of its presence in 1946, Australia provided almost 12,000 troops to BCOF. Diplomatically, Australia contributed: the British Commonwealth representative to the advisory body, the Allied Council for Japan (ACJ), based in Tokyo; the president of the International Military Tribunal of the Far East, Sir William Flood Webb; and a separate delegation to the policy-making body for the Occupation, the Far Eastern Commission (FEC), based in Washington DC.

In addition to male service personnel, Australian women came to Japan as wives, mothers, teachers, nurses, medical corps and volunteers, the latter including the Women's Voluntary Service, the Red Cross, and the YWCA. Women began to arrive from April and May 1946, first as nurses and medical corps, then as teachers and civilian volunteers, and finally as wives of servicemen along with their children. As Roma Donnelly has argued, the presence of women in the Australian area was meant to have a 'civilising' influence on the Australian soldiers – that is, to prevent or at least minimise them from 'fraternising' with Japanese women and help maintain an acceptable spatial barrier between the occupier and the occupied to reinforce the power hierarchy. It is the role of Australian women as occupiers, particularly in relation to the domestic workers they were assigned by BCOF authorities, that this chapter seeks to elucidate by placing the experience within a longer term colonial discourse and practice.

Creating a feminised 'neo-colonial' occupation space

Many writers have argued that the Allied Occupation of Japan was an exercise in neo-colonialism and orientalism, both generally and specifically in relation to the female occupier/occupied. John W. Dower, author of *Embracing Defeat*, calls the occupation the 'last immodest exercise in the colonial conceit known as "the white man's burden"' (Dower 1999: 23). Mire Koikari argues that 'US and European women's reform efforts in Asia, including "feminist" interventions, were inextricably intertwined with Western imperial and colonial endeavour in the region', and this too is reflected in the Occupation of Japan (Koikari 2002: 27). Lisa Yoneyama, in a critique of feminist reforms in Japan during the occupation, called the occupation a 'colonized space' linked to the western image of Japanese women as 'submissive yet licentious' (Yoneyama 2005: 895-898). Yet there are also differences between the Occupation of Japan and Western imperialism/colonialism that need to be noted. Japan had itself been a colonising power in Asia and very quickly found itself in the reverse position after the war. Australia had been a British colony; had pursued a colonising role in Papua and New Guinea after Federation in 1901 and, particularly, following World War I; had colonised/occupied indigenous lands in Australia; and actively played the neo-coloniser/occupier role in Japan. Therefore, Japan and Australia experienced, to some extent, both positions as the coloniser/occupier and colonised/occupied.

Postcolonial studies are useful in informing interpretations of the Occupation as a colonised, or neo-colonised, space, and in the construction of asymmetrical power relations within that space. As Pierson and Chaudhuri state,

> [T]he power relations of gender have intertwined with those of class, race, and sexuality and ... these technologies of power have been at the heart of the histories of imperialism, colonialism and nationalism shaping our modern world (Pierson & Chaudhuri 1998: 1).

This chapter is interested in the asymmetrical relationship constructed with the 'technologies of power' between occupier women and the occupied in the domestic or 'private' spaces of the occupation. While there were non-white occupiers (for example African-Americans, British-Indians, New Zealand Maoris, Australian Aboriginals and Torres

Strait Islanders, Australian-Asian), occupation power was defined and controlled by white men, and white women's roles defined in relation to that power, ostensibly designed to 'protect' them from the occupied. Yet, the relationship between white male and white female in the occupation space provided access to a 'borrowed' power: white female occupiers 'often gained opportunities lacking at home and played a central role in shaping the social relations of [occupation] because of the contradictory experiences of being "members of the inferior sex within the superior race" in [an occupation] setting' (Strobel in Janiewski 1998: 57).[4] It was their race, combined with victory in war, rather than, or in spite of, their gender that gave Australian women access to power. The role of women as occupiers therefore shares similarities with that of coloniser women in terms of the relations of power as shaped by gender, race and class.

One of the implicit tasks of the occupiers was to create tangible border markers between occupier women and the occupied similar to those found in colonial contexts. These border markers functioned to make visible the hierarchies of power between the victor/vanquished and the occupier/occupied. In November 1946, the Australian government approved a policy to allow the wives and children of soldiers serving in Japan to join them if the soldiers continued to serve at least one year in Japan after his family's arrival (Donnelly 1994). Five hundred and sixty-one new western-style buildings built especially for the 'BCOF families' and a further 134 Japanese homes were taken over and renovated to suit Western tastes and household practices (Donnelly 1994).[5] The largest dependents' development was just outside the Australian base of Hiro, where a whole village was built especially for the BCOF families. It was named Nijimura, or rainbow village, after the colourful pastel buildings. Built with Japanese labour under BCOF supervision, the village boasted a church, a school, a library, a shop, a cinema, the fire brigade, a medical post, a sporting field and a playground – a complete mini-suburb (Donnelly 1994). It was not only the house, but, in that terribly English-style, the garden that was seen to differentiate Australian, or Western homes from those of the surrounding devastated and/or rural Japanese homes (Dawson 1994).

The Western-style architecture of Nijimura contributed to the creation of an 'occupation landscape' by emphasising the 'modernity' of the occupier over the 'traditional' occupied, who were part of a rural landscape (despite, of course, the fact that the Japanese had very modern buildings elsewhere, including in nearby Kure). It created an architectural barrier to keep the occupied out (except those authorised to enter in their appropriate roles, for example, as domestic workers and labourers), and keep the occupier women in – they could not move freely through the occupied zone without occupier males escorts, especially after dark, quite unlike the men. Therefore, while the occupation created opportunities for women to access ancillary power, it also limited their activities in relation to white male power. The arrival of larger numbers of mostly white occupier women in Japan threatened the previous white male homo-social occupation space, and feminised domestic spaces such as Nijimura, combined with rules of non-fraternisation and requirements to have escorts after dark, helped to limit feminine intrusion into that space. The home was the appropriate designated and controlled place for occupier women to exert their ancillary occupation power.

Figure 5 *Dependents' housing built for BCOF families by Japanese labour in Niji-mura, complete with western-style gardens and streets (Photo courtesy of Mr Len Chapman, originally appearing in a publication for soldiers called As You Were, published by the Australian War Memorial).*

White women and 'the Home' as markers of 'civilisation'

Australian women, particularly the wives of soldiers, were sent to Japan as agents of 'civilisation' and 'modernity'. 'The Home' is an integral component of nationalist discourse in that it represents an imagined microcosm of the dominant gender narratives of the nation, and the occupier women in Japan were part of a 'showcase' of the perceived superiority of western/Australian culture, as vindicated by victory in war, through their role in a transplanted Australian domestic space. The linking of the home to the state, the private-domestic to the public-political, had also been an integral component of Japanese nationalist discourse, with the idealised role of the housewife, or *shufu*, seen as determining the quality of the home that in turn determined the quality of the nation – the 'good wife, wise mother' (*ryōsai kenbo*) discourse (Uno 2005). Thus, the gendered national discourse of the occupier was not very different from that of the now occupied when the Japanese state had pursued its own imperialist/nationalistic vision in Asia and the Pacific. This similarity was not acknowledged by the occupier, and instead, the Japanese woman was framed by the occupier's orientalist stereotypes. In fact, in the discourse of the occupier, the entire history of Meiji modernisation-westernisation was ignored and the occupied instead were constructed as feudal, backward and barbaric. This discourse, or the silences within it, was necessary to justify the occupation and the extraordinary levels of intervention into Japanese social, political and economic life, and to claim victory for the Allies as based on a 'good' versus 'evil' dichotomy. The possible war crimes of the victors, including the atomic and incendiary bombings of Japanese cities, were thus also silenced, justified, or 'whitewashed'.

Australian women as occupiers in their purpose-built occupier homes combined to exhibit the occupier's self-perceived superior civilisation – a 'glass display case' of Australian society and nation. Australian women were provided with a handbook called *BCOF Bound* to aid them in their occupation role. The forward to this handbook informed them that they were

> bringing once more to members of the Force the ties of home and family on which our Western civilization has been built.

> You are coming to live in a country whose people, together with their ways of living and their ways of thinking, are vastly different from our own (AWM114 130/2/58 1947).

These women were further warned and simultaneously comforted:

> Japan is still a primitive country populated by a primitive people, and the Japanese scene is only partially coated with a thin veneer of Occidental civilization....

> Initially, everything will be strange to you, but you will find that as long as you conform to the various Occupation Force instructions and live the life of the community of which you are now a member, life should be pleasant (AWM114 130/2/58 1947).

The 'community' was the BCOF community and excluded the Japanese, and 'instructions' included rules of non-fraternisation with Japanese locals (other than for work purposes) and architectural segregation. The creation of segregated domestic spaces for the occupier women reinforced idealised notions of the Australian occupier woman as more civilised than the occupied, and, at the same time, ostensibly protected her and her children – the future white Australian citizens – from the 'uncivilised' 'Other'.

Constructing self to 'Other': domestic workers and occupier women

In occupied Japan, the Japanese government supplied female, and some male, domestic workers to BCOF and their families. Domestic workers' wages were paid by the Japanese government, but the BCOF Labour Unit allocated them to occupation families, barracks and dormitories. Worker duties included housekeeping, cooking, childcare and gardening. As a rough guide to the numbers employed, an Australian officer without children was entitled to three, officers with children to four, other ranks without children to two, other ranks with children to three, and men in barracks or women in dormitories shared one or two between them. Donnelly provides one reason for the use of domestic labour: 'it was considered undesirable for [Australian] wives to perform menial and domestic tasks, particularly as it was thought that they would be unable to cope with such duties in the hot, humid months' (1994: 111).[6] The types of work undertaken were an expression of occupation power relations. Domestic and other forms of labour were generally considered the work of the occupied, while occupiers served in supervisory roles. The treatment of domestic workers was subject to the post-war labour reforms and workers were entitled to a forty-hour week, paid leave of two days per month, three days of menstrual leave per month, and six weeks pre-and-post natal leave. They received between ¥150-250 a month. It is difficult to determine from the available records how well these rights were upheld. It can be surmised, however, that the unequal power relationship, occupier/occupied and victor/vanquished, allowed at least some violations to be overlooked or excused, and prevented some workers from making complaints against their employers. Domestic workers were required to undergo regular medical examinations to check for contagious and sexually transmitted diseases (Donnelly 1994) (the Japanese woman as unclean/diseased and immoral), and if they failed the test, they could lose their jobs (Warner-Bishop 2006).[7]

Many Australians in the 1940s still aspired to be more British, and the Occupation gave them an opportunity to pretend this through the 'rituals of domesticity' in a racialised/occupied domestic space (McClintock 1995: 35-36). Race, class and gender combined to inform the Australian female occupier's role. As Hobsbawm has noted, the 'widest definition of the middle class ... was that of keeping domestic servants' (cited in McClintock 1995: 85). Most Australian women were unlikely to have domestic workers in their homes in Australia, but the Occupation allowed them to 'class jump' through a transient, upward mobility. Domestic workers were constructed as the inferior 'Other' in that domestic space, where the occupier woman could perform on a daily basis the idealised role of the victorious, civilised, superior self – a self that also contributed to the wider nationalist discourse of Australia as victor nation in Japan. The occupier woman could perform occupation power over occupied women and men and enjoy a privileged, high-status lifestyle that she would have been unlikely to have had in Australia. She could play the role of the 'coloniser' and participate in a (declining) British Empire.

The relationship constructed between Japanese and Australian women in the domestic occupation space conforms to Anderson's description of Victorian English 'values':

> The employment of domestic workers meant women could negotiate the contradiction between domesticity, requiring physical labour and dirtiness, and the cleanliness and spirituality of feminine virtue. 'Ladies' need servants ... once established this relationship helped to maintain difference: workers proved their inferiority by their physicality and dirt, while female employers proved their superiority by their femininity, daintiness, and managerial skills (Anderson 2000: 18).

The Occupation hierarchy was further reinforced through language, including references to domestic workers as one's 'servants'. That is, even though the workers were paid by the Japanese government, possession was taken of the domestic worker and justified by Australia's status as an occupier. Discursive distinctions between white Australian women as occupiers and Japanese occupied reflected that of the master-slave relationship. As Anderson describes of southern slavery in the United States, the 'master gains honour through the slaves dishonour,' and in Japan that dishonour came with defeat and was reinforced through the types of tasks and duties the Japanese performed for the occupiers (2000: 143). 'Servants' in the home raised the status of the white occupier women. This status was discursively reinforced by the widespread use of 'housegirl' or 'houseboy' to describe domestic workers in occupier homes. These diminutive labels were an integral part of Western colonial discourse where a woman is described as a girl and a man as a boy, and constructed and named the unequal domestic relationship between the occupier and the occupied. These terms removed the individual identity of the Japanese worker, their personal and family name, and instead referred to them through a 'labour category'... and the identity of servitude' (McClintock 1995: 268), thus further reinforcing their lower status as the vanquished.

Figure 6   *Ruth Warner-Bishop outside her Nijimura home standing over her three Japanese domestic workers (c. 1947) (photo courtesy of Ruth Warner-Bishop).*

Having a domestic worker allowed Australian occupier women to pursue other 'middle-class' activities during the Occupation that she usually could not have participated in, at least not as often. She could play tennis, go on outings with her family, host a cocktail party or engage in philanthropic activities. Domestic help 'liberated' her from household chores and childcare responsibilities. The occupation wives also often acted in the orientalist role of 'tutor' to their domestic workers, teaching Western ways of housekeeping. One BCOF child remembers her mother teaching their domestic workers about housekeeping and cooking:

> I remember how they watched with surprise when my mother made her deliciously light sponge cake. How did that sloppy mixture become that beautiful cake? There were several comical results from misunderstood directions from my mother. I recall some confusion about the starching of my father's uniform which eventuated in his undies also being starched (Ladyga 2004: 10).

Through this relationship, Australian women participated in the wider occupation discourse and practice of democratisation/westernisation by extending it to the domestic space, thus taking the public/political aims of military occupation into the private space of the Home.

Women's newspapers in Australia reflected orientalist stereotypes and the privileged role of Australian women as occupier. A group of Australian nurses interviewed on their way to Japan said that they were 'hopeful of getting Japanese labour to do their washing' (Powe 1946: 17). They were not disappointed, but some took on the role of 'tutor' to the occupied 'Other'. In a follow up article, it was noted that 'Jap girls [sic] wash out the quarters using plenty of water and much energy, but Sister Kath O'Bryan gave some in our dormitory a lesson on the correct technique' (Drain 1946: 19). Another article, titled 'Shopping in Japan presents few difficulties,' proudly declared: 'No crowds. No queues. No waiting. Instead a carefully planned system to make their [Australian women's] lot happy and comfortable'. Australian women came with 'their shopping lists and housegirls' (Jackson 1948). The article implied that Australian women were 'making it big' on the world-occupation stage, and the role of the occupied was to serve the Australian women. However, another article lamented:

> Japanese servants have been so accustomed to paying deference to boys that it's just as well [Australian] fathers are around to counteract their indulgence.

> Sensible parents are keeping the training of their children in their own hands (*Australian Women's Weekly* 1947).

There was a perceived negative side to the presence of domestic workers in occupier's home where there were children – the Japanese could corrupt that 'home and family on which ... Western civilisation has been built' with their 'feudal' ways, potentially affecting idealised Australian gender roles. Overall, the articles informed their female readership of the positives and perils of occupation life for Australian women, but, more importantly, participated in a discourse that privileged an Australian female self as constructed against the inferior female Japanese 'Other'.

Domestic workers were often the only source of contact with the Japanese for many Australian women as they were forbidden to have any other contact, such as informal socialising.[8] Relationships often developed between Australian and Japanese women, and also between BCOF children and their Japanese caretakers. For instance, one Australian woman recalled that she 'really liked the Japanese, especially the old mama-sans, they were really nice and they were lovely to the children. Our housegirls were really good ... we had young housegirls and ... they really enjoyed the children' (O'Brien 2006). Gifts were often exchanged and sometimes contact was maintained, at least for a short while, after the family returned to Australia. The development of bonds between domestic workers and their employers is common everywhere, but Anderson points out that it is still an asymmetrical, 'maternalistic' relationship: 'Maternalism is based on the supraordinate-subordinate relationship with the female employer caring for the worker as she would a child or a pet, thereby expressing, in a feminized way, her lack of respect for the domestic worker as an adult worker' (2000: 144).

For Australian women, one of the positive legacies of close contact with Japanese women (and men) was that at the same time that stereotypical gendered, raced and classed images of the Japanese were reinforced to construct a national and self image of the Australian woman as victor and occupier, other stereotypes were challenged or subverted. When they returned to Australia, many Australian women spoke about Japan and the Japanese in a positive way, which shocked and disappointed many other Australians who were still influenced by wartime images and orientalist stereotypes. Rose O'Brien conducted talks about Japan to the Country Women's Association (CWA), a conservative rural women's organisation, when she returned to Australia:

> they used to be amazed that I spoke kindly of the Japanese because their idea was of the war and all the very vindictive things that had happened during the war, that's what I felt, I felt that I could speak as I knew them. ... I felt we were giving them first hand information which I was able to project to them instead of the suppositions that they had before we went away.

> I used to tell them [CWA] how I was living in Japan and they used to wonder how I could speak decently about the Japanese. They thought it was stupid, they thought that there was no way you could speak nicely about the Japanese at all and yet living with them made you feel like that...because you saw them in a different light (2006).

Thus, the positive legacy of the Occupation and contact between Australian women and their domestic workers was that Australian women (and men) acted as a vanguard of changed attitudes towards the Japanese in post-war Australia. Their experiences in Hiroshima allowed them to deconstruct many of the stereotypical cultural representations of the Japanese that had been created and exacerbated by fear, racism and war.

Many Australian women were reluctant to leave the 'British style, upper-class colonial lifestyle' behind to return to Australia after their sojourn in Japan had ended (Woodward 2006). One Australian woman upon returning to Japan said: 'We wives all wondered what we were heading for in Japan, but none of us imagined things would be so nice' (source provided by Hogg, c. 1950). The *Melbourne Sun* reported that 'Many Australian wives in Japan would be reluctant to leave their comfortable home and abundant home help for a servantless Australia' (*Melbourne Sun* 1950). But, despite the fond relationships that developed between many Australian and Japanese women, their positions in the Occupation power hierarchy were never contested. As one Australian woman informed, 'they [Japanese domestic workers] were a thing apart from us, if you know what I mean ... they were just treated as the servants. ... A lot of us were possibly nice to them as we weren't used to people as servants all the time' (O'Brien 2006). There is little, if any, evidence of awareness amongst Australian female occupiers of the 'emancipation' of Japanese women, an aim of, and a justification for, the Allied Occupation of Japan. Rather, it is the power that they remember: 'we were the "top dog" over there'; 'we were the head of the occupation forces'; 'there was a superiority feeling of "we are the occupiers"'; 'we were the ones they had to kowtow down to' (O'Brien 2006; Olney 2006). The main role of occupied women, particularly in the domestic space, was to reinforce the status and power of occupier women and, ultimately, that of the Australian nation.

Conclusions and postscript

An examination of Australian women as occupiers, and especially their relationship with Japanese women as domestic workers, reveals a number of factors. First, it demonstrates the imperative of increased social and class status for Australian women offered by the Occupation (albeit a transient one). Australian women constructed a national image and a self-image in relation to the Japanese 'Other', one that distracted them from their own subordinate position in Australian society in terms of gender and class. Second, it demonstrates the racialised, neo-colonial attitudes prevalent in the Occupation, not just at Occupation centres such as Tokyo, but within the daily practices and interactions between occupier and occupied at the grassroots level.

Third, Australian women were constructed as 'bearers of morality and modernity', the Japanese women as traditional, oppressed, submissive, and in need of tuition by the 'modern' Australian woman. This includes the construction of the occupied 'Other' as the inferior other through language as well as practice – 'servants', 'girls', 'boys', and 'Japs'. Fourth, the Occupation reinforced orientalist racial stereotypes previously held (even contradictory ones) – clean, dirty, submissive, arrogant, child-like, dangerous, and warlike – and, at the same time, challenged previous stereotypes and even changed attitudes towards the Japanese from those of wartime propaganda to one that at least acknowledged the humanity of the Japanese people.

Lastly, the role of the occupied domestic worker in Australian occupier homes served to construct and reinforce a wider narrative of Australian national identity as victor nation through the performance of the victor over the vanquished in the domestic realm. This representation evoked the dominant gender stereotypes in Australian national narratives, including, for Australian women, the middle-class imaginary of the woman in the home serving family and nation. Victory in war had enhanced this imaginary further to allow the Australian woman a number of domestic 'servants' and thus she could participate in the wider collective imagining of a strong Australian post-war nation and, concurrently, in the British empire with its privileged 'colonial lifestyle'. But what of the legacy of Japanese women and men in these domestic occupation encounters? Perhaps most informative is the fate of the BCOF family village of Nijimura – bulldozed and replaced today by an industrial complex and hospital.[9] The erasure of the physical memory of the occupier silences the difficult, probably humiliating, public and private memories of the occupied, especially those of the workers in the domestic space of occupier homes. 'Nijimura' has now been relabelled with a more palatable public memory that instead narrates the success of Japan's post-war economic and industrial growth.

Notes

1   This essay is based on a paper presented at ICAS 5, Kuala Lumpur, 2-5 August 2007. Some parts also appear in De Matos, 'A very gendered Occupation: Australian women as 'conquerors' and 'liberators', *US-Japan Women's Journal*, 33, 2007: 87-112, and De Matos, 'Gender, nation and power in occupied Japan', part of a forthcoming collection of essays on Australia and military occupations, edited by De Matos & Gerster, to be published by Cambridge Scholars Publishing (2009).

2   The end date for the Australian presence in Hiroshima prefecture was actually 1956, as part of the British Commonwealth Force Korea (BCFK), which replaced the BCOF after the peace treaty was signed in 1952.

3   This is the statistic usually given, however, there is some dispute over its accuracy and whether it includes only service personnel, or also their families and other civilian occupiers.

4   Note that the original words pertaining to colony/colonial/colonisation in this quote have been replaced by 'occupation' to demonstrate the synchronicity between gendered power relations in colonial and occupation settings.

5   Other early statistics on housing suggest the following: 80 houses erected at Etajima; 157 at Hiro; 55 at Okayama; 41 at Iwakuni; and 5 at Tokushima (total of 348) (AWM 114: 130/1/23 Pt II, 1947).

6   There was a similar idea about Australian women unable to work in tropical conditions amongst the Australian colonial residents in Papua and New Guinea. See Chilla Bulbeck (1992), *Australian Women in Papua New Guinea: Colonial Passages 1920-1960*. Cambridge: Cambridge University Press: 64.

7   A domestic worker in the household of Mrs Warner-Bishop lost her job this way (the decision was made by male BCOF authorities, not Mrs Warner-Bishop, who regretted losing a good worker).

8   There were some instances where this rule was broken, particularly by the Australian women who worked for the YWCA in Kure, who often developed closer relationships with Japanese women. However, these relationships were still marked by the inevitable power inequities that existed between occupier and occupied.

9   Only the original Nijimura park remains and is now used for baseball games.

Decolonisation and the Origin of Military Business in Indonesia[1]

Bambang Purwanto

Military business has been an attractive theme for foreign and local researchers in the literature on Indonesia, especially those studying Indonesian politics and Indonesian political economy during the New Order (Robison 1986; Muhaimin 1990; Iswandi 1998; Samego et al. 1998; Singh 2001; Widoyoko et al. 2003). The abovementioned studies tend to suggest that military business evolved and operated solely during the New Order, a time of military dominance in the socio-political life of the country. Those who do discuss pre-New Order military business tend to argue that the earliest of Indonesia's military business occurred no earlier than 1950, and developed especially during the period of the 1950s when the nationalisation policies, *nasionalisasi*, were enacted.

Harold Crouch's text on the Indonesian military business, one of the earliest studies ever conducted on the topic, clearly concurs with the general opinion that the 1950s were the starting point for military business in Indonesia (Crouch 1975/1976). Even further, Richard Robison's oft-quoted book explicitly avoids the economic reality of the period 1945-1949. To Robison, the discussion of the process of early capital formation and military involvement in Indonesian economic and political history only needed to start with colonial capitalism and the failure of domestic private capital in the period 1948-1957. Robison also considers the period of the Japanese occupation and the subsequent revolution to be of no value to the country's economic history (Robison 1986). Even in the two chapters discussing the period of 1949-1965, Robison is mostly silent on the topic of military business, despite the fact that he argues that the most significant development of the relation between power and capital occurring from 1957 to 1965 was the emergence of the military as the most powerful 'politico-bureaucratic' force in the country (Robison 1986). Instead, Robison focuses more on political party business activities, indigenous entrepreneurs, and government economic policies. A similar rendering can furthermore be seen in two books published in Indonesia, which admit the importance of the period of 1945-1949 for the process of Indonesian military business formation. Unfortunately, not much information on military business can be gleaned from the two books in question (Samego et al.

1998; Widoyoko et al. 2003). Despite the fragmentary facts, several studies have shown that the process of military involvement in the economic and capital formation process occurred during an even earlier
period, in conjunction with the process of decolonisation since the
middle of August 1945.

This paper will discuss the formation of Indonesian military business during the process of decolonisation between 1945 and the early
1960s. Despite the fact that the Dutch relented and officially acknowledged Indonesia's independence in 1949, and despite the differences
of opinion among historians as to the status of Indonesia's independence prior to the signing of the Round Table Conferent, one undeni-
able fact remains, that the early process of Indonesian decolonisation,
politically, socially and economically, started immediately after Soekarno and M. Hatta proclaimed Indonesia independent on 17 August
1945. Several basic questions arise from this, such as: When did the Indonesian military first become involved in the practical economic and
capital formation initiatives? Why did the Indonesian military conduct
business functions outside of its core function as an institution of defence? Who or what military groups conducted these businesses? Were
there different goals among the various military departments in their
responses to the opportunities available for conducting business?

Generally speaking, the decolonisation process leading to the weakening of colonial influence and a strengthening of the identity and
authority of Indonesia's character between 1945 and the early 1960s
can be divided into at least five general periods: First, we have the short
period between the proclamation of Indonesian independence and the
coming of the Dutch-Allied troops. Second, we have the war period,
starting with the arrival of Allied-Dutch troops, and ending in the ac-
knowledgement of independence in 1949. Third, we have the period of
the Republik Indonesia Serikat (RIS), until just prior to the adoption of
the state of war and siege policy. Fourth, is the period starting with the
widespread takeover of Western, especially Dutch, economic assets in
1957. Fifth, is the period after the *nasionalisasi* policy had been officially
introduced. This is why this essay, in contrast with previous studies
that focus on the development of the Indonesian military business only
through the lens of the *dwifungsi* (dual function) principle (Singh
2001), will also address the significant meaning of decolonisation for
the formation of the Indonesian military business complex of the next
period. The word military or soldier in this text will not only cover the
official military apparatus through its evolutionary transformation from
the *Badan Keamanan Rakyat* (BKR), *Tentara Keamanan Rakyat* (TKR),
Tentara Rakyat Indonesia (TRI) to the *Tentara Nasional Indonesia* (TNI),
but also armed groups such as youth militias involved within the decolonisation process.

The war and the emergence of the military business

The process of Indonesian decolonisation resulted in the creation of a unique historical creature in the form of the Indonesian military, unique in comparison with the military history of most other Western colonial possessions in Asia. On the one hand, the creation of the BKR on 22 August 1945 and the TKR on 5 October 1945, as the initial organs that formed the Tentara National Indonesia, did not come from groups that fought for independence during the colonial period. Nor was it a continuation of the previous colonial army, neither personnel-wise nor institutional-wise. Although the BKR and TKR members were sociologically a combination of the manpower trained in the military during the colonial period and the Japanese occupation, these soldiers had never fought against the colonial rulers to uphold independence. Suddenly, however, they faced new challenges that forced them to work together with newly armed civilian groups, in order to fight against their former Japanese and Dutch masters who were aided by the Allied British, to once again shore up colonial power after the proclamation of Indonesian independence by civilian leaders.

In the context of the Indonesian national enlistment movement, the war suddenly transformed the army from what was once a sociological and political non-existence, into one of the most dominant aspects in the formation of the image and identity of Indonesian nationhood. Civilian politicians, in the process of creating Indonesian nationalism forty years prior, had to face the fact that their role had been marginalised or replaced because of the war. The war made the military into the new symbol of Indonesian nationalism and, at the same time, made them the new dominant elite of the country. As explained above, the state of affairs could only happen because Indonesia's early decolonisation process had to deal with a stronger military opponent bent on recreating Western colonial dominance. This was further enforced by the sociological impact of the Japanese occupation and the formation of a new elite and socio-cultural conditions which were adapted to the subsequent war.

During the war, personnel and institutional consolidation of the Indonesian military occurred. The various differences inherited from the diverse social and ideological backgrounds, and the unique role played by the army in protecting the independence movement, has, on the one hand, resulted in political conflict and competition within the army itself and with other parties as well, including the government. On the other hand, the military grew to become a corporation that not only functioned as an institution of the state that handled protection and defense, but also conducted matters of practical politics, bureaucracy and economy. Under Soedirman's leadership, the Indonesian military since its inception identified itself as the representative of the people while at the same time functioning as an apparatus of the state responsible for the freedom of the newly proclaimed Indonesian state and a party that would ensure independence (Said 1991). Its civilian policies were clearly mirrored by the principle of the system of total popular defense and security, *sistem pertahanan dan keamanann rakyat semesta.*

The combination of the civilian and military roles of the soldier as a freedom fighter started as early as the BKR period, not after the formation of the TKR as many experts believe. Many believe that the BKR had neither a military organisation in place nor a clear recruitment policy, and thus could not be called an army in its own right. However looking at the development of the BKR on the regional level, such as the development engineered by Soedirman in Banyumas, A.K. Gani in South Sumatra or Dahlan Jambek in West Sumatra, it is difficult to maintain that the BKR was an unstructured armed organisation without a command line. In many areas, the BKR functioned as more than just as a keeper of the peace and also engaged in active self-defense against foreign enemies that threatened its borders. Although the BKR membership was mostly dominated by young people with military training gained during the Japanese occupation, in other areas, it was very difficult to distinguish between the BKR and the youth militias or struggling organisations, or those who were members of the provisional parliament of *Komite Nasional Indonesia* (KNI) in charge of running the civilian government.

Besides acting as soldiers, BKR members and the militias were routinely involved in political, social and economic activities. Most members of the KNI in regional areas were also members of the BKR or militias. On the other hand, the Hizbullah or Barisan Pelopor, militarily trained under the Japanese, also had people with dual membership in the BKR and KNI. Nationally speaking, historical facts have also proven that the TKR was merely a superficial transformation of the BKR, given that the ranks and certain fixed structures accorded with the professional military organisation. One prominent historical fact that needs to be considered is that almost all of the TKR units in the regions formed after 5 October 1945 came from the BKR. The TKR commanders, including Soedirman in Banyumas, had been BKR commanders. Furthermore, the formation of the TKR as an official army did not instantly mean that the armed youth groups or militias affiliated with certain political or ideological powers would disappear (Purwanto 2000).

The decolonisation process placed the army in a dominant position and led to a lack of separation between the military and civilian sectors; this played an important role in determining the involvement of the military in the nation's economic sector. This process was furthered along by battles with the Dutch army that weakened Indonesia's civilian government and its ability to function effectively following the arrival of the Allied forces at the end of September 1945. The government actually had to be moved from Jakarta to Yogyakarta on January 1946. As the war raged on, logistical support was needed to uphold the government, the people and especially the army, both the formal units and the militias. According to current historical records, logistics were provided exclusively via community support because of the Dutch blockade. This statement is not entirely incorrect, but through further investigation, we discover that the statement functions more as a proof of community support for the military than as an accurate view of the larger situation. The statement basically disregards other aspects that indicate various sources used for logistic support, the conduct of the government and continuance of the armed struggle. One of these was the involvement of the army in the economic arena, whether that was large or small, legal or illegal.

The involvement of the army – both official and the militia – in the management of economic resources began when the BKR and subsequently TKR members and the militia in many areas took over strategic economic sources such as factories, telephone offices, estates, power generators and installations, transport companies, mines, and various daily necessities previously controlled by the Japanese army.

In Wonosobo, Central Java, for example, the military took over the Dutch privately owned tea estates and factories from the Japanese, who had used these tea facilities to supplement their economic needs during the occupation. In Yogyakarta, the military took over the Dutch-owned tool factories and even requisitioned several Chinese owned companies, factories and warehouses. Similar events occurred in many other cities such as Surabaya, Semarang, Surakarta, Cirebon, Jakarta, Palembang, Padang, Medan and Makassar. Some of these armed forces even acted as if they were official branches of the Indonesian government, despite the fact that their actions were mostly focused on personal or group economic gains.

The important role of the military in Indonesia's economy can also be clearly seen in the distribution of the Indonesian currency, the *Oeang Repoeblik Indonesia* (ORI) in October 1946. Other similar currencies were issued by various regions to replace the Japanese currency and compete with that issued by the Netherlands Indies Civil Administration (NICA). The chaos and confusion caused by each region trying to print and circulate their own currenciy led to the involvement of practical economic activities in several regions. For instance, when the *Oeang Repoeblik Indonesia Propinsi Sumatra* (ORIPS) started printing money in Bukittingi, after being moved from Pematang Siantar, the

printing of currency came under the direct control of local military leaders (Zed 1997). Although the civilian government and local banking
authorities formally kept an eye on these activities, in reality no explicit
control over military management of currency printing, which was
needed to meet the needs of each region, was ever implemented. In
fact, in several places, the army purposefully produced low quality currency, using ink that had a tendency to wash away easily. Consequently,
this resulted in unavoidable inflation as too much money was produced with no control (Zed 2003; Kahin 1997).

Other episodes, in other areas, also show how military involvement
in the economy was an important fact of decolonisation as a whole, in
areas such as Sumatra and Sulawesi. For instance, although A.K. Gani,
resident of Palembang after the proclamation of independence, was a
civilian, he was also a major general and held the title of Coordinator
of the Sumatra Military since November 1945 (Zed 2003). His double
function resulted in the absence of a clear division between civilian
and military involvement in the economic activities of Palembang and
other parts of Sumatra within his jurisdiction. In reality, the military
played an important role not just on the battlefield against Dutch military action, but also fielding the area of fund raising to support the activities of the civilian government and the military struggle. This is
clearly shown in the 'oil diplomacy' policy and the presence of 'oil militias' and 'oil battalions' that made quite a few economic contributions
to both the local and the central government. The fund acquisition
through tax and tariffs, known as the *iuran perang* (war contribution),
was conducted by the local government of West Sumatra, which was
dependent on the military and had to justify its actions before the local
military leader; this was another example of military involvement in
the business activities of Sumatra.

One very important policy issued by A.K. Gani in support of military
business in Palembang was the creation of a Liaison Body, a body
formed in January 1947 to function as a liaison for oil and coal sales
and to distribute the vital needs of the Indonesian government and
military (Zed 2003). A.K. Gani also gave opportunities to many young
TRI officers to conduct trading activities through the *Usaha Muda*, an
organisation fully under the control of the military leaders situated at
Bukittinggi. The policies he had chosen had become a stimulant for
the creation of military-owned corporation groups that controlled a
large part of Sumatra's trade economy. Other trade organisations, such
as Soematera Import and Export (SOEIMEX), which had subsequently
been formed and become an important element in Palembang's economy, were also part of the military influence. A similar thing occurred
when the Central Trading Corporation and the Sumatra Banking and
Trading Corporation (SBTC) was formed in 1948. The trading organi-

sations were under the control of army traders who had also assumed the role of military leaders in each area. This can be verified by merely looking at the military-dominated board of directors of each trading company, with members coming from both the army and navy (Zed 2003).

In South Sulawesi and surrounding areas, the various militias, such as *Laskar Pemberontak Republik Indonesia Sulawesi Selatan* (LA-PRIS) and *Badan Pemberontak Republik Indonesia* (BPRI), focussed on the city of Pare Pare, and were involved in inter-island trade, especially in numerous areas in Kalimantan and Surabaya, and with trading in the Sulawesi area. Copra was a major commodity traded by army groups at the time. Moreover, many BPRI army groups, for instance, had run other businesses such as land and sea transport companies, grocery stores, and even a barbershop. While the other groups of soldiers incorporated within the *Gabungan Pemberontak Indonesia Soppeng* (GAPPIS) had done the same. Besides copra, the military had also brought coffee and rice up to Kalimantan to sell or trade for other necessities, including firearms. Although the military groups were formally integrated into the TRI in January 1947, the business activities of these groups did not cease (Limbagau 2000). There is even strong evidence to suggest that the business activities of the military widened in conjunction with the organisational consolidation and the appearance of young officers capable of taking advantage of the condition of military dominance for business gains, whether for their men or for personal gains.

The presence of oil diplomacy, oil militias and oil battalions, as stated above, is important to keep in mind when we reconstruct and explain the important role of the military in large-scale economic processes during decolonisation. As Mestika Zed notes, since the year 1946 'the role of the militias and the TRI was no longer warfare, but actually trading and other productive activities for logistical support and supplies for civilian and the military of all the areas of Sumatra' (Zed 2003). The military controlled all of the productive oil fields and oil refineries present in the hinterland of South Sumatra, including its distribution. They not only supplied the oil for all of South Sumatra, but also for the republic's supporters in West Sumatra and Java. Although the Plaju and Sungai Gerong oil refineries were handed over to the allies in the month of August 1946, the military's oil business continued unabated in many other oil-producing areas in the interior. Therefore it comes as no surprise that the period was coloured by the appearance of 'oil barons' in the many oil producing areas of South Sumatra who also happened to be military rulers of the areas. Prabumulih, an area controlled by the republican army, which also functioned as the Second TRI Division command headquarter, developed to become the main centre of Indonesian oil production in the Palembang area at the start of 1947 under the management of *Perusahaan Minyak Republik Indonesia* (PERMIRI), an oil company dominated by the military. The same situation was paralleled in Aceh and East Sumatra. The Indonesian Army controlled oil production and distribution in the area through the oil company *Perusahaan Tambang Minyak Negara Republik Indonesia* (PTMNRI). In the subsequent development, most of the individuals involved in the oil business had military backgrounds; people like Hasymi A. Taher and Ibnu Sutowo headed the state oil company, Permina, which eventually became the present-day Pertamina.

In other areas, the military also played an important role in the area of barter trade, especially the trade between Sumatra and the trade area along the Malay Peninsula, in particular Singapore (Yong 1997; Muchtar, ed. 1992). Audrey Kahin in one of her books wrote that through the first years after the proclamation of independence, barter trade between West Sumatra and the Malay Peninsula was effectively dominated by the IX Army Division centred in Bukittinggi (Kahin 2003). In exchange, aside from providing daily provisions, the soldiers in the division also supplied guns and distributed them to the republican resistance groups, as they had done in Riau through Pekanbaru. In Palembang, these trader-soldiers succeeded in making rubber, coffee and quinine a lucrative economic source capable of contributing a large sum of money to the republic, aside from the traditional oil and coal. Aside from the above commodities, opium also became one of the major trade items to cross the Malacca Strait. Sumatran opium traded via the Strait by the army, but, according to Dutch intelligence, Javanese opium was brought in as well. In Java, Dutch military intelligence reports that many of the regular and militia army, including those under the command of Soeharto regularly traded opium from Yogyakarta in the centre of the Republic, to occupied territories in cooperation with Chinese middlemen (Elson 2001).

The explanation above attempts to prove that the business activities conducted by the military during that period not only built up a strong economic source for local military rulers, but also had a huge political influence that would greatly affect the trajectory of the next period. The involvement of the military in economic activities cannot be explained away as the mere activities of a war economy; instead, it prospered to become a large business on both group and individual levels in the period after Dutch recognition of the Indonesian independence, a new phase in Indonesia's decolonisation.

The final stage of decolonisation, chaos and the strengthening of military business

In conjunction with the cessation of hostilities, the Dutch acceptance in December 1949 of Indonesian independence and the unilateral dissolution of the United States of Indonesia in 1950 marks a new period of Indonesian decolonisation. Economically speaking, on the one hand, there was a great desire by the Indonesian government and community to change the present colonial economy into a national economy concurrent to the rising dominance of the nationalists. But, on the other hand, in a relatively short period time, the dominance of foreign corporations in the economy was again cemented as a result of the weaknesses inherent in the state and local businessmen in running the local economy. That is why two major patterns marked the macro-economic decolonisation process after 1950. First, the takeovers of corporations previously owned by the colonial government into a public or state company were conducted, whether they were compensated or not. Aside from Bank Indonesia, acquired from de Javasche Bank, most of the other large corporations were public utilities such as the trains, ports, bus transport, water supply, post offices, telephone companies, pawnshops, electricity company, and hospitals, while the rest were commercial companies. Second, there was support for the development of indigenous Indonesian businessmen, leading to an indigenisation or *pribumisasi* policy (Sutter 1959; Robison 1986; Muhaimin 1990).

The policy of takeovers and *pribumisasi* provided a good opportunity for the military to get involved in business after 1950. This condition was strengthened by the fact that the government was unable to provide sufficient funds for the costs of military operations. The *pribumisasi* policy within the Benteng Policy tried to limit the opportunities of Chinese businessmen. In fact, however, it did not seriously affect their role in the economy. With some exceptions, these policies had an impact on producing dependent groups or individuals of military or indigenous civilian businessmen, rather than independent indigenous merchant capitalists. The military not only functioned as patrons but also as actors directly involved in the economic activity of the time. The policy of giving preferential license to indigenous copra traders to compete with their Chinese counterpart in other areas of Sulawesi, for instance, inadvertently created a trading alliance between the military and Chinese traders, and the increasing strength of local individual military leaders in business activities. The cooperation paved the way for the trading of copra between Sulawesi and Singapore. In fact, after several more years, similar business ventures involving the military and Chinese middlemen appeared in many other areas. Using the excuse of routine and military operations and soldier welfare costs as reason to seek funds, the military business activities, which involved most of the local elite military rulers, developed to become a neat and profitable commercial enterprise. This is why, to a certain extent, the decolonisation process must be considered an important factor used to justify the military business activities.

The opportunity for soldiers to conduct business activities widened as a result of political conflict and labour problems in some areas, creating uncontrollable security conditions from the start of the 1950s in several areas such as West Java, Central Java, the Moluccas, most of Sulawesi, Aceh and North Sumatra. Armed political conflict involving Andi Aziz and Kahar Muzakkar in South Sulawesi, for instance, resulted in the control of the trade in copra, rice and other daily necessities by one of the battalions in the VII Territory Army. The army forced the growers of copra, rice and other export commodity crops to sell their produce cheaply to certain companies chosen by the military or directly to the military itself. The military also forbade the populace to sell their produce to other parties and did not hesitate to react violently against those who were connected to other buyers, or did not want to sell their produce. There is even some evidence that the army or their henchmen themselves harvested coconuts from growers' fields, taking the coconuts and turning them into copra from growers' groves left unattended because of unsafe conditions. Moreover, the military also had trading companies centred in Majene and controlled the import and export trade between Sulawesi and Singapore, so it is no surprise that the battalion was renowned as the 'dollar battalion' (Limbugau 2000).

The involvement of the military in the business arena became more widespread as the government decided to proclaim a state of emergency and war in the country in the first quarter of 1957, being the result of the appearance of armed movements in Sumatra and Sulawesi, increasingly uncontrollable labour problems and land conflicts, and the fall of the elected 1955 cabinet lead by Ali Sastroamidjojo in the month of March 1957. These business ventures gained even stronger legitimacy after the diplomatic failure of Indonesia on the matters of West Papua (Irian) in the United Nations, the issuing of the 5 July 1959 Presidential Decree, and the start of the confrontation with Malaysia. Similar to the hostile conditions after the proclamation of Independence and the arrival of the Allied-Dutch troops, the declaration of a state of war and emergency, long running conflicts among civilian politicians and political instability that interfered with the next phase of decolonisation, gave the military a very important position, since the situation provided them with political as well as social and economic authority.

In Semarang, for example, Soeharto devised an economic policy and founded an institution to run the businesses of the Diponegoro division, explained as a fund raiser needed for the troops to keep guard over the safety of the country and sustain Indonesia's sovereignty. During a fairly limited time, several companies that ran various forms of businesses – agricultural trading, fishing, shipping lines and sugar factories, all of which involved Chinese businessmen – were able to provide lucrative profits for the Diponegoro Division. It is therefore no surprise that at the beginning of 1959, the capital owned by the corporation reached 35 million rupiah, or the equivalent of a little less than eight hundred thousand US dollars (Elson 2001). Besides the official businesses, the development of the Diponegoro Division military business was also supported by the ability to manage illegal barter trade in the form of sugar traded for rice between Semarang and Singapore. In connection with the capital accumulation of the Diponegoro Division above, not all of it was conducted openly or officially. There is evidence that shows that many military businessmen in many other parts of Indonesia consciously created a condition whereby civilian traders, especially Chinese traders, had to pay certain forms of taxes or levies for each economic activity they conducted, apart from the official taxes they paid to the government. Furthermore, civilian traders also faced conditions that forced them to build alliances with the military businessmen. This clearly shows that manipulation and corruption had always been the hallmarks of military business, and was always considered a normal thing from the very start.

Robert Elson, in his biography of Soeharto, notes in connection with Soeharto and the Chinese businessmen that the business development of the Diponegoro Division was not so much determined by the personal relations between Soeharto and Liem Sui Liong, as stated by many previous experts, but through other Chinese trade groups such as Bob Hasan and Sukatia. This was because Lim Sui Liong had moved from Kudus to Jakarta when Soeharto began developing his military business. Even if that had happened, the business relations between the Diponegoro soldiers and Lim Sui Liong took place through Sujono (Elson 2001). Moreover, Bob Hasan, a businessman deeply involved in the business ventures of the Diponegoro Division, was the adopted son of Gatot Subroto, a very influential army general in Central Java.

As mentioned above, a similar military business development occurred in Sulawesi and Sumatra, although, to a certain extent, this was based on a different set of reasons than the Javanese situation. The trade activities conducted by army groups who defied the economic centralisation policy and demanded that the central government should distribute economic resources to the regions, resulted in armed conflicts with the central government and with other army groups loyal to the central government. Way before an open political and military conflict erupted with the central government, the army leaders of Sulawesi

that supported the local civilian government routinely conducted trade
or condoned smuggling, especially copra from Sulawesi to Singapore.
They used the excuse that they were supporting the regional government and the military budget, an issue never addressed by the central
government. It was a similar thing with the military leaders of Sumatra, where rubber and oil exports helped raise necessary cash or barter
for various other necessities (Widoyoko et al. 2003).

The army continued to try to monopolise the copra trade of Sulawesi. The formation of the *Yayasan Kopra* created an opportunity for businessmen outside the army but these efforts garnered fairly negative re-
actions, which resulted in the regulations signed by the Teritorium VII
commander and the Copra Board (Badang Urusan Kopra), an organisation that took direct orders from the military governor, to monopolise
the copra purchase in March 1957, just after the Permesta proclamation of 2 March 1957. Meanwhile, at the same time, several individual
soldiers from the 710th Battalion of South Sulawesi, which supported
the central government in Jakarta, became influential businessmen in
the 1950s and early 1960s (Limbugau 2000). These soldier-business-
men from South Sulawesi, along with other business soldiers from
many other parts of the nation, became the main element in the formation of a new social group present in each region and at the national level. It first appeared in the 1950s and was known as the *Orang
Kaya Baru*, New Rich. Awareness of this process opens for the possibi-
lity of a better understanding of the political revolt in Sulawesi at the
end of the 1950s, and to a certain extent in Sumatra as well. The armed
revolts appear to have been caused by more than just the problems that
arose between the local government and the military on the one hand,
and the central government on the other; they were also caused by the
competition for economic resources among the soldiers, or with other
interest groups which also involved soldiers.

The policy of the state in a state of emergency and a time of war, as
well as deteriorating political sentiments toward the Dutch in connection with the problems of West Papua, resulted in massive takeovers of
Western corporate interests, especially those owned by the Dutch. The
takeovers took place from 1957 and reached their climax in 1959. Labourers, especially labour unions with political ties to various parties,
specifically the Indonesian Communist Party (PKI), initiated these takeovers. In several areas, the takeover process began much earlier,
while talks between Indonesia and the Netherlands were still taking
place. Anti-Dutch sentiments were expressed by President Soekarno in
his many speeches demanding the repatriation of the territory of West
Papua, and boosted the confidence of the labours to demand the process of *indonesianisasi* of foreign corporations that had previously employed them. The labour actions that began in December 1957, espe-

cially those of leftist labourers, increased in scope and depth and in-
curred the interest of the soldiers, especially the army which was increasingly involved in the process due to safety issues and the attitude
of rivalry it developed towards the PKI. The army's involvement was
not solely to keep the peace during the process of Dutch economic takeovers, but also functioned to deny economic resources to its most
important political rivals. In their effort to control the labour unions,
the military formed alliances such as the Military Labour Cooperation
Body or *Badan Kerjasama Buruh dan Militer* (BKSBM) (Pikiran Rakjat,
11 December 1957).

The widespread involvement of the military, especially the army, in
connection with the takeover process was clearly demonstrated in the
many regulations and actions that were not just conducted by the central military leaders but repeated in each individual territory as well.
The II Territory Army leader who was responsible for the West Java territory had garnered a lot of foreign-owned plantations, and issued regulations specifying that all transfers of rights of foreign corporations in
the area could only be conducted via the military (Keng Po, 9 December 1957). One day later, the same military leader announced that all
Dutch-owned companies in West Java would come under military control to avoid chaotic takeovers (Keng Po, 11 December 1957; Pikiran
Rakjat, 11 December 1957). Prior to that, the Bandung military commander of *Pelaksana Kuasa Militer Bandung* took over the 'Fateru' company, 'Vorkink' and 'De Kleyne' publisher, which had already been taken over by labourers (Pikiran Rakjat, 7 December 1957). The V Territory Army had already conducted similar actions in Malang, East Java
and the Greater Jakarta Military Commandery. Both of them issued
proclamations stating that all Dutch-owned companies in the two provinces were under the supervision of the military (Keng Po, 10 and 12
December 1957). Prior to that, in September, the military leaders of
East Java even managed to take over the distribution of Gresik Cement
in the area (Keng Po, 17 September 1957). In South Sulawesi, the 710th
Battalion, which had developed their business since independence,
took over the Dutch-owned coconut and coffee *ondernemers* in the areas
of Polewali, Mamasa, Majene and Mamuju. During December 1957,
the West Java military commander of *Pembantu Utama Pelaksana Militer* conducted a similar act by taking over the tea plantation in Ciawi,
Bogor (Keng Po, 5 December 1957). These takeovers were not only limited to companies, but also included company-owned houses, as happened in Jakarta. Until February 1958, the military commander of Jakarta expropriated no less than 321 houses; the houses were subsequently distributed among civil service and military personnel (Keng
Po, 20 February 1958). The position of the military in the takeover process became politically stronger after president Soekarno issued his de-

cree in the month of July 1959, an action Douglas Paauw has characterised as 'having opened the opportunity for real takeovers of important economic and political function by the military elite' (Paauw: 1960).

The takeover process of foreign oil companies, and the formation of a national oil company, strengthened the accusation of widespread military business participation in the process of Indonesian economic decolonisation (Muhaimin 1990; Kanumoyoso 2001). Although the government began to pay more attention to the oil industry, beginning in at least 1954, it did not do a lot prior to 1957. At the time, the decolonisation or *indonesianisasi* of the oil fields was mostly influenced by group activities related to oil labour unions. But a large shift that favoured the military took place when labour unrest in the oil companies became more radical, with the appearance of initiatives to take over foreign corporation to support the build-up of the national economy. The Department of Industry, that was responsible for issues relating to the oil industry, passed the responsibility for the country's oil companies, such as *PT Exploitasi Tambang Minyak Sumatra Utara*, directly over to the army under General A.H. Nasution, which was to eventually be consolidated under P.T. Permina. Colonel Ibu Sutowo was subsequently appointed the President-Director, while Major S.M. Geudong became Director in October 1957 (Humas Unit I PN. Permina: 1966). Ibnu Sutowo then appointed Major Harijono, Major Pattiasina and Capten Affan to run the newly created national oil company. The first headquarters of the company were even located within the army headquarters complex (Bartlett III et al. 1972). The activities of the national oil company, which began with Pangkalan Brandan, developed swiftly, especially because it had gained capital from a Japanese consortium (Karma 2001). The problem was not merely that PT. Permina (which became PN. Permina and, eventually, the present-day Pertamina, which was the result of a merger of Permina and Pertamin in 1968) was controlled by the military. The *indonesianisasi* process toward the Indonesian oil business since 1957 appeared to come hand in hand with the process of increasing the strength of military business ventures, which also played an important role for the military in the decolonisation process, especially in the cases of West Papua and Malaysia. The nationalisation of the NIAM oil company, previously owned by Shell, into the *Pertambangan Minyak Indonesia* (PERMINDO) in the year 1958, and also that of *Sorong Petroleum Maatschappij* and *Nederlands Nieuw Guinea Petroleum Maatschappij*, for instance, resulted in the opening up of large military business participation in Indonesia's oil sector during other periods, at the personal as well as group level.

In Java, Western-owned sugar and tobacco companies, once among the major contributors of foreign trade on the island, were inevitably taken over by the military as the nationalisation policy continued. In Central Java, in accordance with the stipulation that the military would become the highest commander of the area in a state of war, the Diponegoro IV Territory Army swiftly issued a notification of the takeover of all Dutch-owned companies in the region on the 10 December 1957. The Gondangwinangun sugar factory in Klaten for instance, was immediately taken under the command of the Klaten Regency Supervision Officer (Perwira Pengawas Perusahaan Kabupaten Klaten) and Surakarta's 15th Infantry Regiments (Suyitno 1996). The Cipiring sugar factory in Kendal, which was taken over by farmers and labourers on 15 December 1957, immediately came under the control of the Kendal military commander (Afandi 2004). It was from these factories that the Diponegoro Division soldiers got their sugar that they bartered, as mentioned above. The takeovers of those sugar factories were part of the actions of the Diponegoro Division which took over 31 plantations and 13 sugar factories owned by 6 Dutch companies in the area on 26 December 1957. Similar conditions occurred in Cirebon, West Java's sugar producing centre, where all the sugar and *spiritus* factories in the Paliaman regency were taken over by the local military just before Christmas 1957 (Pikiran Rakjat, 24 December 1957).

Closing remarks

The appointment of Colonel Suprijogi as the Minister for Economic Stability, and Colonel Suhardiman as the Head of the Nationalisation Board in charge of handling the nationalisation process, within the new cabinet of Prime Minister Djuanda in 1958, shows that the military had truly taken over a large part of Indonesia's economic activities as the decolonisation process of the nation drew to a close. The once political party-controlled banking sector began to change hands as a result of the initiation of the guided economy, when military businessmen started to control Dutch-owned banks. At the same time, the military also expanded their business activities to cover such things as rice monopolies, trading companies, shipping lines, plantations, sugar factories, oil fields, foreign exchange and many other economic activities previously controlled by Western- and Chinese-owned companies.

The decolonisation process, which placed the military in a central position, compounded by the inability of the civilian government to manage the politics and economic resources of the nation, stimulated the interests of the soldiers and officers to conduct business, either at a group or personal level. In the context of Dutch company takeovers since 1957, for instance, it was not just a question of military involvement in the takeover process as the result of the national state of war. It also involved the domination that military personnel wielded over the board members of companies, and the expansion of control of military organisation into every aspect of business policy. This resulted in the positioning of the military as the main power in the business world of the country, whether via the private sector or government bureaucracy.

When General A.H. Nasution realised the gross violations of the army in their business affairs, and reacted by calling for an investigation of the culpable soldiers in mid-1959, it was already too late. The military officers had already slotted themselves into dependent positions with regard to their business activities, and were reaping large profits – socially, economically and politically. The army as an institution had also become dependent on the financial benefits gained from the military business conducted by these soldier businessmen. As the decolonisation process wound down, the business community and the military had become two sides of the same coin.

The army was not the sole violator in the field of military business activities. Every other aspect of the military, including the police force, was involved in similar business activities, whether directly or indirectly. The navy, for instance, conducted its business ventures with the official support of the cabinet meeting of June 1958, which allowed it to own companies and to militarise trade-based shipping lines (Kedaulatan Rakjat, 6 June 1958). In the end, decolonisation provided a firm base from which the military could carry on its business activities in Indonesia, eventually supporting the creation of the new and more sophisticated military business network that emerged during the 1960s, especially during the period of the New Order.

Notes

1   This was originally a paper presented at the 4th International Convention of Asian Scholars, in the panel entitled 'Social and Economic Decolonization in Southeast Asia, in Particular Indonesia' in Shanghai, China, 20-24 August 2005. I would like to thank Farabi Fakih for the English, and Rika and Beti for their assistance. The author is a staff member at Department of History, Universitas Gadjah Mada Yogyakarta Indonesia. For further information and any comments, please contact: purwantougm@yahoo.co.uk.

Contributors

Rachana Chakraborty is a Reader at the Department of History, Bethune College, Calcutta University in India. She has been researching the history of educational management and administration, gender studies, and caste politics in an Indian context. Her main published work is *Higher Education in Bengal 1919-1947: A Study of its Administration and Management* (Calcutta: Minerva Associates 1997). She has presented, and presided over, sessions of the IAHA and ICAS conferences in Bangladesh, Taipei and Malaysia, as well as contributing to numerous international and national journals.

Hans Hägerdal studied history at Lund University, Sweden, and got his Ph.D. in 1996. He has twice been a fellow at the IIAS, Leiden, and since 2000, he is a senior lecturer in history at Växjö University in Sweden. He has written extensively on East and Southeast Asian history, in particular Indonesia, publishing among other titles *Hindu Rulers, Muslim Subjects: Lombok and Bali in the Seventeenth and Eighteenth Centuries* (Bangkok: White Lotus 2001) and *Vietnams historia* (Lund: Historiska Media 2005).

Victoria Haskins is a lecturer in Australian history at the University of Newcastle, in New South Wales, Australia. She has researched and published widely on the histories of Australian Aboriginal domestic service and relationships between white and Aboriginal women, work that includes a comparative study of Native American and Australian Aboriginal child removal, and her 2005 book, *One Bright Spot*, on Joan Kingsley-Strack, a white feminist activist for Aboriginal rights. She is particularly interested in the historical roles and representations of white and Indigenous women in the colonial histories of settlers. Her studies of Indigenous domestic service have broadened her research outlook to encompass Southeast Asia under British colonial rule, and the United States of America.

Vincent Houben studied history and Indonesian languages at Leiden University, the Netherlands, where he got his Ph.D. degree. His thesis was published as *Kraton and Kumpeni: Yogyakarta and Surakarta 1830-1870* (Leiden: KITLV Press 1994). Since 1994, he has been a professor in Southeast Asian studies, first in Passau University and since 2001, at Humboldt University, Berlin. He has published extensively on various historical themes connected with Southeast Asia and particularly Indonesia.

Daniel Leplat is *agrégé d'histoire* and a Ph.D. candidate at Sorbonne University, Paris, France. His field of academic interest includes Asia, financial conditions, and crime.

Sandra Khor Manickam is a Ph.D. candidate at the Australian National University, Division of Pacific and Asian History, Research School for Pacific and Asian Studies. Her main interest is the history of colonial British Malaya, exploring themes such as race, the production of knowledge and Malay manuscripts. She is currently working on a history of the anthropology of indigenous groups in British Malaya and the interactions between the British, Malays and indigenous groups in the formation of anthropological knowledge.

Christine de Matos is a research fellow in the Centre for Asia Pacific Social Transformation Studies (CAPSTRANS) at the University of Wollongong, Australia. She is currently researching the everyday practice of power in relations between Australians (occupier) and Japanese (occupied) during the Allied Occupation of Japan (1945-1952) using gender, race and class. Her book, *Imposing Peace and Prosperity: Australia, Social Justice and Labour Reform in Occupied Japan*, which examines the policies of the Australian government towards the labour movement in occupied Japan, is forthcoming from Australian Scholarly Press.

Bambang Purwanto was educated at Gadjah Mada University, Yogyakarta, Imdonesia, and later at SOAS, London, where he got his Ph.D. in history in 1992. Since 2004, he has been a professor at the Department of History, Faculty of Cultural Sciences, Gajah Mada University. He has published extensively on modern Indonesian political and economic history, and historiographical issues. Among his publications is *Gagalnya historiografi Indonesiasentris?!* (Jogjakarta: Ombak 2006).

Ram Krishna Tandon is a reader at the Department of Defence & Strategic Studies, University of Allahabad, India. He has two masters in Medieval Indian History and Defence Studies, and has studied cartography. He earned his Ph.D. in defence studies with a work on European military adventurers in India. He has served at the universities of both Madras and Allahabad. Dr. Tandon has published two books and several research articles in journals and monographs. His present research and teaching interests lie in Indian military thought, Maratha history, and Indian Ocean affairs.

References

Afandi, Zaenuri (2004), 'Perkembangan Pabrik Gula dan perubahan Ekonomi Pedesaan Cepiring, Kendal Tahun 1948-1966', Skripsi Sarjana, Yogyakarta: Jurusan Sejarah Fakultas Ilmu Budaya UGM.

Ahmed, Raffiuddin, (2001), *Understanding the Bengal Muslims*. New Delhi: Oxford University Press.

Alphonsus Adrianus and Fettor Ebenoni, letter to the Dutch authorities in Kupang, 3 August 1798, LOr 2238, Department of Eastern Letters, University Library, Leiden.

Andal, N. (2002), *Women and Indian society: Options and constraints*. Jaipur and New Delhi: Rawat Publications.

Anderson, Bridget (2000), *Doing the Dirty Work? The Global Politics of Domestic Labour*. London: Zed Books.

ANRI Timor, Arsip Nasional Republik Indonesia, Jakarta.

Archer, M. (1980), *Early Views of India: The Picturesque Journeys of Thomas and William Daniell 1786-1794*. London: Thames and Hudson.

Armorin, J.L. (n.d.), *Son dernier reportage*. Paris: n.p.

Arnold, David and Hardiman, David (eds.) (1994), *Subaltern Studies*, vol. 8. New Delhi: OUP.

Asad, T. (1991), 'Afterword: From the History of Colonial Anthropology to the Anthropology of Western Hegemony', in Stocking Jr., G.W. (ed.) (1991), *Colonial Situations: Essays on the Contextualization of Ethnographic Knowledge*, 314-24. Madison: University of Wisconsin Press.

Australian War Memorial (1947), 114: 130/2/58, 'BCOF Bound'.

Australian War Memorial (c. 1947), 114: 130/1/23 Pt II, 'Introduction – Dependents Housing'.

Author and title unknown. (1947), *Australian Women's Weekly*, 6 December.

Author unknown. (1950), 'Family home from Japan will miss help', *Melbourne Sun*, 1950, copy provided to author by Barbara Hogg (Queensland, Australia) in 2006.

Author unknown. (c. 1950), 'Dandenong Woman Likes Life in Japan', unknown newspaper provided by Barbara Hogg (Queensland, Australia) in 2006.

Baker, D.W.A. (ed.) (2006), Godfrey Charles Mundy, *Our Antipodes* (originally published 1852). Canberra: Pandanus.

Ballantyne, Tony (2002), *Orientalism and Race: Aryanism in the British Empire*. Hampshire: Palgrave.

Ballard, C. (2006), 'Strange alliances: Pygmies in the colonial imaginary', *World Archeology* 38(1): 133-151.

Bandyopadhyay, Sekhar (2004a), *From Plassey to Partition – A History of Modern India*. New Delhi: Orient Longman Ltd.

Bandyopadhyay, Sekhar, (2004b), *Caste Culture and Hegemony – Social Dominance in Colonial Bengal*. New Delhi: Sage publications.

Banerjee, Swapna M. (2004), *Men women and Domestics: Articulating middle class identity in colonial Bengal*. New Delhi: Oxford University Press.

Barrow, J. (1822), 'The Indian Archipelago', *The Quarterly Review* 28 (55): 111-138.

Bartlett III, A.G., et al. (1972), *Pertamina Indonesian National Oil*. Djakarta: Amerasian.

Bayly, C.A. (1989), *Imperial Meridian: The British Empire and the World 1780-1830*. London: Longman.

Benjamin, G. (2002), 'On Being Tribal in the Malay Worlds' in Benjamin, G. and Chou, C. (eds.), *Tribal Communities in the Malay World: Historical, Cultural and Social Perspectives*, 7-76. CITY: International Institute of Asian Studies.

Bethune School, Praktani Samiti (ed.) (2001), *Education and Empowerment: Women in South Asia*. Kolkata: Bethune School Publications.

Bethune School, Praktani Samiti (ed.) (2006), *Bethune: His School & Nineteenth Century Bengal*. Kolkata: Bethune School Publications.

Bhagwat, A.K. (ed.) (1977), *Maharashtra – A Profile*. Kolhapur: Visnu Sakharam Khandekar Amrit Mahotsav Satkar Samiti.

Bhargava Meena and Dutta Kalyani (2005), *Women Education and Politics – The Women's Movement and Delhi's Indraprastha College*. New Delhi: Oxford University Press.

Bhatia, H.S. (1977), *Military History of British India (1607-1947)*. New Delhi: Deep and Deep Publications.

Blair, E.H. and Robertson, J. (eds.) (1973), *The Philippine islands, 1493-1898* with historical introduction and additional notes by Edward Gaylord Bourne, translated from the originals. Mandaluyong, Rizal: Cachos Hermanos.

Blunt, Alison (1999), 'Imperial Geographies of Home: British Domesticity in India 1886-1925', *Transactions of the Institute of British Geographers* 24 (4): 421-440.

Bodard, Lucien (1997), *La guerre d'Indochine*. Paris: Grasset.

Borthwick, M. (1984), *The changing Role of Women in Bengal, 1849-1905*. Princeton: Princeton University Press.

Boxer, C.R. (1947), *The Topasses of Timor*. Amsterdam: Koninklijk Vereeniging Indisch Instituut. (Mededeling no. 73.)

Brendon, Vyvyen (2006), *Children of the Raj*. London: Phoenix.

Bryant, G.J. (2004), 'Asymmetrical Warfare: The British Experience in Eighteen Century India', *Journal of Military History*, 68 (2): PP?.

Bulbeck, D. (1999), 'Current Biological Anthropological Research on Southeast Asia's Negritos', *SPAFA Journal* 9 (2): 15-22.

Burke, Peter (2001), 'Overture. The New History: Its Past and its Future', in Burke, Peter (ed.), *New Perspectives on Historical Writing*. Cambridge: Polity.

Butalia, Urvasi (ed.) (2002), *Speaking Peace: Women's voices from Kashmir*. London: Zed Books.

Casalilla, Bartolomé Yun (2007), '"Localism", global history and transnational history. A reflection from the historian of early modern Europe', *Historisk tidskrift* 127 (4): 659-78.

Castro, A. de (1867), *Os possessões portuguezas na Oceania*. Lisboa: Imprensa nacional.

Central India Gazetteer (1908), *Gwalior State, vol. I*.

Chakraborty, Dipesh (2007), *From the colonial to the post colonial*. New Delhi: Oxford University Press.

Chakraborty, Rachana (1997), *Higher Education in Bengal 1919-1947: A Study of its Administration and Management*. Calcutta: Minerva Associates.

Chaudhuri, Nupur (1994), 'Memsahibs and their Servants in Nineteenth-century India', *Women's History Review* 3 (4): 549-562.

Chijs, J. A. van der (1872), 'Koepang omstreeks 1750', *Tijdschrift voor Indische Taal-, Land- en volkenkunde* 18, pp. 209-27.

Chowdhury, Indira (2001), *Frail Hero and Virile History: Gender and the Politics of Culture in Colonial Bengal* New Delhi: Oxford University Press.

Christiansen, E. (2006), *The Norsemen in the Viking Age*. Malden, etc.: Blackwell.

Compton H. (1892), *A Particular Account of the European Adventurers of Hindustan from 1784 to 1803*. London: T. Fisher Unwin, Paternoster Square.

Coolhaas, W. Ph. (ed.) (1968), *Generale missiven van Gouverners-Generaal en Raden XVII der Verenigde Oostindische Compagnie*, vol. 3. 's-Gravenhage: M. Nijhoff. (Rijks Geschiedkundige Publicatien, Grote Serie 125.)

Cotton, E. (1927), 'Benoit de Boigne,' *Calcutta Bengal Past & Present, Journal of Calcutta Historical Society* vol. XXXIII S. no. 65-66.

Crane Ralph (ed.) (2007), *Daughters of India: Margaret Wilson*. New Delhi: Oxford University Press.

Crawfurd, J. (1820; 1972), *History of the Indian Archipelago, containing an account of the manners, arts, languages, religions, institutions, and commerce of its inhabitants*. London: Frank Cass & Co. Ltd.

Crawfurd, J. (1856; 1971), *A Descriptive Dictionary of the Indian Islands & Adjacent Countries*, with an introduction by M.C. Ricklefs. Kuala Lumpur: Oxford University Press.

Crawfurd, J. (1866), 'On the Physical and Mental Characteristics of the Negro', *Transactions of the Ethnological Society of London* 4: 212-239.

Crouch, Harold (1975/1976), 'Generals and business in Indonesia', *Pacific Affairs* 48: 4.

Curtin, P.D. (1964), *The Image of Africa: British Ideas and Action, 1780-1850*. Madison: University of Wisconsin Press.

Daniels, K. and Murnane, M. (eds), *Uphill All the Way: A Documentary History of Women in Australia*. St Lucia: University of Queensland Press.

Davis, D.B. (1984), *Slavery and Human Progress*. New York: Oxford University Press.

Dawson, Graham. (1994), *Soldier Heroes: British Adventure, empire and the imagining of masculinities*. London and New York: Routledge.

Debi, Sarala (2007), *Jibaner Jharapata*. Kolkata: Subarnarekha Publications.

Dentan, R.K. (1981), 'Batek Negrito Religion: The World View and Rituals of a Hunting and Gathering People of Peninsular Malaysia', *Journal of Asian Studies* 40(2): 421-423.

De Souza, Eunice and Pereira, Lindsay (2002), *Women's Voices: Selections from Nineteenth and early Twentieth century Indian Writing in English*. New Delhi: Oxford University Press.

Despuech, Jacques (1953), *Le trafic des piastres*. Paris: Ed. des Deux Rives.

De Vries, Susanna (2005), *Great Pioneer Women of the Outback*. Sydney: HarperCollins.

Diamond, J. (1997), *Guns, Germs and Steel: The Fates of Human Societies*. New York: Norton.

District Gazetteer Central India State (1908), *Indore State vol. II.*

Doko, I.H. (1981), *Pahlawan-pahlawan suku Timor*. Jakarta: PN Balai Pustaka.

Donnelly, Roma (1994), 'A Civilising Influence? Women in the British Commonwealth Occupation Force in Japan 1946-1952', MA thesis: Swinburne University.

Dower, John W. (1999), *Embracing Defeat: Japan in the Wake of World War II*. New York: W.W. Norton & Company.

Drain, Dorothy (1946), 'New Hospital Moves in on Eta Jima Island', *Australian Women's Weekly*, 20 April.

Duiker,William J. (2000), *Ho Chi Minh*. New York: Hyperion.

Duplay, Philippe and Pedroncini, Guy (1992), *Leclerc et l'Indochine (1946-1947)*. Paris: Albin Michel.

Dupuy R.E. and Dupuy, T.N. (1977), *Encyclopedia of Military History*. New York: Harper and Row.

Earle, E.M. (1944), *Makers of Modern Strategy: Military Thought From Machiavelli to Hitler*. Princeton: Princeton University Press.

Edwards, Penny (2003), 'On Home Ground: Settling Land and Domesticating Difference in the 'Non-Settler' Colonies of Burma and Cambodia', *Journal of Colonialism and Colonial History* 4 (3): electronic journal.

Eisenstadt, S.N. (2002), *Multiple Modernities*. New Brunswick and London.

Ellinghaus, Kat (1997), 'Racism in the Never-Never: Disparate readings of Jeannie Gunn', *Hecate* 23 (2): 76-95.

Elson, R.E. (2001), *Suharto. A Political Biography*. Cambridge: Cambridge University Press.

Endicott, K. (1983), 'The Effects of Slave Raiding on the Aborigines of the Malay Peninsula', in Reid, A. and Brewster, J. (eds.), *Slavery, bondage, and dependency in Southeast Asia*, 216-245. New York: St. Martin's Press.

English Records Maratha History (1936), *Poona Residency Correspondence, vol. I*. Bombay: Central Press.

Errington, Shelly (1979), 'Some Comments on style in the Meaning of the Past', in Reid, Anthony and Marr, David (eds.), *Perceptions of the Past in Southeast Asia*, 26-72. Singapore: Heineman.

Fildes, Valerie (1988), *Wet Nursing: A History from Antiquity to the Present*. Oxford: Basil Blackwell.

Finnegan, R. (1996), 'A Note on Oral Tradition and Historical Evidence', in Dunaway, D.K., and Baum, W.K. (eds.), *Oral History: An Interdisciplinary Anthology*. Walnut Creek etc.: Altamira Press.

Florida, Nancy K. (1995), *Writing the Past, Inscribing the Future: History as Prophecy in Colonial Java*. Durham and London: Duke University Press.

Fobia, F.H. (1984), Sonbai dalam kisah dan perjuangan. Unpublished manuscript, Soe.

Fobia, F.H., n.d., (Legendary history of Oecusse). Unpublished manuscript, Soe.

Forbes, Geraldine (1998), *The New Cambridge History of India*, iv. 2: Women in Modern India. Cambridge: Cambridge University Press.

Forbes, Geraldine (2005), *Women in colonial India Essays on Politics, Medicine and Historiography*. New Delhi: Chronicle Books.

Fox, J.J. (1982), 'The Great Lord Rests at the Centre', *Canberra Anthropology* 5: 2, pp. 22-33.

Fox, J.J. (1997), 'Place and Landscape in Comparative Austronesian Perspective', in Fox, J.J. (ed.), *The Poetic Power of Place: Comparative Perspectives on Austronesian Ideas of Locality*. Canberra: Department of Anthropology.

Frank, Andre Gunder (1998), *ReOrient: Global economy in the Asian age*. Berkeley: University of California Press.

Gathorne-Hardy, Jonathon (1972), *The Unnatural History of the Nanny*. New York: Dial Press.

Ghosh, Dhurba (2006), *Sex and the Family in Colonial India: The Making of Empire*. Cambridge: Cambridge University Press.

Giddens, Anthony (1995), *The Consequences of Modernity*. Stanford, CA: Stanford University Press.

Godden, Judith (1979) 'A new look at the pioneer woman', *Hecate* 5 (2) 1979: 6-21.

Goscha, Christopher E. (2000), Le contexte asiatique de la guerre franco-vietnamienne, Paris: Thèse EPHE.

Gothard, Janice (1991), '"Pity the Poor Immigrant": Assisted Single Female Migration to Colonial Australia', in Richards, Eric (ed.), *Poor Australian Immigrants in the Nineteenth Century. Visible Immigrants: Two*, 97-116. Canberra: Australian National University.

Gothard, Jan (2001), *Blue China: Single Female Migration to Colonial Australia*. Melbourne: Melbourne University Press.

Grimshaw, Patricia and Standish, Ann (2007), 'Making Tasmania Home: Louisa Meredith's Colonizing Prose', in Haskins, Victoria and Jacobs, Margaret (eds.), *Domestic Frontiers: The Home and Colonization*. Frontiers 28 (1-2): 1-17.

Grimshaw, Patricia and Evans, Julie (1996), 'Colonial Women on Intercultural Frontiers: Rosa Campbell Praed, Mary Bundock and Katie Langloh Parker,' *Australian Historical Studies* 27 (106): 79-95.

Großheim, Martin (2007), The Year 1956 in Vietnamese Historiography and Popular Discourse: the Resilience of Myths. Unpublished Paper Humboldt University.

Guha, Ranajit (2000), 'On Some Aspects of the Historiography of Colonial India', in Chaturvedi, Vinayak (ed.), *Mapping Subaltern Studies and the Postcolonial*. London and New York: Verso.

Gunn, Mrs Aeneas (1924), *The Little Black Princess of the Never-Never*. Melbourne: Robertson and Mullens.

Haga, A. (1882), 'De slag bij Penefoeij en Vendrig Lip', *Tijdschrift voor Indische Taal-, Land- en volkenkunde* 28, pp. 389-408.

Hägerdal, H. (2007), 'Rebellions or Factionalism? Timorese Forms of Resistance in an Early Colonial Context', *Bijdragen tot de Taal-, Land- en Volkenkunde* 163: 1, pp. 1-33.

Hasan, Morshed Safiul (2006), *Rokeya Rachanabali*. Dhaka: Maola Brothers.

Hasan, Zoya and Menon, Ritu (2004), *Unequal Citizens: A study of Muslim Women in India*. New Delhi: Oxford University Press.

Hasan, Zoya and Menon, Ritu (2005), *In a Minority: Essays on Muslim Women in India*. New Delhi: Oxford University Press.

Haskins, Victoria (2004), '"A Better Chance'? Sexual abuse and the apprenticeship of Aboriginal girls under the NSW Aborigines Protection Board', *Aboriginal History* 28: 49-52.

Haskins, Victoria (2005), *One Bright Spot*. Hampshire: Palgrave.

Hatalkar, V.G. (1958), Relations between the French and the Marathas (1668-1815). Bombay: University of Bombay.

Heijmering, G. (1847), 'Bijdragen tot de geschiedenis van Timor', Tijdschrift van Nederlandsch Indië 9: 3, pp. 1-62, 121-232.

Hering, Bob (2002), *Soekarno. Founding Father of Indonesia 1901-1945*. Leiden: KITLV Press.

Higman, B.W. (2002), *Domestic Service in Australia*. Melbourne: Melbourne University Press.

Hodder, Rupert (1996), *Merchant princes of the East: cultural delusions, economic success and the overseas Chinese in Southeast Asia*. New York, Chichester and Singapore.

Houben, Vincent (2008), 'Historische Repräsentationen des Eigenen und Nationenbildungsprozesse in Südostasien', in Baberowksi, Jörg et al. (eds.), *Selbstbilder und Fremdbilder. Repräsentationen sozialer Ordnungen im Wandel*. Frankfurt am Main and New York: Campus.

Howard, M. (1976), *War in the European History*. Oxford: Oxford University Press.

Humas (1966), *Humas Unit I PN Permina*. Permina. Dulu, Sekarang dan Dimasa Datang. Medan: Humas Pusat PN. Permina.

Hussin, Nordin (2007), *Trade and Society in the Straits of Melaka: Dutch Melaka and English Penang, 1780-1830*. Singapore and Copenhagen: NUS Press and NIAS Press.

Hutchinson, L. (1964), *European Freebooters in Mughal India*. Bombay: Asia Publishing House.

Jackson, Alice (1948), 'Shopping in Japan Presents Few Difficulties', *Australian Women's Weekly*, 3 January.

Jahoda, G. (1999), *Images of Savages: Ancient Roots of Modern Prejudice in Western Culture*. London: Routledge.

Janiewski, Dolores E. (1998), 'Gendered Colonialism: The "Woman Question"; in Settler Society', in Roach Pierson, Ruth and Chaudhuri, Nupur (eds.), *Nation, Empire, Colony: Historicizing Gender and Race*. Bloomington: Indiana University Press: 57-76.

Jasanoff, Maya (2005), *Edge of Empire: Lives, Culture and Conquest in the East 1750-1850*. New York: Vintage.

Jhunjhunwala, Bharat and Jhunjhunwala, Madhu (2004), *Indian approach to Women's empowerment*. New Delhi: Rawat Publications.

Johns, H. (1979), 'The turning image: myth and reality in Malay perceptions of the past', in Reid, Anthony and Marr, David (eds.), *Perceptions of the Past in Southeast Asia*, 43-67. Singapore: Heineman Reid and Marr.

Jomo, K.S. (1999), 'Development Planning in Malaysia: A Critical Appraisal', in Ghosh, B.N. and Syukri Salleh, Muhammad (eds.), *Political Economy of Development in Malaysia*. Kuala Lumpur: Utusan.

Joseph, Betty (2006), *Reading the East India Company, 1720-1840: Colonial currencies of Gender*. New Delhi: Orient Longman.

Kahin, Audrey (1997), 'Perdagangan dan Pajak: Aspek Ekonomi Sumatra Barat di Masa Revolusi', in Abdullah, Taufik, et al. (eds.), *Denyut Nadi Revolusi Indonesia*. Jakarta: Gramedia.

Kanumoyoso, Bondan (2001), *Nasionalisasi Perusahaan Belanda di Indonesia*. Jakarta: Sinar Harapan.

Karlsson, K.G. (1999), *Historia som vapen: Historiebruk och Sovjeunionens upplösning 1985-1995*. Stockholm: Natur och Kultur. (with summary in English.)

Karma, Mara (2001), *Ibnu Sutowo Mengabdi Misi Revolusi Sebagai Dokter, Tentara, Pejuang Minyak Bumi*. Jakarta: Sinar Harapan.

Kartodirdjo, S., et al. (eds.) (1973), *Ikhtisar keadaan politik Hindia-Belanda, tahun 1839-1848*. Jakarta: Arsip Nasional Republik Indonesia.

Kedaulatan Rakjat, September 1956-April 1959.

Keng Po, Januari-Desember 1957.

Khoo Kay Kim (1979), 'Local Historians and the Writing of Malaysian History in the Twentieth Century', in Reid, Anthony and Marr, David (eds.), *Perceptions of the Past in Southeast Asia*, 299-311. Singapore: Heineman.

Koikari, Mire (2002), 'Exporting Democracy?: American Women, "Feminist Reforms," and Politics of Imperialism in the U.S. Occupation of Japan, 1945-1952', *Frontiers*, 23 (1): 23-45.

Kosambi, Meera (2003), *Returning the American Gaze: Pandita Ramabai's The People of the United States (1889)*. New Delhi: Permanent Black.

Krishnamurty, J. (ed.) (1989), *Women in Colonial India: Essays on Survival, Work and the State*. New Delhi: Oxford University Press.

Kumar, Deepak (1995), *Science and the Raj*. New Delhi: Oxford University Press.

Ladyga, Elaine (2004), *Memories of BCOF in Japan, 1947-1952*. Self-published.

Lal, Brij Vilash (ed.) (2006), *The Encyclopedia of the Indian Diaspora*. Singapore (1st Edition).

Leyden, J. (1811), 'On the Languages and Literature of the Indo-Chinese Nations', *Asiatic Researches* 10: 158-289.

Limbugau, Daud (2000), 'Keterlibatan TNI dalam Perdagangan di Sulwaesi Selatan dari Masa Revolusi Sampai Tahun 1970-an', in E.L. Polinggoman, E.L., dan Mappangara, Suriadi (eds.), *Dunia Militer di Indonesia. Keberadaan dan Peran Militer di Sulawesi*. Yogyakarta: Gadjah Mada University Press.

Macmillan, Margaret (1988, 1996), *Women of the Raj*. London: Thames and Hudson.

Majumdar, R.C. (ed.) (1977), *The History & Culture of the Indian People vol. 8: The Maratha Supremacy*. Bombay: Bhartiya Vidya Bhawan.

Malleson, G.B (1885), *The Decisive Battles of India from 1746 to 1849*. London: W.H. Allen and Company.

Mani, A. et Sandu, K.S. (eds.) (1993), *Indian Communities in South East Asia*. Singapore.

Marr, David (1979), 'Vietnamese Historical Reassessment 1900-1944', in: Anthony Reid and David Marr (eds.), *Perceptions of the Past in Southeast Asia*, 313-338. Singapore: Heineman.

Marr, David (1981), *Vietnamese Tradition on Trial 1920-1945*. Berkeley: University of California Press.

Mason, P. (1974), *A Matter of Honour*. London: Jonathan Cape.

Masudjjaman Selina Hossain (2006), *Narir Kshamatayan: Rajniti O Andolan*. Dhaka: Maola Brothers.

Matheson, V. and Hooker, M.B. (1983), 'Slavery in the Malay texts: Categories of Dependency and Compensation', in Reid, A. and Brewster, J. (eds.), *Slavery, bondage, and dependency in Southeast Asia*, 182-208. New York : St. Martin's Press.

Matos, A.T. de (1974), *Timor português 1515-1769: Contribução para a sua história*. Lisboa: Faculdade de Letras da Universidade de Lisboa.

Maynard, John (2007), *Fight for Liberty and Freedom: The origins of Australian Aboriginal Activism*. Canberra: Aboriginal Studies Press.

McClintock, Anne (1995), *Imperial Leather: Race, Gender and Sexuality in the Colonial Contest*. New York: Routledge.

McGregor, Katharine E. (2007), *History in Uniform. Military Ideology and the Construction of Indonesia's Past*. Singapore: NUS Press.

McGuire, Madeline E. (1990), 'The Legend of the Good Fella Missus', *Aboriginal History* 14 (2): 124-151.

McKenzie, Kirsten (2004), *Scandal in the Colonies: Sydney and Cape Town, 1820-1850*. Carlton: Melbourne University Press.

McPherson, Mrs Alan (1860), My Experiences in Australia. Being Recollections of a Visit to the Australian Colonies in 1856-7. By a Lady. London: J F Hope.

McVey, Ruth (1979), 'History and Action in an Indonesian Communist Text', in: Anthony Reid and David Marr (eds.), *Perceptions of the Past in Southeast Asia*, 340-358. Singapore: Heineman.

McWilliam, A. (2002), *Paths of Origin, Gates of Life: A Study of Place and Precedence in Southwest Timor*. Leiden: KITLV Press (Verhandelingen van het Koninklijk Instituut voor Taal-, Land- en volkenkunde 203.)

Menon, Nivedita (ed.) (1999), *Gender and the Politics in India*. New Delhi: Oxford University Press.

Metcalf, Barbara D. and Metcalf, Thomas R. (2005) (Reprint), *A Concise History of India*. UK: Cambridge University Press.

Metcalf, Thomas R. (2005), *Ideologies of the Raj*. U.K: Cambridge University Press (Reprint).

Misra, Kamal K. and Lowry, Janet Huber (eds.) (2007), *Recent studies on Indian women*. New Delhi: Rawat Publications.

Middelkoop, P. (1938), 'Iets over Sonba'i, het bekende vorstengeslacht in Timor', *Tijdschrift voor Indische Taal-, Land- en volkenkunde* 78, pp. 392-509.

Middelkoop, P. (1939), 'Amarassisch-Timoreesche teksten', *Verhandelingen van het Bataviaasch Genootschap* 74:2, pp. 1-105.

Minault, Gail (1998), *Secluded Scholars: Women's education and Muslim social reform in colonial India*. New Delhi: Oxford University Press.

Mochtar, Kustiniyati (ed.) (1992), *Memoar Pejuang Republik Indonesia Seputar "Zaman Singapura" 1945-1950*. Jakarta: Gramedia.

Montross, L. (1946), *War Through the Ages*. New York: Harper and Brothers Publications.

Muhaimin, Yahya. A. (1990), *Bisnis dan Politik. Kebijaksanaan Ekonomi Indonesia 1950-1980*. Jakarta: LP3ES.

Murshid, Ghulam (1983), *Reluctant Debutante: Response of Bengali Women to Modernisation 1849-1905*. Rajshahi: Sahitya Samsad.

Müller, S. (1857), *Reizen en onderzoekingen in den Indschen Archipel*, vol. I-II. Amsterdam: F. Muller.

Nadkarni, R.V (1966), *The Rise & and Fall of the Maratha Empire*. Bombay: Popular Praka-shan.

Nanda, Reena (2002), *Kamaladevi Chattopadhyay- A Biography*. New Delhi: Oxford University Press.

Neogy, Ajit K. (1997), *Decolonization of French India, Liberation Movement and Indo-French relations, 1947-1954*. Paris and Aix: Institut français de Pondichéry.

O'Brien, Rosina (2006), Interview with Christine de Matos in Macgregor Queensland, Australia, 13 September.

Olney, Patricia (2006), Interview with Christine de Matos in Waitara New South Wales, Australia 22 August 22.

Ormeling, F.J. (1956), *The Timor Problem*. Djakarta and Groningen: Wolters.

Ospina, S, and Hohe, T. (2002), *Traditional Power Structures and Local Governance in East Timor: A Case Study of the Community Empowerment Project (CEP)*. Genève: Institut universitaire d'études de developpement. (Etudes courtes no. 5.)

Paauw, D.S. (1960), *Financing Economic Development. The Indonesian Case*. Glencoe: The Free Press.

Pan, Lynn (2000), *Encyclopédie de la diaspora chinoise*. Paris: Éd. du Pacifique.

Pant, G.S. (1970), *Studies in Indian Weapons and Warfare*. New Delhi: Army Educational Stores.

Parera, A.D.M. (1969), *Portugis dan Belanda di Kota Kupang*. Unpublished manuscript, Kupang.

Parera, A.D.M. (1994), *Sejarah pemerintahan raja-raja Timor*. Jakarta: Pustaka Sinar Harapan.

Pieterse, J.N. (1992), *White on Black: Images of Africa and Blacks in Western Popular Culture*. New Haven: Yale University Press.

Pikiran Rakjat, Desember 1957-Januari 1958

Plates to Raffles' History of Java, preface by John Bastin (1988), Singapore: Oxford University Press.

Poeze, H.A. (2007), *Verguisd en vergeten. Tan Malakka, de linkse beweging en de Indonesische revolutie 1945-1949*. Leiden: KITLV.

Powe, Joan (1946), 'Australian Nurses and AAMWS Leave for Japan'. *Australian Women's Weekly*, 23 March.

Powell, Avril A. (2006), *Rhetoric and reality-Gender and the colonial experience in South Asia*. New Delhi: Oxford University Press.

Prakash, Gyan (2000), 'Writing Post-Orientalist Histories of the Third World: Perspectives from Indian Historiography', in Chaturvedi, Vinayak (ed.), *Mapping Subaltern Studies and the Postcolonial*. London and New York: Verso.

Prasad, Leela (2003), 'The authorial other in folktale collections in colonial India: Tracing Narration and its Dis/Continuities', *Cultural Dynamics* 15 (1): 5-39.

Procida, Mary A. (2003), 'Feeding the Imperial Appetite: Imperial knowledge and Anglo-Indian discourse', *Journal of Women's History* 15 (2): 123-151.

Purwanto, Bambang (2000), 'Historiografi dan Legitimasi Peran Sosial Politik Militer di Indonesia', in Polinggoman, E.L., dan Mappangara, Suriadi (eds.), *Dunia Militer di Indonesia. Keberadaan dan Peran Militer di Sulawesi*. Yogyakarta: Gadjah Mada University Press.

Raffles, T.S. (1817; 1988), *The history of Java*: complete text, introduction by John Bastin. Singapore: Oxford University Press.

Rahmann, R. (1963), *The Negritos of the Philippines and the Early Spanish Missionaries*. Wien: St. Gabriel.

Ranade, M.G. and Telang, K.T. (1961), *Rise of the Maratha Power and Gleanings from Maratha Chronicles*. Bombay: University of Bombay.

Ransel, David. L. (2007), 'Reflections on transnational and world history in the USA and its applications', *Historisk tidskrift* 127 (4): 625-42.

Ray, Bharati, (2002). *Early feminists of colonial India* New Delhi: Oxford University Press.

Ray, Bharati (ed.) (2005), *Women of India, Colonial and postcolonial periods.* New Delhi: Sage Publications Ltd.

Ray Bharati and Basu Aparna (eds.) (1999), *From Independence Towards Freedom, Indian Women since 1947.* New Delhi: Oxford University Press.

Raza, Rosemary (2006), *In Their Own Words: British Women Writers and India 1740-1857.* Oxford: Oxford University Press.

Razali Kidam and Amidah Hamim (compilers) (1999), *Collection of Mahathir's Speeches. January-December 1998.* Kuala Lumpur: Jabatan Penerangan Malaysia.

Reid, Anthony (1979), 'Nationalist Quest for an Indonesian Past', in: Reid, Anthony and Marr, David (eds.), *Perceptions of the Past in Southeast Asia,* 281-298. Singapore: Heineman.

Reill, P.H. (1996), 'Seeing and Understanding: A commentary', in Miller, D.P. and Reill, P.H. (eds.) (1996) *Visions of Empire: Voyages, botany, and representations of nature,* 293-304. Cambridge: Cambridge University Press, 1996.

Roever, A. de (2002), *De jacht op sandelhout: De VOC en de tweedeling van Timor in de zeventiende eeuw.* Zutphen: Walburg Pers.

Roo van Alderwerelt, J. de (1904), 'Aanteekeningen over Timor en Onderhoorigheden 1668 tot en met 1809', *Tijdschrift voor Indische Taal-, Land- en volkenkunde* 47, pp. 195-226.

Roy, K. (2005), 'Military Synthesis in South Asia: Armies, Warfare and Indian Society 1740-1849, *Journal of Military History* 69 (3).

Rude, G. (1972), *Europe in the Eighteenth Century.* London: Weidenfeld and Nicholson.

Russell, Penny (1994), *A Wish of Distinction: Colonial Gentility and Femininity.* Melbourne: Melbourne University Press.

Rutter, O. (1930; 1986), *The Pirate Wind: Tales of the Sea-Robbers of Malaya.* Singapore: Oxford University Press.

Saha, Chandana (2003), *Gender Equity and Equality.* New Delhi: Rawat Publications.

Sangari, Kumkum and Vaid, Sudesh (eds.), (2006.), *Recasting Women.* New Delhi: Kali for Women.

Said, Edward (1978), *Orientalism.* London: Routledge and Kegan Paul.

Said, Salim (1991), *Genesis of Power. General Sudirman and Indonesian Military in Politics, 1945-1949.* Singapore: Institute of Southeast Asian Studies.

Samego, Indria, et al. (1998), *Bila Abri Berbisnis.* Jakarta: Kronik Indonesia Baru.

Sardesai, G.S. (1946), *New History of the Marathas vol. I.* Bombay: New Phoenix Publications.

Sarkar, J.N. (1973), *Shivaji and His Times.* Calcutta: Orient Longman

Sarkar, J.N. (1984), *The Art of War in Medieval India.* New Delhi: Munishram Manoharlal Publications.

Schenk, Catherine R. (2001), *Hong Kong as an international financial centre: emergence and development, 1945-65.* London and New York: Routledge.

Schoonevelt-Oosterling, J.E. (1997), *Generale missiven van Gouverneurs-Generaal en Raden aan Heren XVII der Verenigde Oostindische Compagnie,* vol. XI. Den Haag: Instituut voor Nederlandse Geschiedenis. (Rijks Geschiedkundige Publicatië, Grote Serië 232.)

Schulte Nordholt, H.G. (1971), *The Political System of the Atoni of Timor.* The Hague: M. Nijhoff. (Verhandelingen van het Koninklijk Instituut voor Taal-, Land- en volkenkunde 60.)

Sen, S.N. (1958), *The Military System of the Marathas.* Calcutta: Orient Longman

Siegel, James (1976), 'Awareness of the Past in the Hikajat Potjoet Moehamat', in Cowan, C.D. and O.W. Wolters (eds.), *Southeast Asian History and Historiography. Essays presented to D.G.E. Hall.* Ithaca and London: Cornell University Press.

Simon, P.J. (1981), *Rapatriés d'Indochine. Une village franco-indochinois en Bourbonnais*. Paris: Harmattan.

Singh, Bilveer (2001), *The Indonesian Military Business Complex Origins, Course and Future*. SDSC Working Paper no. 354. Canberra: Australian National University.

Slater, David (1998), 'Globalization and questions of Post-colonial Theory', in Marcussen, H. and Arnfred, S. (eds.), *Concepts and Metaphors: Ideologies, Narratives and Myths in Development Discourse*. Roskilde: International Development Studies.

Smith, J. (2006) *Charles Darwin and Victorian Visual Culture*. Cambridge: Cambridge University Press.

Smithies, M. (1983), 'A New Guinean and the Royal Society', *Hemisphere* 27 (6): 365-371.

Spaulding, L. (1937), *Warfare*. Washington: Infantry Journal Press.

Spillett, P.G. (1999), *The Pre-Colonial History of the Island of Timor, Together with Some Notes on the Makassan Influence in the Island*. Unpublished manuscript, Darwin.

Stafford, B.M. (1996), 'Images of ambiguity: eighteenth-century microscopy and the neither/ nor', in Miller, D.P. and Reill, P.H. (eds.), *Visions of Empire: Voyages, Botany, and Representations of Nature*, 230-257. Cambridge: Cambridge University Press.

Staum, M.S. (2003), *Labeling People: French Scholars on Society, Race, and Empire 1815-1848*. Montreal: McGill-Queens University Press.

Stocking, Jr., G.W. (1987), *Victorian Anthropology*. New York: The Free Press.

Sufi, Motahar Hossain (2001), *Begum Rokeya: Jiban O Sahitya*. Dhaka: Maola Brothers.

Sutter, John O. (1959), *Indonesianisasi: Politic in a Changing Economy, 1940-1955*. Ithaca: Cornell University Press.

Sutton, T. (1954), *The Daniells: Artists and Travellers*. London: Bodley Head.

Suyitno, Heru (1996), 'Pabrik Gula Gondangwinangun Sebelum dan Sesudah Nasionalisasi Tahun 1950-1963', Yogyakarta: Jurusan Sejarah Fakultas Sastra UGM.

Tarling, Nicolas (2001), *Southeast Asia. A Modern History*.

Taylor, J.G. (2007), 'Meditations on a Portrait from Seventeenth-Century Batavia', *Journal of Southeast Asian Studies* 37 (1): 23-44.

Thapar, Suruchi (2006), *Women in the Indian National movement*. New Delhi: Sage Publications Ltd.

'The Rediscovery of Our Revolution'. Address by the President of the Republic of Indonesia on the seventeenth of August, 1959 (Jakarta: Ministry of Information 1959).

Thomas, Joan (ed.) (1984), *The Sea Journals of Annie and Amy Henning*. Sydney: Halstead Press.

Tomlinson (ed.) (1993), *The New Cambridge History of India: The Economy of Modern India*. Cambridge: Cambridge University Press.

Traube, E.G. (1986), *Cosmology and Social Life: Ritual Exchange among the Mambai of East Timor*. Chicago: University of Chicago Press.

Tsai Maw Kuey (1968), *Les Chinois au Sud Vietnam*. Doctorat d'université sous la direction de J. Delvert. Paris: Bibliothèque Nationale.

Uno, Kathleen (2005), 'Womanhood, War and Empire: Transmutations of "Good Wife, Wise Mother" before 1931' in Barbara Moloney and Kathleen Uno (eds.), *Gendering Modern Japanese History*. Cambridge, MA: Harvard University Asia Center: 493-519.

Valentijn, F. (1994), 'The Slave Trade and Relations with the Dutch', in Vickers, A. (ed.), *Travelling to Bali: Four Hundred Years of Journeys*. Kuala Lumpur: Oxford University Press.

Vansina, J. (1961), *Oral Tradition: A Study in Historical Methodology*. London: Routledge & Kegan Paul.

Vansina, J. (1985), *Oral Tradition as History*. London: Currey.

Vivers, Meg (2002), 'Dealing with Difference: Evidence of European Women in Early Contact History,' *Journal of Australian Colonial History* 4 (2): 72-93.
VOC, The archive of the, no. 1.04.02, Nationaal Archief, The Hague.

Walden, Inara (1995), '"That was slavery days": Aboriginal Domestic Servants in New South Wales in the Twentieth Century', in Ann McGrath and Kay Saunders (eds.), *Labour History: Aboriginal Workers* 69: 196-207.
Wallace, A.R. (2000 (1869)), *The Malay Archipelago*. Singapore: Periplus.
Warner-Bishop, Ruth (2006), Interview with Christine de Matos in Toorak Victoria, Australia, 11 July.
Weidner, C.T. (1932), *Nota van toelichting betreffende het landschap Mollo*. KIT 1289, Open collection microfiches, Nationaal Archief, The Hague.
Widoyoko, Danang et al. (2003), *Bisnis Militer Mencari Legitimasi*. Jakarta: Indonesia Corruption Watch.
Wieringa, E.P. (1999), 'An Old Text brought to Life again. A Reconsideration of the "Final Version" of the Babad Tanah Jawi', in: *Bijdragen tot de Taal-, Land- en Volkenkunde* 155-2: 244-263.
Woodward, Gretel (2006), Interview with Christine de Matos in Carlton New South Wales, Australia, 19 June.
Woollacott, Angela (2003), 'Creating the White Colonial Woman: Mary Gaunt's Imperial Adventuring and Australian Cultural History', in Hsu-Ming Teo and White, Richard (eds.), *Cultural History in Australia*, 186-200. Sydney: UNSW Press.
Wright, H.R.C. (1960), 'Communication: Raffles and the Slave Trade at Batavia in 1812', *The Historical Journal* 3 (2): 184-191.

Yeager, R.M., and Jacobson, M.I. (2002), *Textiles of Western Timor: Regional Variations in Historical Perspective*. Bangkok: White Lotus. (Studies in the Material Cultures of Southeast Asia no. 2.)
Yoneyama, Lisa (2005), 'Liberation under Siege: U.S. Military Occupation and Japanese Women's Enfranchisement', *American Quarterly*, 57 (3): 885-910.
Yong, Mun Cheong (1997), 'Koneksi Indonesia di Singapura, 1945-1948', in Abdullah, Taufik, et al. (eds.), *Denyut Nadi Revolusi Indonesia*. Jakarta: Gramedia.

Zed, Mestika (1997), 'Ekonomi Indonesia Pada Masa Revolusi: Mencari Dana Perjuangan (1945-1950)', in Abdullah, Taufik, et al. (eds.), *Denyut Nadi Revolusi Indonesia*. Jakarta: Gramedia.
Zed, Mestika (2003), *Kepialangan Politik dan Revolusi. Palembang 1900-1950*. Jakarta: LP3ES.

 PUBLICATIONS SERIES

Monographs

Marleen Dieleman
The Rhythm of Strategy. A Corporate Biography of the Salim Group of Indonesia
Monographs 1
2007 (ISBN 978 90 5356 033 4)

Sam Wong
Exploring 'Unseen' Social Capital in Community Participation. Everyday Lives of Poor Mainland Chinese Migrants in Hong Kong
Monographs 2
2007 (ISBN 978 90 5356 034 1)

Diah Ariani Arimbi
Reading the Writings of Contemporary Indonesian Muslim Women Writers. Representation, Identity and Religion of Muslim Women in Indonesian Fiction
Monographs 3
2009 (ISBN 978 90 8964 089 5)

Edited Volumes

Sebastian Bersick, Wim Stokhof and Paul van der Velde (eds.)
Multiregionalism and Multilateralism. Asian-European Relations in a Global Context
Edited Volumes 1
2006 (ISBN 978 90 5356 929 0)

Khun Eng Kuah-Pearce (ed.)
Chinese Women and the Cyberspace
Edited Volumes 2
2008 (ISBN 978 90 5356 751 7)

Milan J. Titus and Paul P.M. Burgers (eds.)
Rural Livelihoods, Resources and Coping with Crisis in Indonesia.
A Comparative Study
Edited Volumes 3
2008 (ISBN 978 90 8964 055 0)

Marianne Hulsbosch, Elizabeth Bedford and Martha Chaiklin (eds.)
Asian Material Culture
Edited Volumes 4
2009 (ISBN 978 90 8964 090 1)